CIPS STUDY MATTERS

PROFESSIONAL DIPLOMA IN PROCUREMENT AND SUPPLY

COURSE BOOK

Leadership in procurement and supply

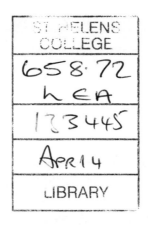
© Profex Publishing Limited, 2012

Printed and distributed by:

The Chartered Institute of Purchasing & Supply, Easton House, Easton on the Hill, Stamford, Lincolnshire PE9 3NZ
Tel: +44 (0) 1780 756 777
Fax: +44 (0) 1780 751 610
Email: info@cips.org
Website: www.cips.org

First edition November 2012

Contents

Preface

Welcome to your new Study Pack, consisting of two elements.

- A **Course Book** (the current volume). This provides detailed coverage of all topics specified in the unit content.
- A small-format volume of **Revision Notes.** Use your Revision Notes in the weeks leading up to the exam.

For a full explanation of how to use your new Study Pack, turn now to page xi. And good luck in your exams!

A note on style

Throughout your Study Packs you will find that we use the masculine form of personal pronouns. This convention is adopted purely for the sake of stylistic convenience – we just don't like saying 'he/she' all the time. Please don't think this reflects any kind of bias or prejudice.

November 2012

The Unit Content

The unit content is reproduced below, together with reference to the chapter in this Course Book where each topic is covered.

Unit purpose and aims

On completion of this unit, candidates will be able to critically appraise influencing and leadership skills and behaviours, to help achieve commitment from across the organisation, including senior management, as well as customers and suppliers.

This unit emphasises the leadership skills and behaviours required for the achievement of the objectives and improvements sought by effective procurement and supply chain management.

Learning outcomes, assessment criteria and indicative content

Chapter

1.0 Understand the main leadership skills and behaviours that are appropriate for improving procurement and supply chain management

1.1 Critically evaluate the differences between leadership and management

• Defining leadership	1
• The role of a leader and the activity of leadership	1
• The importance of leadership	1
• The differences between management and leadership	1

1.2 Critically analyse the main approaches to leadership for improving procurement and supply chain management

• The qualities or traits approach to leadership	2
• The functional or group approach, including action-centred leadership	2
• Styles of leadership including the authoritarian or autocratic, democratic and *laissez-faire* styles	2
• Contingency theories for leadership such as path-goal theory	2

1.3 Evaluate the main skills and behaviours that contribute to effective leadership for improving procurement and supply chain management

• The continuum of leadership behaviour	2
• The main forces in deciding the type of leadership	2
• Situational leadership	2
• Transformational and inspirational leadership	2

4.0 Understand the main methods to lead change in the supply chain

4.1 Evaluate the main methods of change management that can be used to develop the supply chain

4.2 Critically assess the main methods for resolving conflict with internal and external stakeholders to support change in the supply chain

4.3 Evaluate the importance of effective delegation to implement change successfully

How to Use Your Study Pack

Organising your study

'Organising' is the key word: unless you are a very exceptional student, you will find a haphazard approach is insufficient, particularly if you are having to combine study with the demands of a full-time job.

A good starting point is to timetable your studies, in broad terms, between now and the date of the examination. How many subjects are you attempting? How many chapters are there in the Course Book for each subject? Now do the sums: how many days/weeks do you have for each chapter to be studied?

Remember:

- Not every week can be regarded as a study week – you may be going on holiday, for example, or there may be weeks when the demands of your job are particularly heavy. If these can be foreseen, you should allow for them in your timetabling.
- You also need a period leading up to the exam in which you will revise and practise what you have learned.

Once you have done the calculations, make a week-by-week timetable for yourself for each paper, allowing for study and revision of the entire unit content between now and the date of the exams.

Getting started

Aim to find a quiet and undisturbed location for your study, and plan as far as possible to use the same period each day. Getting into a routine helps avoid wasting time. Make sure you have all the materials you need before you begin – keep interruptions to a minimum.

Using the Course Book

You should refer to the Course Book to the extent that you need it.

- If you are a newcomer to the subject, you will probably need to read through the Course Book quite thoroughly. This will be the case for most students.
- If some areas are already familiar to you – either through earlier studies or through your practical work experience – you may choose to skip sections of the Course Book.

The content of the Course Book

This Course Book has been designed to give detailed coverage of every topic in the unit content. As you will see from pages vii–ix, each topic mentioned in the unit content is dealt with in a chapter of the Course Book. For the most part the order of the Course Book follows the order of the unit content closely, though departures from this principle have occasionally been made in the interest of a logical learning order.

Each chapter begins with a reference to the assessment criteria and indicative content to be covered in the chapter. Each chapter is divided into sections, listed in the introduction to the chapter, and for the most part being actual captions from the unit content.

All of this enables you to monitor your progress through the unit content very easily and provides reassurance that you are tackling every subject that is examinable.

Each chapter contains the following features.

- Introduction, setting out the main topics to be covered
- Clear coverage of each topic in a concise and approachable format
- A chapter summary
- Self-test questions

The study phase

For each chapter you should begin by glancing at the main headings (listed at the start of the chapter). Then read fairly rapidly through the body of the text to absorb the main points. If it's there in the text, you can be sure it's there for a reason, so try not to skip unless the topic is one you are familiar with already.

Then return to the beginning of the chapter to start a more careful reading. You may want to take brief notes as you go along, but bear in mind that you already have your Revision Notes and Passnotes – there is no point in duplicating what you can find there.

Test your recall and understanding of the material by attempting the self-test questions. These are accompanied by cross-references to paragraphs where you can check your answers and refresh your memory.

The revision phase

Your approach to revision should be methodical and you should aim to tackle each main area of the unit content in turn. Read carefully through your Revision Notes. Check back to your Course Book if there are areas where you cannot recall the subject matter clearly. Then do some question practice. The CIPS website contains many past exam questions. You should aim to identify those that are suitable for the unit you are studying.

Additional reading

Your Study Pack provides you with the key information needed for each module but CIPS strongly advocates reading as widely as possible to augment and reinforce your understanding. CIPS produces an official reading list of books, which can be downloaded from the bookshop area of the CIPS website.

To help you, we have identified one essential textbook for each subject. We recommend that you read this for additional information.

The essential textbook for this unit is *Management and Organisational Behaviour,* by Laurie Mullins.

CHAPTER 1

Leadership and Management

Assessment criteria and indicative content

 Critically evaluate the differences between leadership and management

- Defining leadership
- The role of a leader and the activity of leadership
- The importance of leadership
- The differences between management and leadership

Section headings

1. Leadership and management
2. The importance of leadership
3. Leadership roles and activities
4. Leadership in procurement and supply

Introduction

The terms 'management' and 'leadership' are often used interchangeably – and indeed, many 'management' theories and models have simply been relabelled using the more fashionable term 'leadership' in recent years.

What then is leadership – and is it meaningfully different from management? To the extent that it is different from management, why might it be important or valuable for managers to be developed as leaders or to exercise leadership functions and behaviours? What is the role of a leader – and what do leaders actually *do?*

In this chapter we begin by surveying definitions of the term 'leadership', and evaluating the differences between leadership and management. We then go on to examine aspects of the leadership role and leadership activities.

In the final section, we look at some of the distinctive values and behaviours that are said to characterise leadership. This discussion will be followed up in Chapter 2, as we explore various theories, models and styles of leadership.

1 Leadership and management

Defining leadership

1.1 Laurie Mullins *(Management and Organisational Behaviour)* emphasises the multi-faceted nature of the leadership concept, and the ways in which it can be interpreted.

- Leadership may be seen as an interpersonal process of 'getting others to follow' or 'getting people to do things willingly'.
- Leadership may be exercised as an attribute of a person's position in a group or organisation (eg by appointment or election), or some other source of power and influence (eg personal charisma, knowledge or expertise, or access to valued resources).
- Leadership may be seen as a role (achieving effective performance through others), a set of functions (planning, organising, communicating, developing and so on) or a cluster of behaviours (goal articulation, direction, facilitation, assertive communication and so on).

1.2 All definitions and interpretations of leadership, however, emphasise processes of interpersonal influence: all leaders have 'followers'. Mullins argues that the process of leadership is therefore inseparable from group activity and team building – but, as we will see in Chapter 3, leadership influencing may be used in a range of contexts and relationships within internal and external supply chains.

1.3 The following is a representative sample of definitions of leadership.

- 'Leadership defines what the future should look like, aligns people with that vision and inspires them to make it happen despite the obstacles' (John Kotter, *Leading Change).*
- 'Leadership is the art of mobilising others to want to struggle for shared aspirations' (Jim Kouzes and Barry Posner, *The Leadership Challenge*).
- 'Leadership is a process that involves: setting a purpose and direction which inspires people to combine and work towards it willingly; paying attention to the means, pace and quality of progress towards the aim; and upholding group unity and individual effectiveness throughout' (James Scouller, *Three Levels of Leadership).*
- 'Leaders have followers, and that's it. If you inspire people to follow you then you are a leader' (Chartered Institute of Personnel and Development).

The relationship between leadership and management

1.4 There are many different definitions of the terms 'manager' and 'leader'. Here are two (from Mullins) to begin with.

- Management is 'the process through which efforts of members of the organisation are co-ordinated, directed and guided towards the achievement of organisational goals: the clarification of objectives, planning, organising, directing and controlling other people's work.'
- Leadership is 'a relationship through which one person influences the behaviour or actions of other people'.

1.5 The terms are often used interchangeably – although 'leader' is now the more fashionable term (and you'll find management theories relabelled more or less unchanged, as 'leadership' theories). However, a number of efforts have been made to distinguish meaningfully between the two concepts.

1.6 For example, Kotter *(A Force for Change: How Leadership Differs from Management,* 1990) has made a detailed and helpful distinction between leadership and management. He suggests that management involves the following activities.

- Planning and budgeting: target-setting, establishing procedures and processes for reaching targets, and allocating the resources necessary to meet the plans

- Organising and staffing: designing the task structure, hiring people, allocating tasks and establishing rewards and incentives
- Controlling and problem-solving: monitoring results against plan, identifying problems, evaluating options and implementing decisions

In other words, management is about coping with complexity: managerial functions are to do with logic, structure, analysis and control. Management can be exercised over processes, projects, resources, time and so on.

1.7 Leadership, on the other hand, requires a rather different set of activities.

- Creating a sense of direction: finding a vision for something new out of the challenge of dissatisfaction with the *status quo*
- Communicating the vision: meeting the needs of other people, giving the vision credibility
- Energising, inspiring and motivating: stimulating others to translate the vision into achievement

Leadership is about creating and coping with change. It can, essentially, only be exercised over people. (The change management aspects of leadership are covered in detail in Chapter 8.)

1.8 The following are some other influential attempts to distinguish between the concepts.

- Gary Yukl *(Leadership in Organisations,* 1998*)* suggests that while management is defined by a formal role and position in the organisation hierarchy, leaders are given their roles by the perceptions and choice of others. Management is an authority relationship, while leadership is an influencing relationship. Managers have 'subordinates': leaders have 'followers'.
- R Meredith Belbin (*Changing the Way We Work,* 1997) similarly argues that 'leadership is not part of the job, but a quality that can be *brought* to the job'. In other words, a leadership role may not be clearly defined or assigned, but comes about through the exercise of leadership qualities and skills.
- Abraham Zaleznik ('Managers and leaders: are they different?' in *Harvard Business Review,* 1997) suggests that while managers are primarily concerned with order and maintaining the *status quo,* focusing on impersonality, diplomacy and decision-making processes in the organisation, leaders are more concerned with introducing new ideas and approaches, focusing on personal engagement, excitement, vision and empathy for people.
- David Katz and Robert L Kahn *(The Social Psychology of Organisations,* 1974) suggest that while managers aim to secure compliance with routine organisational objectives, leaders aim to secure willingness, enthusiasm and commitment.

1.9 David Boddy *(Management: An Introduction,* 2005) sums up the differences between managers and leaders as follows.

'Most commentators view an "effective manager" as someone who "gets things done" to ensure order and continuity. They maintain the steady state – keeping established systems in good shape and making incremental improvements. People generally use the term "effective leader" to denote someone who brings innovation, moves an activity out of trouble into success, makes a worthwhile difference. They see opportunities to do new things, take the initiative to raise the issue and do something about it.'

1.10 In other words: leadership is about 'where are we going?' – while management is about 'how do we get there?' This has sometimes been expressed in the (rather value-laden) formula: 'Managers do things right; leaders do the right things'.

Do managers need to be leaders – and *vice versa*?

1.11 David Whetten and Kim Cameron *(Developing Management Skills,* 2002) argue that the distinction between managers and leaders is no longer very useful. 'Managers cannot be successful without being good leaders, and leaders cannot be successful without being good managers.'

1.12 Mullins similarly argues that leadership is part of effective management. 'An essential part of the process of management is coordinating the activities of people and guiding their efforts towards the goals and objectives of the organisation. This involves the process of leadership… The manager needs to understand the nature of leadership influence, factors that determine relationships with other people, and the effectiveness of the leadership relationship.'

1.13 Kotter, while distinguishing between management and leadership (as discussed above) stressed that organisations need *both,* for effective performance: organisations still require a measure of order and control (supported by management) in the process of change (supported by leadership).

1.14 Terry Gillen *(Leadership Skills for Boosting Performance,* 2002) also points out that 'You do not have to be the best technician or manager to be a credible leader, but you need to be good enough to avoid making a fool of yourself and losing too much time doing things and managing processes.' In other words, it's all very well having 'vision' and 'values' – but you also have to invest time and energy taking action to support them by making things happen, efficiently and effectively.

1.15 The trend in modern management literature is to emphasise that leadership can be exercised by any individual: not just managers or designated team leaders. However, in practice there is usually a greater weighting towards leadership in senior management roles, and towards management in junior or front-line management roles.

Hard and soft aspects of organisation

1.16 An alternative framework for looking at this, with which you might be familiar, is the **McKinsey 7S framework**. Developed by the McKinsey management consultancy group and popularised by Tom Peters and Robert H Waterman (*In Search of Excellence*), the 7S framework is a handy mnemonic for a range of organisational elements which can be controlled by managers to bring about change: Figure 1.1.

Figure 1.1 *The 7S framework*

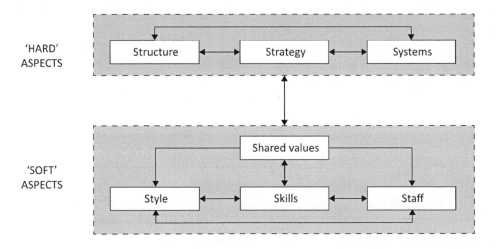

1.17 Taking each element in turn:

- **Strategy** is a chosen course of action leading to the allocation of the firm's resources over time in order to reach defined goals
- **Structure** refers to the formal organisation structure of division of labour, authority, reporting relationships and communication channels
- **Systems** refer to procedures, tools and processes that standardise work and information flow in the organisation (including IT systems, but also business processes, policies and rules and so on)
- **Staff** are the human resources of the organisation: their abilities and motivation, team dynamics, flexibility, turnover rates and so on

1

- **Style** refers to corporate image, organisation culture and management style: patterns and norms of behaviour
- **Skills** refer to the distinctive capabilities of key personnel or of the organisation as a whole (eg in knowledge transfer, innovation and so on)
- **Shared values** are the underlying guiding beliefs and assumptions that shape the way the organisation sees itself and its purpose. These are sometimes called **super-ordinate goals**: the over-arching goals which all sub-units of the organisation share.

1.18 The 7S network is a tool for strategic management, but in our present context, it is important to note that organisations require attention to:

- Strategy, Structure and Systems: 'hard' or technical aspects – which are arguably the focus of management *and*
- Style (or culture), Staff, Skills and Shared values: 'soft' or people-oriented aspects – which are arguably the focus of leadership.

1.19 This is a useful checklist for considering a scenario, at work or in an exam: what problems are evident, and what changes need to be made, in each aspect of the situation? Kenneth Lysons and Brian Farrington helpfully highlight the implications for procurement managers and leaders of the seven dimensions – which may be useful for exam scenarios – as follows: Table 1.1.

Table 1.1 *The purchasing implications of the 7S framework*

Strategy	• How can procurement contribute to the achievement of growth, diversification, outsourcing and other strategies?
Structure	• The breaking down of functional barriers to integrate procurement into seamless logistics and supply chain processes
Systems	• The development of procedures and information flows and the facilitation of e-procurement
Style	• The building of internal and external supply chain co-operation, value addition and innovation, through relationships based on trust, courtesy, information sharing and ethical principles
Staff	• Securing the right mix of procurement and support staff • Developing, motivating and rewarding staff
Skills	• The development of procurement and supply chain management knowledge and competencies • The sharing of best practice with internal and external supply chains
Shared values	• The importance of procurement sharing in the corporate culture • The recognition by the organisation that procurement is a key contributor to organisational performance • The relating of all procurement activities to the ethical and environmental policies of the organisation

2 The importance of leadership

2.1 Why then might it be important to distinguish between managers and leaders – or for managers to become leaders in a given team, organisation or supply chain?

Leadership as 'that something extra'

2.2 As we have seen, leadership offers an added extra dimension to management, in several ways – which are particularly relevant to the modern business environment and world of work.

- Leaders energise and support **change**, flexibility and adaptation in organisations. This is an essential capability for survival in highly competitive and fast-changing business environments.
- Leaders secure **commitment** (over and above mere compliance with organisational directives). Commitment mobilises the energy, ideas, creativity, experience and initiative of team members, which are willingly offered in the service of shared goals and values. This in turn contributes to key organisational success factors such as innovation, and improved quality and customer service.

- Leaders set **direction**, helping teams and organisations to understand their purpose and goals. This facilitates teamworking and empowerment, without loss of co-ordination. Or, conversely, it facilitates unity of purpose and direction, co-ordination and control, without the potentially deadening and restrictive effect of 'tight' managerial controls (such as programmed activities, supervision, and continuous monitoring and correction).
- Leaders **support, challenge and develop people**, maximising their contribution to the organisation. This reflects a major shift in the business environment, whereby the contribution of human resources (in terms of ideas, knowledge, service, flexibility and innovation) is increasingly recognised as a key source of long-term value, and competitive differentiation and advantage, for many organisations in knowledge-based and service-based sectors.
- Leaders use a **facilitate-empower style** rather than a command-control style. This is better suited to the needs and expectations of increasingly educated, skilled and professional workers, and therefore enhances motivation, morale, job satisfaction, commitment and loyalty. It is also better suited to the increasing need for information-sharing and collaboration, in business environments where co-ordination is critical to the flow of value to the customer (eg in customer service and supply), and where learning, best practice sharing and innovation are critical to competitive advantage and continuous improvement.
- As an explicitly **interpersonal process**, based on qualities such as interpersonal sensitivity, rapport and emotional intelligence, leadership supports relationship and trust building – in a way that the managerial focus on processes and resources may not. Relationships and trust are increasingly recognised as a critical success factor in cross-functional and inter-organisational processes: optimising the linkages in the value chain which secures the flow of value to the customer (Michael Porter, *Competitive Strategy*).
- Leaders use **influence**, rather than positional, structural or hierarchical power (authority) to change the behaviour and attitudes of other parties in a relationship or interaction. As we will see in Chapter 3, this is an important factor in the context of non-authority-based relationships, such as managing upwards (influencing strategy, policy or more senior individuals in the organisation or supply chain) and managing across (influencing colleagues and collaborators in the internal and external supply chains). It also enables the leader to secure the change, attitudes and behaviours he requires – without the potentially relationship-damaging or resistance-causing side effects of more coercive approaches such as the imposition of authority.

2.3 Each of these attributes is important for business in general – but you should also be able to see their particular relevance to procurement and supply chain management, in which some of the key distinguishing features are as follows.

- The importance of horizontal, non-authority-based relationships (in the internal and external supply chains)
- The need for skills in non-authority-based influencing (to suit procurement's role as a service and consultancy function with a potential strategic contribution to make)
- The potential role of procurement as an agent of change and innovation in the supply chain (eg in regard to make/do or buy decisions, sustainable and responsible procurement, waste and cost reduction and continuous improvement).

Leadership and competitive advantage

2.4 One of the cornerstones of the leadership concept is that corporate productivity, added value and competitive advantage are not gained solely through programmes and activities, but through *people*: people add value to material, financial, informational and other resources. Why do we need to influence, motivate and inspire people to work effectively? Why do we need to help them develop their skills and contributions? Because that is the source of competitive advantage and added value in an ever-changing, networked, knowledge-based, customer-focused business environment.

2.5 Personnel practitioners have long argued this viewpoint. Peters and Waterman *(In Search of Excellence,* 1982) argued that it was a key characteristic of 'excellent' companies, such as IBM, McKinsey and 3M: they called it simply 'success through people'. Employees are increasingly being regarded not as a cost to be controlled, but as human assets to be nurtured, developed and empowered in order to maximise their contribution and commitment to the organisation's objectives.

2.6 People are the key resource of businesses in an age where value is added through knowledge, creativity and interpersonal relations. ICL *(The ICL Way)* affirm that: 'Our attitude to people is created by the fact that we are in a knowledge industry. Our business success will therefore be led by people first and products second. We are no longer mainly selling boxes of computer equipment. We are selling creative solutions to business problems. If we are to be successful, to excel in all we do, to win rather than merely compete, then the full capabilities of all ICL people must be realised and released into action. That is the business of our managers, who are expected to cultivate employees' skills continuously and systematically.'

2.7 This is the cornerstone of what has come to be known as a **human resource management** (HRM) orientation to management and leadership. HRM tends to focus on managing people for key strategic aims such as quality, innovation, organisational flexibility and learning, and employee commitment. It tends to be associated with leadership behaviours such as:

- Replacing rules and controls with vision, cultural values and customer focus
- Open communication and employee involvement
- Collaborative employee relations
- Empowered teamworking
- A facilitative (rather than directive) style of leadership
- Continuous learning and development, at an individual, team and organisational level.

Leadership and the 'new organisation'

2.8 Organisation and management theory – as well as the concept of supply chain management – has increasingly emphasised the importance of effective business processes in optimising the flow of value to the customer. Hand in hand with this is the recognition that processes (such as product development, supply, customer service, quality management and learning and innovation) are essentially **horizontal**, cutting across functional and organisational boundaries. This emphasises the need for horizontal structures and systems of management, facilitating collaboration in pursuit of shared goals and values.

2.9 Horizontal, process-focused structures include:

- Chunked (team) structures: creating and empowering smaller and more flexible units (eg teams) within the overall structure
- Cross-functional structures, such as matrix organisation, multi-skilled and cross-functional teams, quality and innovation circles and other mechanisms for communication and collaboration across the 'vertical' barriers created by specialisation, departmental role demarcations and formal communication channels
- Project management: temporary structures, organised to focus on specific outputs or results, and drawing on cross-functional expertise and resources
- Network structures: loose, dynamic, informal affiliations of autonomous and broadly equal units or organisations, which exchange information and pursue ongoing (typically long-term) relationships for mutual benefit – as in supply networks
- Virtual structures: special forms of the network concept, in which individuals, teams and organisations operate, collaborate and co-ordinate their activities – regardless of physical location or distance – primarily through the use of ICT networks and tools (such as the internet, intranet and extranets).

2.10 All these structural forms place a premium on *leadership* (in addition to management of the processes and resources involved), for the following reasons.

- They involve teamworking: encouraging identification with a shared vision and values, facilitating people in 'getting along with others', creating an open climate of information sharing and communication – and so on.
- They emphasise that, in the words of team leadership guru Ken Blanchard, 'no one of us is as wise as all of us': in other words, they seek to maximise the realisation of both individual *and* collective potential.
- They break down the formal business hierarchies which have traditionally given managers and team members a sense of their relative position in the organisation and what was expected of them (on the basis of their job or role description). Rob Goffee and Gareth Jones (*Why Should Anyone Be Led By You?* 2006) argue that 'personal leadership is beginning to replace organisational structure', as leaders help people to understand their roles and contributions in the more fluid, horizontal, 'career'-less structures of today.

Leadership, organisational culture and values creation

2.11 Geert Hofstede *(Cultures and Organisations,* 2010) summed up culture as 'the collective programming of the mind which distinguishes the members of one category of people from another'. It represents all the shared assumptions, beliefs, values, behavioural norms, symbols, rituals, stories and artefacts that make our society (or ethnic group, or organisation) distinctively 'us'.

2.12 Different countries and regions may have significantly different cultural norms, values and assumptions which influence how they do business and manage people. It is important to understand this, since procurement professionals are increasingly likely to work in organisations that have multi-national or multi-cultural elements – and with multi-cultural or cross-cultural supply chains. (These aspects are touched on in Chapter 7, in the context of leading diverse teams.)

2.13 However, *organisational* culture has also increasingly been recognised as a vitally important element of organisational infrastructure, with a pervasive effect on the attitudes, perceptions and behaviours of members. Identified performance gaps or problems in organisations (and supply chains) may well have a cultural basis, and may require cultural change – or at least the bringing of cultural values, assumptions and norms into the open, where they can be discussed and dealt with more intentionally. Values such as 'quality' or 'sustainability', for example, are most powerful when they are expressed and internalised as core cultural values of the organisation: part of 'the way we do things around here' (Edgar Schein, *Organisational Culture and Leadership*).

2.14 Organisation culture has been defined as 'a pattern of beliefs and expectations shared by the organisation's members, and which produce norms which powerfully shape the behaviour of individuals and groups in the organisation' (H Schwartz and SM Davis, 'Matching corporate culture and business strategy', in *Organisational Dynamics*).

2.15 The importance of organisation culture for business performance was highlighted by Tom Peters and Robert Waterman, in their influential study of successful corporations: *In Search of Excellence* (1982). One of the key features of excellent companies (which consistently produce commercially viable new products and respond effectively to change) was their use of organisation culture to guide business processes and to motivate employees. A handful of widely shared, strongly held guiding values can replace rules, guidelines and supervision: focusing employees' attention on strategic aims such as quality, innovation and customer service, and empowering them to take initiative and responsibility in pursuit of those aims. This reduces rigidity, increases flexibility, enables change (on the basis that if values change, behaviour will follow) and develops people.

2.16 Leadership has a crucial role in the creation, shaping, maintenance – and, where necessary, change – of corporate culture, through the following processes.

- Acting as exemplars and role models for the values and behavioural expectations and norms of the culture
- Encouraging examination and expression (and where necessary, challenging) of underlying assumptions and paradigms: why do we do what we do?
- Expressing the values and beliefs of the culture (or the *desired* values and beliefs of the organisation, where the current culture is dysfunctional), through a wide range of leadership communications: stories, mottoes, instructions, briefings, value statements and so on
- Encouraging team members (and suppliers) to 'own' desirable values, beliefs and behaviours: eg through incentives, co-opting people to coach others, recognition and affirmation
- Using human resource management mechanisms (with team members) or supplier management mechanisms (with suppliers) to reinforce desirable changes: making new values and behaviours criteria for selection, appraisal, reward, promotion (or preferred supplier status); including them in employee and supplier development needs assessment and continuous improvement agreements; and so on.

2.17 Explicit **value statements** are increasingly used in organisations, for the following purposes.

- To define what is meant by value-laden concepts such as procurement ethics, professionalism and commitment, rather than assuming that they will be understood in the same way by everyone
- To specify the key values and behaviours which are considered desirable for the organisation (taking into account stakeholder values and expectations) – and those which are not – so that everyone knows where they stand
- To encourage ongoing discussion about value definitions, conflicts, dilemmas and issues, as they arise – in order to foster an integrity-based (rather than a merely compliance-based) approach to managing corporate ethics
- To highlight areas where people's 'true' values (reflected in their behaviour) diverge from the organisation's 'ideal' or 'preferred' values, as a basis for programmes of value (and therefore behaviour) change.

2.18 The range of values that might be promoted to create a positive culture of procurement and supply chain management may include: personal and professional ethical values (such as integrity, confidentiality, objectivity, fair dealing, and a duty of service to one's employer); teamworking and leadership values (such as courtesy, respect, openness, trust, loyalty and co-operation); and values which specifically reflect the department's mission and culture (in regard to cost, quality, adding value, customer and supplier relationships and so on).

Leadership and innovation

2.19 Innovation has been defined simply as 'the successful exploitation of new ideas'.

2.20 Innovation capability and leadership is a key source of competitive advantage for organisations, based on differentiation from competitors through distinctive competencies and resources such as: technology leverage; excellent product functionality and design; unique product features; continually 'new', adapting and improving features; and a loyal brand following among early adopters and style leaders.

2.21 A firm with strong innovation capability may gain competitive advantage by the following means.

- Capturing new ideas and technological developments, and recognising market opportunities more creatively or swiftly than competitors
- Translating new ideas into business process (re)design more swiftly and effectively than competitors (eg the early adoption of e-commerce, e-distribution or social media marketing)
- Translating new ideas into deliverable and marketable products and services more swiftly or appealingly than competitors (eg the Apple iPad)

- Getting new products and services to market more swiftly or cost-effectively than competitors

2.22 Meanwhile, frequent product innovation and modification, due to shortening product lifecycles, requires flexible sourcing and supply chain management strategies – among other challenges. In the context of supply markets, therefore, innovation is mainly about exploiting new processes and technologies and their applications by suppliers to deliver more effective, efficient and sustainable products and services.

2.23 Leadership can have a key role in supporting supply chain innovation, through dynamics such as the following.

- **Motivating and inspiring people** to 'think outside the box' or 'transcend the ordinary': encouraging confidence in experimentation, celebrating mistakes as learning opportunities and so on
- **Designing and developing an organisational environment** which enables people to be innovative. This may include:
  - Creating **structures** which facilitate multi-directional and cross-functional communication, synergies and the use of initiative (eg cross-functional or multi-skilled teamworking)
  - Creating an **organisational climate** which is open to new ideas, criticisms, problem identification and feedback; facilitates the gathering and sharing of knowledge and information; continually scans the external environment for good ideas and performance benchmarks; encourages personal development and experimentation; tolerates risk taking mistakes as tools of learning; and values continuous learning and improvement
  - Developing innovation-relevant **skills and capabilities** in people and teams (eg facilitating ideas-generation processes such as brainstorming)
  - Mobilising organisational resources to support innovation (eg R & D funding, rewards for suggestion schemes, time and equipment for personal experimentation and so on).

2.24 Such an innovation-friendly organisation is often identified as a **learning organisation.**

2.25 In addition, a buying organisation may exercise leadership to drive and support innovation in its supply chain and/or industry, by measures such as the following.

- Supporting supply market innovation by signalling strong demand for innovative products and services (for example, through **forward commitment procurement**)
- Supporting supply market innovation by development activities, such as technology transfer and supplier development
- Prioritising innovation capability in supplier pre-qualification and selection
- Rewarding supplier innovation with long-term partnership and co-investment, innovation awards, gain-sharing arrangements and so on.

Leadership and supply chain management

2.26 Each of the learning outcomes for this syllabus emphasises the application of leadership models, skills and behaviours:

- To improve procurement and supply chain management
- To influence personnel involved in a supply chain
- To overcome common challenges faced by procurement and supply chain managers
- To lead change in the supply chain.

2.27 You should try to contextualise everything we say about leadership in this Course Book to potential procurement and supply chain management scenarios – both in your study (as you consider the implications of generic theoretical points) and in the exam (as you apply theory to specific case study scenarios and your own examples). We will do some generic context setting at key points: considering issues in supply chain improvement later in this chapter, for example, and highlighting some 'common challenges' in Chapter 3.

2.28 For the moment, in the context of the 'importance of leadership', we will just emphasise – again – that the distinctive attributes and focus of leadership make it an essential tool for:

- **Supporting innovation in supply chains**: by articulating, and securing 'buy-in' to, challenging objectives; by empowering and inspiring supply chain partners to contribute ideas and initiative in support of those objectives; and by supporting a culture of continuous learning and flexibility within the organisation
- **Improvement of supply chain processes and performance**: by developing supportive interpersonal competencies, relationships and collaborations; by inspiring and empowering supply chain partners to contribute meaningfully to improvement (and cost reduction); by providing role models of best practice; and by applying power and influence, as required, to overcome barriers and resolve problems
- **Developing sustainability, responsibility and ethics** in supply chains: by setting clear expectations and standards for the supply chain; by role modelling best practice; by creating incentives, rewards and mutual benefits for compliance or improvement; and by empowering the supply chain for compliance (eg through transparency, supplier development and best practice sharing). This is one area in which an organisation may become an industry or supply chain leader: seeking to use influence to raise standards and conditions beyond the boundaries of the enterprise.

3 Leadership roles and activities

3.1 We have already emphasised that 'roles and activities' are only one way of looking at leadership. Leaders are generally distinguished not just by 'what they do' – but by *how* they do *everything* they do.

3.2 However, we have also highlighted various definitions of leadership focused on roles and activities – and will follow up on this when we explore the 'functional' model of leadership in Chapter 2. Key leadership roles and activities have been identified as follows.

- Creating a sense of direction, or finding a vision for something new
- Communicating the vision, in a credible and compelling way
- Energising, inspiring and motivating people, to translate the vision into achievement
- Developing people, to enhance the long-term capability of the organisation: directing, supporting, challenging, training and empowering team members
- Creating, articulating, maintaining or changing organisational culture and values

What do leaders do?

3.3 Research by Henry Mintzberg *(The Nature of Managerial Work)* suggested that – contrary to the classical, rational view of managers as organisers and planners – managers are not separate from, or 'above', the demands of everyday work. Their work is sometimes routine and often disjointed and discontinuous: they are not always able to be reflective, systematic thinkers. Despite the development of formal management information systems, managers generally prefer verbal and informal information.

3.4 Mintzberg suggested that in their daily working lives, managers fulfil a range of roles: Table 1.2. Despite the fact that 'leader' (in this classification) is rather narrowly defined, you should be able to see how a leader (in the wider sense) may exercise the full range of roles suggested by Mintzberg.

Table 1.2 *Mintzberg's managerial roles*

NATURE OF ROLE	ROLE DEFINITION
Interpersonal Arising from a manager's formal authority or position in the organisation and unit	• *Figurehead*: a ceremonial role, representing the organisation in public • *Leader*: hiring, supervising, developing, motivating, team building and so on • *Liaison*: networking and co-ordinating with peers in other units and functions
Informational Arising from a manager's access to internal and external contacts	• *Monitor*: gathering information • *Spokesperson*: giving information on behalf of the unit or organisation • *Disseminator*: sharing information with relevant stakeholders or interested parties
Decisional Arising from a manager's formal authority and access to information, which places him in the best position to solve problems relating to the unit or department as a whole	• *Entrepreneur*: initiating action to exploit opportunities • *Disturbance handler*: responding to threats and pressures, taking corrective action • *Resource allocator*: distributing limited resources where they will be most effective • *Negotiator*: resolving conflicts and securing favourable outcomes in matters involving others

3.5 In terms of roles (the 'hats' they wear as tasks are performed), procurement leaders may be: figureheads (at a CIPS conference, say); leaders (directing the Procurement and Supply department); liaisons (at cross-functional management or quality meetings); information handlers (analysing supply market risks and costs, and managing procurement information systems); entrepreneurs (initiating new quality initiatives, perhaps); disturbance handlers (responding to unforeseen supply problems or team conflicts); resource allocators (selecting suppliers, empowering teams); and negotiators (not just on price, but to get procurement policy approved by senior management, say).

3.6 Mullins *(Management & Organisational Behaviour)* cites a summary of 14 functions of the leader.

- Executive
- Planner
- Policy-maker
- Source of expertise
- External group representative
- Controller of internal relations
- Purveyor of rewards and punishment
- Arbitrator and mediator
- Exemplar or role model
- Symbol of the group
- Substitute for individual responsibility
- Ideologist (source of values and standards)
- Ideal parent figure (focus of positive emotions)
- Scapegoat (focus of blame)

What positions are leaders in?

3.7 As the distinction between management and leadership has become blurred (in part by the more fashionable perception of 'leadership'), leadership 'roles' may be associated with particular positions in a team or organisation. We will look at some of the roles in which leadership may be exercised in a procurement and supply context, for example, in the next section.

3.8 However, it is an important aspect of leadership theory to recognise that leadership functions (what leaders do) and attributes (how leaders operate) can be exercised by individuals at *any level* of the organisation, in any formal role, job or position.

4 Leadership in procurement and supply

Leadership roles or positions in procurement and supply

4.1 Any member of a procurement team may exercise leadership functions, or display leadership attributes, in the ways described by Kotter or Mullins. However, there will probably be **designated leadership roles** in the procurement and supply chain function. These will vary, according to the size and type of organisation, and the status and role of procurement within it (and you will need to bear this in mind when tackling exam case studies...). You may be able to think of specific examples from your own experience. However, typical leadership roles include the following.

4.2 At the strategic level, the procurement director (or Chief Procurement Officer or Head of Procurement) will have a role in determining the strategic approach of the function: providing strategic leadership through policy formulation, and creating the direction, culture and values of procurement and supply chain management in the organisation. Increasingly, he will also have input to the strategic management of the organisation as a whole, through procurement and supply chain management's potential to add value via such concerns as strategic supply chain development, structural change (through outsourcing or offshoring), make-or-buy and pricing decisions, quality, innovation, corporate social responsibility, sustainability and so on.

4.3 At the business level, there may be a Senior Procurement Manager leading a team of Procurement Managers (or a cross-functional Procurement Council), working within the strategic framework laid down by the Head of Procurement. This group will be responsible for broad decisions on market evaluation, sourcing, appraisal and selection of suppliers, negotiations with suppliers, award of contracts and so on. In large organisations, there may also be a Procurement Leadership Team (PLT), comprised of the Head of Procurement and senior procurement managers, which meets regularly to ensure the 'flow down' of strategic vision, and alignment of all procurement plans and processes.

4.4 At the day-to-day operational level, different areas of purchasing activity may be led by a Contracts Manager, Supplier Manager or Project Managers, with responsibility for contract management; monitoring and controlling purchasing activity; liaising with other departments; leading teams in the procurement and supply chain function; and so on.

Leadership focus in procurement and supply

4.5 Procurement has traditionally been seen as a 'managerial' (or administrative) function, concerned with the planning and control of resources. However, the focus of *leadership* in procurement and supply, particularly at the business and strategic levels, will be on areas such as these.

- Formulating procurement, supply chain and sourcing strategy and aligning it with corporate strategy
- Integrating procurement activity within the organisation (and, increasingly, the wider supply chain)
- Network leadership: drawing together and giving direction to multi-functional and multi-organisational 'teams' (including supply chains); creating and managing partnerships (discussed in Chapter 4)
- Securing internal and external stakeholder buy-in to procurement plans, initiatives and projects (discussed in Chapter 5)
- Establishing and applying meaningful key performance indicators for procurement and supply chain activity: measuring, benchmarking and promoting procurement performance (discussed in Chapter 6)
- Ethical leadership, via procurement's input to environmental and social sustainability and corporate social responsibility goals

4.6 We will look at leadership within the wider supply chain in Chapters 4 and 5, but it is worth re-emphasising immediately that a procurement and supply chain professional may have to exercise leadership not just within the procurement function *and* in cross-functional team or project structures *within* the organisation – but across organisational boundaries. A procurement manager may have a central role in shaping the direction, values, relationships and motivation of teams and organisations throughout the supply chain.

Strategic leadership

4.7 Johnson, Scholes and Whittington *(Exploring Corporate Strategy)* describe a range of approaches to strategic leadership: that is, how senior leaders (such as chief executives or procurement directors) manage higher-level strategy and change in the organisation. Leaders may focus on:

- Their strategic role (the strategy approach). Leaders take personal responsibility for articulating mission, scanning the environment and formulating strategic plans. Day-to-day operations are delegated to other managers.
- Developing people (the human assets approach) who can add value, take responsibility for managing the corporate strategy 'locally', and interface with the market and other stakeholders. Strategy development can then be devolved to empowered local managers.
- Developing 'core competencies' in the organisation (the expertise approach). Leaders cultivate distinctive expertise through planned employee development and supporting systems and procedures: other managers are then expected to utilise competencies for maximum advantage.
- Controlling organisational performance, ensuring efficiency of processes and predictability of outputs (the control approach). Leaders develop and communicate procedures, performance measures and controls, and monitor performance against them: other managers secure stable performance within the plans and controls.
- Their role as change champions or drivers (the change approach), taking personal responsibility for initiating and championing continual cultural and strategic change: the role of other managers is to act as supportive change agents.

Supply chain leadership

4.8 One of the key functions of leaders in procurement and supply is to lead (as well as manage) the supply chain.

- Motivating and inspiring supply chain partners to offer above-compliance levels of service, innovation, support and value addition
- Utilising motivational and relationship-maintaining influencing approaches (eg contract incentives, gain sharing, role modelling, supplier development) to change perceptions, attitudes and behaviours, where required to correct problems or shortfalls in performance or conduct
- Mobilising and developing resources and capabilities within the supply chain (eg through supplier forums, best practice sharing, innovation and quality circles, benchmarking, supplier development, best practice sharing and knowledge management) in support of development and improvement: continuous value addition, waste and cost reduction, process or performance improvement and/or supply innovation
- Introducing changes (to contracts, relationships, processes and systems) in a constructive, supportive, relationship-maintaining and – where possible – collaborative manner: maximising the acceptability and quality of change plans
- Facilitating collaboration and alliance-building between stakeholders in the supply network, in support of improvement and development: emphasising shared goals and mutual benefit; resolving potentially divergent or conflicting interests; encouraging best practice and ideas sharing; and so on
- Leading by example in desired standards of conduct and performance (such as ethical trading or corporate social responsibility policy)
- Utilising influence (including market power, incentives and rewards) to encourage the raising of

standards in the supply chain (especially in regard to minimum acceptable labour and environmental standards in globalised supply chains).

Industry and market leadership

4.9 It is also worth noting that a buying organisation may seek to exercise leadership within its sector, industry or market, both:

- To secure competitive advantage through being 'best in class' in some core competence or success factor. A firm may, for example, seek cost, quality or innovation leadership in its market, or seek to position its corporate brand on ethical leadership (such as The Body Shop or Marks and Spencer).
- To influence other industry or market players, in order to raise overall standards. A firm may, for example, seek to drive alliance-building or technology transfer, in order to improve quality, capacity or innovation in an industry. Or it may seek to act as a champion and role model for corporate social responsibility or sustainable procurement, in order to raise minimum labour, ethical and environmental standards. This is 'leadership' in the sense addressed by this syllabus: the exercise of influence on others to change attitudes and behaviours in desired directions.

Leadership focus in the public and private sectors

4.10 In earlier studies you will have met the differences between procurement objectives, policies and practices in public and private sector organisations. Is there a difference in the kind of leadership exercised? Gino Franco *(Leading and Influencing in Purchasing,* 2006) cites the following key competencies highlighted as crucial in leading public sector organisations.

- Vision for the community and strategy
- Change management
- Motivation
- Innovation and creativity
- Alliance building.

4.11 You should be able to see that each of these competencies is equally applicable to private sector organisations – although you may want to substitute 'business' for 'community' as the prime focus of the private-sector leader's vision. (Even then, it is worth noting that, just as the public sector is being encouraged to adopt commercial disciplines for efficiency and competitive service quality, so the private sector is being encouraged to adopt a greater social responsibility...)

Chapter summary

- Management is the process through which efforts of members of the organisation are co-ordinated, directed and guided towards the achievement of organisational goals'. Leadership is a relationship through which one person influences the behaviour or actions of other people.
- Management is about order and stability and controlling resources; based on positional authority; aimed at securing compliance. Leadership is about change, creating vision; based on interpersonal influence; and aimed at securing commitment. Leadership is 'where we are going': management is 'how we get there'.
- One model for looking at the management and leadership situation is the 7S model: Strategy, Structure, Systems (hard aspects) and Style, Staff, Skills and Shared goals (soft aspects).
- Leadership is important because it specifically addresses key differentiating and success factors for modern business: the need for commitment (rather than compliance); support for change and innovation (rather than the *status quo*); the contribution and development of people (rather than processes); the leverage of horizontal structures for process flow, co-ordination and collaboration (rather than vertical 'silos'); and the creation of positive, adaptive organisation cultures (rather than purely formal aspects of organisation).
- Any individual can exercise leadership functions in a team or informal influencing situation, but designated leadership roles in procurement include the procurement director, procurement managers, procurement council, procurement leadership team (PLT) and project team leaders (PTLs).
- In addition to team and functional leadership, leadership can be exercised at a strategic level, at the level of the supply chain, and at the level of an industry or market.

Self-test questions

Numbers in brackets refer to the paragraphs where you can check your answers.

1   Define leadership. (1.3)

2   Summarise attempts to distinguish between leadership and management. (1.6–1.9)

3   List the seven elements in the McKinsey 7S framework. (1.17)

4   In what respects does leadership 'offer an added extra dimension to management'? (2.2)

5   Why do modern, horizontal organisational structures place a premium on leadership? (2.10)

6   What are the purposes of organisational value statements? (2.17)

7   List the managerial roles identified by Mintzberg. (Table 1.2)

8   According to Mullins, what are the 14 functions of a leader? (3.6)

9   What specific areas within procurement and supply will leadership need to focus on? (4.5)

10   What leadership tasks are involved in leading the wider supply chain? (4.8)

CHAPTER 2

Leadership Theories and Models

Assessment criteria and indicative content

1.2 Critically analyse the main approaches to leadership for improving procurement and supply chain management

- The qualities or traits approach to leadership
- The functional or group approach, including action-centred leadership
- Styles of leadership including the authoritarian or autocratic, democratic and *laissez-faire* styles
- Contingency theories for leadership such as path-goal theory

1.3 Evaluate the main skills and behaviours that contribute to effective leadership for improving procurement and supply chain management

- The continuum of leadership behaviour
- The main forces in deciding the type of leadership
- Situational leadership
- Transformational and inspirational leadership

2.2 Evaluate the main leadership techniques that can be used to influence personnel involved in a supply chain

- Assessing the readiness of followers or groups
- Leaders' attitudes to people

Section headings

1   The trait approach
2   The functional (or group) approach
3   Leadership styles
4   Contingency models
5   Situational leadership
6   Transformational and inspirational leadership

Introduction

In the previous chapter we gave a broad introductory overview of the concept of leadership, and values and behaviours associated with the exercise of leadership. Here, we explore some of the different theoretical perspectives on leadership, in the form of theories of leadership (what leadership is and how it 'works') and models (how to 'do' leadership effectively).

We survey in turn the main strands of thinking on leadership: trait theory; the functional (or group) approach; behavioural (leadership style) theory; and contingency theory. We then look at two influential contemporary models: situational leadership, and transformational leadership.

1   The trait approach

1.1   Traits are attributes or qualities in an individual's personality which create a tendency to behave in certain ways. If we say that someone is 'decisive', for example, we are identifying a personality trait which will make them respond to situations in a relatively predictable way.

1.2   Early leadership theorists suggested that the best way to study leadership was to analyse the personalities of successful leaders, identify their common personality characteristics (or traits) and thus formulate a list of 'leadership traits'. Trait theories of leadership thus seek to identify the personality characteristics or qualities which correlate with successful leadership.

1.3   This reflects a view, widely held at one time, that the great events of history are set in motion by 'great' individuals. They are leaders because of some unique and inherent set of traits that set them apart from normal people. In other words, leaders are 'born, not made': you either have the power to make others follow you, or you don't.

1.4   Various attempts have been made to determine exactly which traits are essential in a leader. A survey of American studies by RM Stogdill ('Personal factors associated with leadership', in *Journal of Psychology*, 1948) includes the following qualities.

- Adaptability to situations
- Decisiveness
- Persistence
- Alertness to social environment
- Dependability
- Self-confidence
- Ambition and achievement orientation
- Dominance (willingness to influence others)
- Willingness to assume responsibility
- Assertive communication
- Tolerance of stress
- Co-operation
- Energy

1.5   The psychologist Edwin Ghiselli suggested that the following six traits are sufficient to characterise effective leadership.

- Supervisory ability
- Occupational achievement
- Intelligence
- Self-actualisation need
- Self-assurance need
- Decisiveness

Evaluating the trait approach

1.6   You may have noticed already that there are certain problems with trait theory!

- It does not take account of the individuality of subordinates, or other factors in the complex leadership situation.
- A hundred years of research have failed to produce a consistent set of qualities that can be used to distinguish meaningfully between leaders and non-leaders.
- The trait approach does not help organisations to make better team leaders (since 'leadership' is innate, and cannot be created, learned or developed): it merely allows them (in theory) to recognise a leader when they see one.

1.7 Trait analysis has remained useful for management **selection**, as a way of expressing the qualities that while not *sufficient*, may at least be *essential* for effective leadership: some mix of the drive to influence and achieve, intelligence and social competence.

2 The functional (or group) approach

2.1 The functional approach to leadership focuses on the role, functions and responsibilities of the leader: in other words, the *content* of leadership, or what the leader actually *does* to create effective performance in a practical context.

2.2 Unlike the trait approach, the functional approach is helpful in drawing attention to:

- The **leadership context**: that is, the task, individual 'followers' and the dynamics of the work group, in relation to which leadership functions are exercised
- The potential for **leadership development** – since leadership functions can be learned and developed as skills and competencies
- The potential for **devolved leadership** – since any individual, regardless of formal position or job role, can develop and exercise leadership functions in a team or supply chain.

2.3 In these kinds of models, leadership is defined by the **functions carried out** (what do leaders *do?*) – not by the attributes or type of person, or by a person's position, title or authority in a group or organisation. Any or all members of a team may, in this sense, exercise leadership if they perform one of these functions within the team.

Action-centred leadership

2.4 UK management and leadership guru John Adair *(Action-Centred Leadership,* 1979) developed a functional model called 'action-centred' leadership, to describe the roles and tasks of leadership in terms of what individual leaders actually *do*.

2.5 Adair argued that the common perception of leadership as 'decision-making' was inadequate to describe the range of action required by the complex situations in which a manager may find himself. He saw the leadership process in a context made up of three basic objectives.

- The achievement of the **task**: defining the task; planning the work; allocating resources; organising duties and responsibilities; controlling performance; and reviewing progress
- The development and satisfaction of **individual group members:** meeting needs; giving praise and status; resolving problems; and training and developing individuals
- The building and maintenance of an effectively functioning **group:** maintaining morale; building team cohesiveness; maintaining discipline; team communication; team training; and developing sub-leaders

2.6 These needs must be examined in the light of the whole situation, which dictates the relative priority that must be given to each of the three sets of needs. Effective leadership is identifying and acting on that priority, and exercising (or mobilising in other group members) a relevant cluster of roles to meet the various needs: Figure 2.1.

Figure 2.1 *Adair's action-centred leadership model*

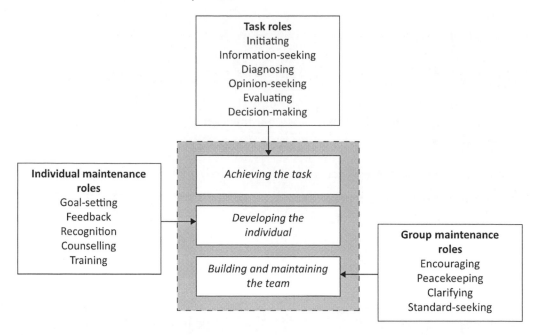

2.7 Our diagram shows that the three sets of needs are interrelated. Success in the task, for example, creates a 'win' mentality which draws the team closer together – and gives satisfaction to the contributing individuals. A team which develops its individuals' skills increases its likelihood of task success *and* team cohesion and satisfaction. A lack of individual growth *or* team cohesion *or* processes which facilitate task success will also impact on the other areas.

2.8 'In any effective work group, the most effective leader is the person who sees that the task needs, the needs of the group and those of the individual are all adequately met. The effective leader elicits the contribution of members of the group and draws out other leadership from the group to satisfy the three interrelated areas of need.' (Mullins)

2.9 In order to meet the three areas of need, certain leadership functions or 'activities' must be performed. Adair developed a scheme of leadership training based on precept and practice in each of eight leadership activities (each of which are applied to task, team and individual needs).

- **Defining the task**: setting out what needs to be done and achieved
- **Planning**: setting goals, standards, targets and schedules
- **Briefing:** sharing goals, instructions and information relevant to the task
- **Controlling:** monitoring and adjusting performance against standards and targets
- **Evaluating:** appraising the efficiency and effectiveness of performance
- **Motivating:** securing and maintaining team member commitment to goals
- **Organising**: allocating tasks, authority and resources
- **Setting an example**: modelling desired behaviours and values.

The challenge-focused approach

2.10 Pedler, Burgoyne and Boydell *(A Manager's Guide to Leadership,* 2004) propose an alternative model, based on their re-definition of leadership as a **collective function** focused on mobilising the resources needed to meet continual personal and organisational challenges. 'Leadership is a doing thing; a performance art. It is not defined by any set of personal qualities or competencies, but by what we actually do when faced with challenging situations.... Leadership is principally concerned with recognising, mobilising and taking action in the face of critical problems and issues.'

2.11 Their three-domain model of leadership reflects the complexity of leadership issues.

- **Challenges** are the critical tasks, problems and issues for the organisation, which must be recognised and against which resources must be mobilised and action taken. They require leadership, making demands on all the people involved in the situation.
- **Characteristics** are the qualities, competencies and skills that individuals can bring to bear on the challenge situation.
- **Context** is the immediate conditions operating in the challenge situation. 'Leadership is always situated: always done here, with these particular people...: what works here and now may not work in another place and at another time.'

2.12 Like Adair's action-centred model, this is a model for developing effectiveness in certain core practices (or leadership practice capabilities) which can be used in combination to meet challenges (some of the typical issues facing modern organisations): Table 2.1.

Table 2.1 *The challenges approach to leadership*

7 CORE PRACTICES	14 KEY CHALLENGES
'Leading yourself': learning and developing leadership practices	Developing direction and strategy
	Creating a 'learning organisation', which is capable of continuous change and learning
'On purpose': having a sense of purpose, defining goals and aims	New, flexible and continually-changing organisational structures
	Working effectively with complex, self-managing and 'virtual' teams
'Power': using power to get things done with, over and through other people	Creating and maintaining cultures of innovation and creativity
	Fostering diversity and inclusion: using and working with different kinds of people and involving a range of stakeholders
'Living with risk': taking difficult decisions on the basis of incomplete information	Promoting collaborative, negotiated partnerships between individuals, groups and organisations (eg in a supply chain).
	Improving the quality and efficiency of work processes throughout the value chain
'Challenging questions': querying existing beliefs and practices, to develop creativity and learning	Streamlining: managing organisational contraction (eg project closure or outsourcing) and its effects on people and resources
	Encouraging social responsibility: pursuing ethical business practices and managing social and environmental impacts
'Facilitation': enabling or empowering individuals to act and learn for themselves, especially in groups or teams	Mobilising knowledge, via both technical and social information systems
	Leading in networks: working via influence, negotiation and diplomacy
'Networking': cultivating informal relationships for information and influence	Managing mergers for added value: integrating separate organisations and projects, both logistically and socially
	Making major change

3 Leadership styles

Behavioural models of leadership

3.1 Leadership theory has begun to revisit the idea of leadership traits or qualities, in a more helpful way, by examining the behaviours and values that contribute to effective leadership dynamics. Unlike 'traits', behaviours and values can be learned, developed and flexibly deployed according to the needs and priorities of the leadership situation. In other words, instead of asking 'What are effective leaders like?', behavioural models ask: 'What do effective leaders *do*?' How do they act and speak and think? (And how can we develop and use those behaviours to become more effective leaders ourselves?) We introduced some leadership behaviours in Chapter 1.

3.2 One of the major strands of behavioural theory is the idea of **leadership style**. Leadership styles are more or less consistent clusters of behaviour, or distinctive ways of behaving that may reflect: (a) a particular purpose or preference on the part of the leader, and (b) the appropriate behaviour in the particular context or situation of leadership. Leadership style may be defined (Mullins) as: 'the way in which the functions of leadership are carried out; the way in which the manager typically behaves towards members of the group'.

3.3 It should be obvious to you from your own experience that not all managers or leaders operate in the same manner. It is possible to identify a wide variety of behaviour patterns which different leaders use more or less consistently as their preferred approach or style. Many attempts have been made both to classify styles and to identify which is the most effective style for a manager to adopt. Leadership style models are usually based on observed real-life leadership practices.

3.4 Some of these models have attempted to suggest that there are **effective and ineffective leadership styles**: that team members prefer some styles to others, and that teams work better under some styles than others. A manager who naturally uses one style should therefore attempt to develop the skills to use a more effective style.

3.5 Other models, however, have reflected the growing realisation that a **range of different styles** might be appropriate – depending on the leadership context: the 'right' style is the one that will work best for a particular task, team and situation. Gillen *(Leadership Skills for Boosting Performance, 2002)* suggests that: 'Using only one leadership style is a bit like a stopped clock: it will be right twice a day, but the rest of the time it will be inaccurate to varying degrees. Leaders need to interact with their team in different ways in different situations. This is what we mean by "leadership style".' We will look at some of the key style models here.

Two-dimensional style models

3.6 In the late 1940s, the Ohio State Leadership Studies asked people to analyse and comment on the behaviour of their superiors in work organisations. From their results (Edwin A Fleishman *et al*, 'The description of supervisory behaviour', in *Journal of Applied Psychology),* it was easy to identify two major dimensions of leadership.

- **Initiating structure** – the concern with organising the work to be done, the definition of roles and the ways of getting jobs done.
- **Consideration** – the concern with the social organisation of the group, maintaining good relations and giving opportunities for group involvement and participation.

3.7 This distinction is more commonly referred to today as the difference between a **task-centred** approach and a **people-centred** approach. This dichotomy has been very influential in suggesting two-dimensional models of leadership behaviour, such as Robert R Blake and Jane Mouton's managerial grid (concern for people, concern for production), Douglas McGregor's Theory X and Theory Y, and the classification of 'directive' and 'facilitative' behaviours.

Directive and facilitative leadership behaviour

3.8 **Directive behaviours** (or leadership styles) are based on letting subordinates know clearly what the leader expects from them (targets and standards); giving specific guidance and instructions; asking subordinates to follow rules and procedures; scheduling and co-ordinating the work; and monitoring and controlling performance against specific criteria.

3.9 A directive style may be effective when subordinates do not share the leader's objectives, or lack ability or confidence; when time is short and results critical; and when subordinates are willing to accept top-down authority.

3.10 **Facilitative behaviours** (or participative or supportive behaviours) are based on giving team members the opportunity to take responsibility and initiative: jointly agreeing objectives and standards; delegating responsibility to the team for day-to-day planning and organisation, monitoring and control; being available as a resource for guidance, information and mediation if required; acting as a champion on behalf of the team (accessing information, resources, contacts and influence on its behalf); and performing the role of 'critical friend' to provide constructive and challenging feedback for individual and team development.

3.11 A facilitative style may be effective where subordinates are willing, able and confident enough to participate in decision making; where subordinate input to (and acceptance of) decisions is important; and where the task or problem is relatively unstructured.

The managerial (or leadership) grid

3.12 The most popular two-dimensional behaviour model is perhaps the **managerial (or leadership) grid**, developed by Blake and Mouton in the US (Blake & Mouton, *The Managerial Grid,* 1964). Managers are classified on the grid in terms of their concern for people (measured along the vertical axis) and their concern for production (measured along the horizontal axis): Figure 2.2

Figure 2.2 *Blake and Mouton's leadership grid*

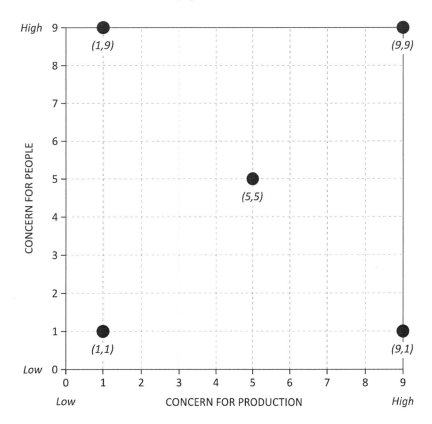

3.13 Table 2.2 picks out some of the defining positions on the grid and explains the main characteristics of each.

Table 2.2 *Key positions on Blake and Mouton's grid*

(1, 1)	*'Impoverished'* The manager exerts (and expects) minimal effort or concern for either staff satisfaction or work targets
(1, 9)	*'Country club'* The manager is attentive to staff needs and has developed satisfying relationships and work culture – but with little attention to results
(9, 1)	*'Task management'* The manager concentrates almost exclusively on achieving results. People's needs are virtually ignored, and work is organised so that human elements interfere to a minimal extent
(9, 9)	*'Team'* The manager achieves high work performance through 'leading' committed people who identify themselves with organisational goals
(5, 5)	*'Middle of the road'* (or *'dampened pendulum'*) A manager achieves adequate performance through balancing the necessity to get work done with maintaining a satisfactory level of team morale. (Alternatively, the manager scores an average of 5, 5 as a result of swinging from one extreme to another!)

3.14 The grid was intended as a tool for management appraisal and development. It recognises that leadership requires a balance between concern for the task and concern for people, and that there is no necessary correlation (positive or negative) between the two. However, it assumes that high concern for both is possible at the same time – and that this is the most effective style of management.

3.15 The grid thus offers a simple and easy-to-use diagnostic tool. It shows where the behaviour and assumptions of a manager may exhibit a lack of balance between the two dimensions and/or an unsuitably low concern in either dimension (or both). This can be used to demonstrate how team leaders might modify their own management style in terms of concern for people and concern for production to become more effective personally, and to develop the synergy inherent in their teams.

3.16 However, critics of the grid complain that it inevitably oversimplifies the leadership role and situation. The grid only has two dimensions: other factors, such as culture, technology, team members, the nature of the task and so on, are not directly considered. Extreme scores may appear polarised and lead to value judgements about individual managers, but they are not a comprehensive description of performance, only a thumbnail sketch of a preferred style of operating.

3.17 The model also assumes that (9, 9) is the optimum style – but in some managerial contexts, this may not be so. A manager may find that a (9, 1) approach, for example, is effective in situations of crisis where survival is at stake, or urgent corrective action must be taken to get a project back on track.

Autocratic, democratic, *laissez-faire*

3.18 Lewin, Lippett & White (1939) identified three basic leadership styles in use in commerce and industry – and while there are many style models, these may still be a useful way of classifying and describing broad types of style.

- **Authoritarian** (or autocratic) style: power and authority for planning, organising and decision making are centralised in the hands of the leader, and all communication and interactions focus on or through him. The expectation of subordinates is simply compliance or obedience.
- **Democratic style**: decision-making is decentralised, shared by team members via participative processes, and there is greater group interaction. Leadership functions are distributed among group members: the manager or designated leader may take on a more facilitative role as part of the team.
- ***Laissez-faire*** ('let them do it') **style**: the team is genuinely autonomous, organising its own work and making decisions (within defined boundaries, such as task objectives, budget spending limits and organisational policies, say). The manager adopts a coaching role within the team: deliberately

supporting freedom of action – while being available to help if needed. Note that this is *not* the same as an 'impoverished' manager who just abdicates responsibility. A *laissez-faire* style is appropriate where the group is genuinely performing well without intervention.

3.19 Other studies and models have identified different style classifications: you may have come across other labels and definitions in your reading. However, style models are often talking about more or less the same things: a range of behaviours on a continuum between completely task-focused, directive behaviours at one end, and completely people-focused, supportive behaviours at the other end. (We'll look at a continuum model a bit later.)

Tells, sells, consults, joins

3.20 The research unit at Ashridge Management College carried out studies in UK industry and identified four styles, which are summarised in Table 2.3.

Table 2.3 *Tells, sells, consults, joins*

STYLE	STRENGTHS	WEAKNESSES
Tells (autocratic) The leader makes decisions and issues instructions which must be obeyed without question	• Quick decisions can be made when required • The most efficient type of leadership for highly-programmed work • May be acceptable in authoritarian cultures	• Communications are one-way, neglecting feedback and potential for upward communication or team input • Does not encourage initiative or commitment from subordinates: merely compliance
Sells (persuasive) The leader still makes decisions, but believes that team members must be motivated to accept them in order to carry them out properly	• Team members understand the reason for decisions • Team members may be more committed • Team members may be able to function slightly better in the absence of instruction	• Communications are still largely one-way • Team members are not necessarily motivated to accept the decision • Still doesn't encourage initiative or commitment
Consults (participative) The leader confers with team members and takes their views into account, although he retains the final say	• Encourages motivation through greater interest and involvement • Enhances the acceptability of the decision to team members • Decision quality may benefit from implementer input • Encourages upward communication	• May take longer to reach decisions (especially if consensus is sought) • Team input may not enhance the quality of the decision • Consultation can be a façade for a basic 'sells' style
Joins (democratic) Leader and team members make the decision together on the basis of consensus	• Fosters motivation and commitment • Empowers team members to take the initiative (eg in responding flexibly and swiftly to customer demands, problems) • Plus strengths of 'consults' style	• May undermine the leader's authority when tough decisions have to be taken • Further lengthens the decision-making process • May cause 'political' decisions

3.21 The Ashridge studies showed a clear preference amongst subordinates for the 'consults' style of leadership – although managers were most commonly perceived to be exercising a 'tells' or 'sells' style. Team members also had more positive attitudes to their work under leaders who were perceived to be exercising a 'consults' style. The least favourable attitudes to work, however, were not found among team members under a 'tells' style, but among those who were unable to perceive a consistent style in their leader. In other words, subordinates are unsettled by a boss who chops and changes between different styles.

A continuum of leadership behaviours

3.22 Tannenbaum and Schmidt's continuum of leadership behaviours ('How to choose a leadership pattern', in *Harvard Business Review,* 1973) is a useful reminder that managers do not adopt extreme either/or styles, but select from a wide repertoire of behaviours: Figure 2.3.

Figure 2.3 *Tannenbaum and Schmidt: a continuum of leadership style*

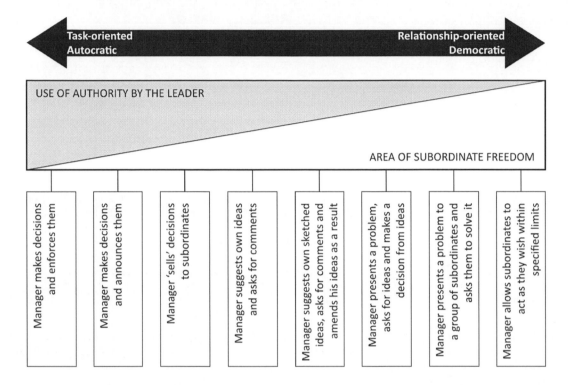

3.23 These behaviours could be classified as four leadership styles. Tannenbaum and Schmidt named their styles as follows.

- **Telling:** the leader makes a decision and communicates it to subordinates, expecting them to implement it.
- **Selling:** the leader makes a decision, but then – recognising the potential for resistance (or the benefits of commitment) – persuades subordinates to accept it
- **Consulting**: the leader presents a problem to the group, and takes their input into account when making the decision
- **Coaching:** the leader defines the problem, offers guidelines and identifies constraints – and then facilitates group decision-making.

3.24 Tannenbaum and Schmidt suggested that the most appropriate (feasible and desirable) leadership style in a given situation would be dictated by three sets of factors or 'forces'.

- **Forces in the manager**: the manager's values and personality preferences (eg in regard to direction or participation); his trust and confidence in the team and its capabilities; and his sense of security and confidence in the situation
- **Forces in the subordinate(s)**: individuals' commitment to the goals of the team and organisation; interest and motivation in regard to the problem; knowledge and experience to contribute to the problem; competence; readiness to assume responsibility; desire for independence; and tolerance for ambiguity and lack of direction. The greater the measure of these attributes in a team, the greater freedom the team will (a) expect and (b) be able to handle.
- **Forces in the situation**: the organisation and management culture of the firm; the effectiveness and capability of the group; the nature of the problem or task; pressures of time (including urgency and

crisis); and other environmental influences (such as increasing employee expectations of discretion and empowerment).

3.25 Effective leaders need to be both perceptive and behaviourally flexible: maintaining a constant awareness of the forces that are most relevant to their leadership at any given time, and able to adapt their behaviour accordingly, 'up and down' the continuum.

3.26 Here are some advantages of a continuum-based view of leadership (emphasising the range of behaviours available).

- Encouraging leaders to be behaviourally flexible, with a range of options according to the situation
- Giving leaders clear decision criteria for the selection of autocratic or democratic styles (three forces, time constraints)
- Supporting employee development and empowerment, given time and opportunity

3.27 The limitations of the continuum are as follows.

- It is still, essentially, a two-dimensional model of leadership (based on leader authority vs subordinate autonomy), and therefore simplifies complex dynamics.
- It only addresses the initial step of assigning tasks to subordinates – without considering how subsequent processes of supervision, control and resourcing may determine the effectiveness of delegation.
- It assumes that managers have sufficient information to determine the most appropriate point on the continuum for a given team or situation.

Leaders' attitudes to people

3.28 A number of classic models propose that the style of leadership chosen by a manager depends, among other things, on the **assumptions** he makes about other people – and what will make them perform effectively. Perhaps the most influential of these models is that of Douglas McGregor: Theory X and Theory Y.

3.29 McGregor *(The Human Side of Enterprise,* 1960) argued that 'every managerial act rests on assumptions, generalisations and hypotheses', whether managers realise it or not. McGregor proposed two extreme sets of assumptions that managers might have about workers, human nature and behaviour. Note that these are *not* descriptions of 'types' of people, but sets of assumptions *about* people.

3.30 **Theory X** asserts that the average human being has an inherent dislike of work and will avoid it if he can. People must therefore be coerced, controlled, directed and/or bribed or threatened with punishment in order to get them to expend adequate effort towards the achievement of organisational goals. This is quite acceptable to the worker, who prefers to be directed, wishes to avoid responsibility, has relatively little ambition and wants security above all.

3.31 **Theory Y** asserts that the expenditure of physical and mental effort in work is as natural as play or rest. The average human being does not inherently dislike work, which can be a source of satisfaction. People can exercise self-direction and self-control to achieve objectives to which they are committed. Commitment to objectives is a result of the rewards associated with achievement: satisfaction of people's self-actualisation needs. The average human being learns, under proper conditions, not only to accept but to seek responsibility. There is widespread capacity to exercise a relatively high degree of imagination, ingenuity and creativity in the solution of organisational problems.

3.32 McGregor's point is that Theory X and Theory Y assumptions are, in essence, self-fulfilling prophecies.

- If employees are treated as if Theory X were true (using carrot-and-stick motivation systems, detailed rules and close supervision, low-discretion jobs and so on: essentially, an authoritarian leadership style) they will begin to behave accordingly. It is negative experience at work that fosters lack of ambition, the need for security and intellectual stagnation.

- If employees are treated as if Theory Y were true (using empowered teamworking, employee involvement schemes and facilitative or democratic leadership styles) they will begin to behave accordingly and rise to the challenge.

Evaluating style theories

3.33 The style approach to leadership has provided useful insights into the nature and processes of leadership. It has usefully stressed the value of democratic and participative leadership and, in identifying styles, it has helped in the perception of leadership as a range of choices open to the manager – rather than one limited and universal set of behaviours.

3.34 However, the approach is also subject to certain criticisms. Despite a level of agreement between different researchers, there are confusions as to style definitions. It has also been argued that the style approach does not consider all the variables that contribute to the operation of effective leadership. In particular:

- The manager's personality (or acting ability) may simply not be flexible enough to utilise style approaches effectively.
- The demands of the task, technology, organisation culture and other managers constrain the leader in the range of styles effectively open to him. (If the leader's own boss practises an authoritarian style, and the team are incompetent and require close supervision, no amount of theorising on the desirability of participative management will make it possible).
- Consistency is important to subordinates. If a manager adopts a style suitable to the changing situation, subordinates may simply perceive him to be fickle, or may suffer insecurity and stress.

3.35 Huczynski and Buchanan *(Organisational Behaviour: An Introduction,* 2001) note that 'There is therefore no simple recipe which the individual manager can use to decide which style to adopt to be most effective. Management style probably can be changed, but only if management values can be changed....'

3.36 It is the consideration of this wider set of variables that has led to the development of contingency or situational approaches to leadership.

4 Contingency models

4.1 Tannenbaum & Schmidt's continuum model introduced a 'situational' approach, arguing that a number of factors in the leadership context influence managerial behaviour – or *should* influence it.

4.2 Contingency leadership models similarly see effective leadership as being dependent on a number of variable or contingent factors. There is no 'one right way' to lead that will fit all situations; no 'one-size-fits all' model. Rather, in order to be effective, it is necessary to lead in a manner that is **appropriate to the dynamics of a particular situation**.

4.3 The four major contingency theories are based on the selection and deployment of leadership behaviours according to:

- The favourability of the leadership situation (Fiedler's contingency model)
- The importance of the quality and/or acceptability of a leader's decisions in a given situation (the Vroom-Yetton model)
- The motivation process of the team (House's path-goal theory)
- The readiness or maturity of the followers (Paul Hersey and Ken Blanchard's situational leadership model) – which will be considered separately in the next section of the chapter.

Fiedler's contingency model

4.4 FE Fiedler studied the relationship between style of leadership and the effectiveness of the work group, and formulated a two-dimensional model of leadership styles.

- **Psychologically distant managers** (PDMs) maintain distance from their subordinates by formalising roles and relationships with the team; being withdrawn and reserved in their interpersonal relationships; and preferring formal communication and consultation methods rather than informal opinion-seeking. PDMs judge subordinates on the basis of performance and are primarily task-oriented. Fiedler found that leaders of the most effective work groups actually tend to be PDMs.
- **Psychologically close managers** (PCMs) do not seek to formalise roles and relationships, and prefer informal contacts to regular formal meetings. They are more concerned to maintain good human relationships at work than to ensure that tasks are carried out effectively.

4.5 Fiedler (*A Theory of Leadership Effectiveness, 1967)* went on to develop a contingency theory, in which he argued that the effectiveness of the work group depended on the leadership situation, made up of three key variables.

- **Leader-member relations:** the relationship between the leader and the group (liking, trust, respect, willingness to follow and so on)
- **Task structure:** the extent to which the task is clearly defined, structured and programmed (able to be carried out to instructions or standard procedures)
- **Position power:** the power of the leader in relation to the group, and specifically the power of the leader to reward and punish the team, with organisational backing.

4.6 The situation is **favourable to the leader** when there are positive leader-member relations, a structured task, and strong position power.

4.7 Fiedler concluded that:

- A structured, task-oriented or psychologically distant leadership style works best when the situation is either *very favourable* to the leader, or *very unfavourable*
- A supportive, relational, participative or psychologically close leadership style works best when the situation is *moderately favourable* to the leader
- 'Group performance will be contingent upon the *appropriate matching* of leadership styles and the degree of favourableness of the group situation for the leader'.

The Vroom-Yetton decision-making model

4.8 Victor Vroom and Philip Yetton *(Leadership and Decision-Making,* 1973) argued that a leader's decision-making style, and the degree of participation required from the team, depend on three main factors.

- **Decision quality**: the importance of coming up with the 'right' solution, or a decision which positively impacts on team performance. Decision quality may be enhanced by involving others with valuable knowledge and information about the problem.
- **Decision acceptance (or subordinate commitment)**: the importance of team motivation and commitment to the effective implementation of the decision. Decision acceptance may be enhanced by involving team members in decision-making.
- **Time constraints**: the time available for the decision process. Longer time frames allow the 'luxury' of involvement, and using a decision as an opportunity for team building and development.

4.9 Vroom and Yetton identified five main **decision styles**: Table 2.4.

Table 2.4 *Vroom and Yetton's decision styles*

STYLE	PROCESS
Autocratic	**A1** The leader makes the decision alone, using the information he already has
	A2 The leader obtains specific information from the team, then makes the decision alone.
Consultative	**C1** The leader shares the problem with individual team members, gathers input, then makes the decision.
	C2 The leader shares the problem with the team as a group, gathers input, then makes the decision.
Collaborative/ group	**G2** The leader shares the problem with the team as a group, then facilitates a process whereby the team generates and evaluates options and works towards a consensus-based decision.

4.10 Any of the five decision styles may be effective in a given situation. Vroom and Yetton formulated seven decision rules (based on yes/no answers to questions), to help a manager select the most appropriate decision-style.

- Is the technical quality of the decision very important? (Quality requirement)
- Does a successful outcome depend on team member commitment to the decision? (Commitment requirement)
- Do you have sufficient information to be able to make the decision on your own? (Leader information requirement)
- Is the problem well-structured so that you can easily understand what needs to be addressed and what defines a good solution? (Problem structure)
- Are you reasonably sure that your team will accept your decision if you make it yourself? (Commitment probability)
- Do team members share the organisational goals which define a successful solution? (Goal congruence)
- Is there likely to be conflict among team members around preferred solutions? (Subordinate conflict).

4.11 The answers to these questions can be plotted on a decision-tree, to derive the recommended decision style: Figure 2.4 (sourced from www.mindtools.com).

Figure 2.4 *The Vroom-Yetton decision tree*

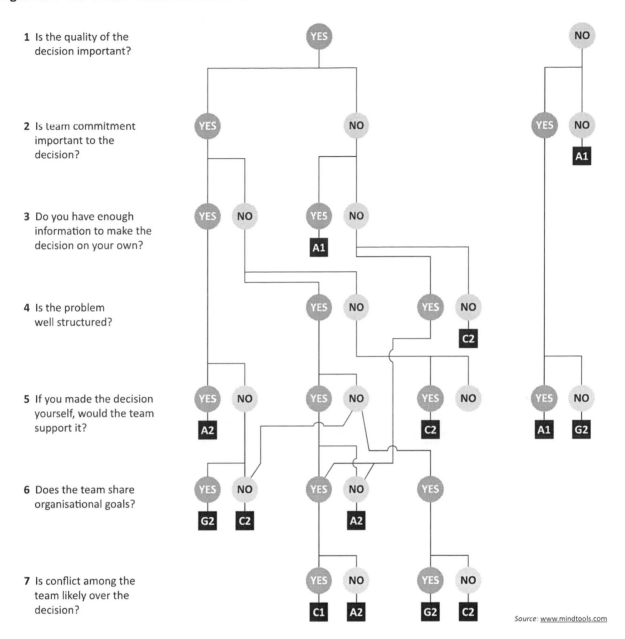

1 Is the quality of the decision important?

2 Is team commitment important to the decision?

3 Do you have enough information to make the decision on your own?

4 Is the problem well structured?

5 If you made the decision yourself, would the team support it?

6 Does the team share organisational goals?

7 Is conflict among the team likely over the decision?

Source: www.mindtools.com

4.12 In general, according to the Vroom-Yetton model:

- A **consultative or collaborative style** is most appropriate where: decision quality will be enhanced by information from others; the problem isn't clearly structured; it is important for team members to 'buy in' to the decision; and there is enough time to manage a team decision-making process

- An **autocratic** style is most efficient when: decision quality will not be enhanced by information from others; the team will accept the leader's decision; and there is little time available for consultation or collaboration.

4.13 Follow-up work by Vroom and Jago (*The New Leadership: Managing Participation in Organisations,* 1988) identified a wider range of questions: quality requirement; commitment requirement; leader information; problem structure; commitment probability; goal congruence; subordinate conflict; *plus* subordinate information; time constraints; geographical dispersion of the group; motivation time; and motivation development.

4.14 Vroom and Jago developed a set of decision-tree models, designed to guide managers through the process of choosing the most appropriate decision style for four generic type of managerial problem: individual problems with time constraints; individual problems where the manager specifically wants to develop the team member's decision-making ability; group problems with time constraints; and group problems in which the manager wishes to develop the team's decision-making abilities.

Path-goal theory

4.15 From your earlier studies you may remember that **expectancy theory** is a process theory of motivation, which basically states that the strength of an individual's motivation to do something will depend on the extent to which he expects the results of his efforts to contribute to his personal needs or goals.

4.16 For example, Victor Vroom (*Work & Motivation,* 1964) suggested that the strength of an individual's motivation is the product of:

- The strength of his preference for a certain outcome (valence)
- His expectation that the outcome will in fact result from a certain behaviour (subjective probability).

4.17 In the expectancy model, the lower the valence *or* expectation, the less the individual's motivation. An employee may have a high expectation that increased productivity will result in promotion (because of managerial promises, say), but if he is indifferent or negative towards the idea of promotion (because he dislikes responsibility), he will not be motivated to increase his productivity. The same would be true if promotion was very important to him, but he did not believe higher productivity would get him promoted (because he has been passed over before, perhaps).

4.18 Robert House ('A Path-Goal Theory of Leadership Effectiveness', *Administrative Science Quarterly,* 1971) argued that **leadership behaviour** can be a motivating influence, to the extent that it strengthens expectancy, by strengthening team members' confidence that:

- Effective performance will lead to satisfaction of their needs or goals (in the form of offered rewards)
- The direction, guidance, training and support required to achieve effective performance will be provided, and obstacles removed
- There is, therefore, a clear path towards satisfaction of their needs or goals.

4.19 House identifies four main types of leadership behaviour.

- **Directive leadership**: establishing clear goals and expectations; giving specific directions and instructions and so on.
- **Supportive leadership**: displaying concern for the needs and welfare of the team; being approachable; coaching and resourcing team members
- **Participative leadership**: consulting with team members, and incorporating their input into decisions
- **Achievement-oriented leadership**: showing confidence in team members' capability, setting challenging goals, and expecting high standards or improvement.

4.20 The most effective of these behaviours in a given context will depend on three main **situational variables**.

- The personality of the team members – including:
  - Their 'locus of control': that is, whether they prefer to be self-controlled (having an internal locus of control: suiting a participative leader) or controlled by others (having an external locus of control: suiting a directive leader)
  - Their perceptions of their own ability, and related confidence. (Individuals with high belief in their own competence are likely to resent directive leadership, whereas less confident individuals may welcome it.)
- The nature of the task: whether it is routine or non-routine, structured or non-structured, and whether task goals are clear or unclear
- The task environment: for example, whether it offers social support (in which case a supportive style of leadership may be less valued).

4.21 Leadership behaviour will be motivational to the extent that the leader:

- Helps to clarify goals and path-goal relationships: making explicit the relationship between the achievement of task goals and the rewards and outcomes team members value.
- Offers team members the degree of help and support they feel they need in order to pursue the path to their goals. If individuals lack experience or confidence, and the task is highly unstructured, the team is likely to welcome directive leadership behaviour – as more likely to help them achieve their goals through task achievement. But if the team is confident, the task structured and its goals clear, the team is likely to resent directive leadership behaviour as patronising, unnecessary and micro-managing: participative or achievement-oriented behaviour will be more motivational.

Evaluating contingency models

4.22 Contingency theory demonstrates that there is no ideal personality nor one best style for a leader. It provides a basis for developing people as leaders. By making people aware of the factors affecting the choice of leadership style and providing a basis for increased self-awareness, it gives a useful starting point for leadership training.

4.23 Contingency approaches have been the object of some criticism, however.

- The key variables of task structure, power and relationships are difficult to measure in practice and may depend more on intuition than on measurement.
- The approach may be seen as manipulative, unless handled with integrity.
- The theory ignores the need for technical competence relevant to the task.

4.24 The major difficulty for any leader seeking to apply contingency theory is actually to modify his behaviour as the situation changes, without inconsistency which may damage team member confidence and security.

5   Situational leadership

Assessing the readiness of followers

5.1 Paul Hersey and Ken Blanchard (*Management of Organisational Behaviour: Utilising Human Resources,* 1988) focus on the readiness (or maturity) of the team members to perform a given task, in terms of their task ability (experience, knowledge and skills) and willingness (whether they have the confidence, commitment and motivation) to complete the task successfully.

- Low-readiness teams (lacking ability and motivation or confidence) require more directive behaviours in order to secure an adequate level of task performance: the most appropriate leadership style may be a 'telling' style. An example might be where staff are new to the organisation or to particular technology or procedures.
- Low-moderate readiness teams (willing and confident, but lacking ability) require both directive and supportive behaviour to improve their task performance without damaging morale: the most appropriate leadership style may be a 'selling' style. An example might be more experienced members of staff taking on new responsibilities for the first time.
- High-moderate readiness teams (able, but unwilling or insecure) are competent, but require supportive behaviour to build morale: the most appropriate leadership style may be a consults or 'participating' style. An example might be a team member returning from training to apply newly-learned skills for the first time; or teams going through a period of low morale or resistance to organisational changes.
- High-readiness teams (able and willing and/or confident) do not need directive or supportive leadership: the most appropriate leadership style may be a joins or 'delegating' style. An example would be any mature and effectively-functioning team which is capable of getting on with performing, only needing to appeal to the leader for guidance in the event of unforeseen problems or new situations.

5.2   The model can be depicted as follows: Figure 2.5 *(Source: Hersey and Blanchard, 1988)*

Figure 2.5 *Hersey and Blanchard's situational leadership model*

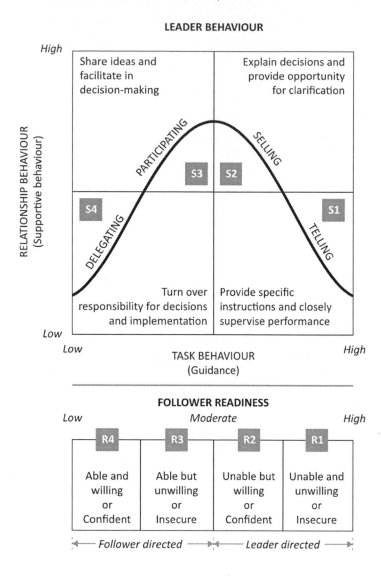

Task behaviour and relationship behaviour

5.3   As Figure 2.5 indicates, four styles of leadership – appropriate to each of the four levels of readiness – reflect a balance between two dimensions.

- **Task (or directive) behaviour** focuses on guidance: setting clear goals, defining roles, providing directions and guidelines for how to undertake tasks and so on.
- **Relationship (or supportive) behaviour** focuses on confidence and team building: providing support and encouragement; building relationships; engaging in two-way communication; resolving conflicts and problems.

5.4   The resulting leadership styles are identified as follows.

- **S1: Telling:** High directive behaviour, low supportive behaviour: providing specific instructions and closely supervising performance
- **S2: Selling:** High directive behaviour *and* high supportive behaviour: explaining decisions – and offering opportunities for clarification
- **S3: Participating:** High supportive behaviour, low directive behaviour: sharing ideas, and facilitating team members in decision-making

- **S4: Delegating:** Low supportive *and* directive behaviour: turning over responsibility for decisions and implementation. (Again, note that this is not 'abdication' of responsibility: an R4 team is likely to be performing well...)

5.5 The key point of Hersey & Blanchard's model is that an effective leader will both:

- Adapt his or her style to the current level of readiness of the team *and*
- Help team members to **develop maturity or readiness** as far as possible (through the process of support and direction that is built into each style).

6 Transformational and inspirational leadership

Transactional and transformational leadership

6.1 Following a 1978 study of political leaders, James M Burns *(Leadership,* 1978) distinguished between two styles of leadership.

- **Transactional leaders** see the relationship with their followers in terms of mutual dependence or exchange: they give followers the rewards they want in return for service, loyalty and compliance. A transactional style tends to focus on directive behaviours and carrot-and-stick motivation. The leader's power is based mainly on his or her authority or position in the organisation.

    This style works well in stable organisations (such as bureaucracies) with security-seeking and authoritarian cultures, operating in stable, slow-change business environments (including highly regulated industry sectors).
- **Transformational leaders** see their role as an interpersonal process of stimulating interest, generating awareness, inspiring higher achievement, and motivating others to work at levels beyond mere compliance and to think about the big picture. A transformational style is charismatic or inspirational. Only transformational leadership is said to be able to change team or organisation culture and performance: 'transforming' the direction and fortunes of the concern.

    This is seen as particularly important in dynamic, fast-changing and competitive environments. It suits lean, flexible organisation structures (such as networks and virtual teamworking) and innovative or learning cultures.

6.2 Transformational leadership is achieved through vision, values and inspiration. Bernard M Bass (*Leadership and Performance Beyond Expectations,* 1985) argues that leaders motivate followers to higher-than-expected levels of commitment and performance by:

- Creating awareness of the significance of the task and task outcomes, and organisational mission and objectives
- Influencing followers to think beyond their own self-interest for the sake of the team or organisation
- Activating followers' 'higher order' motivational needs (for esteem, achievement, satisfaction, personal development and self-actualisation), which are satisfied through higher levels of commitment, engagement and performance.

6.3 Bass and Bruce J Avolio (*Improving Organisational Effectiveness through Transformational Leadership,* 1994) identify transformational behaviours helpfully as Four I's: Table 2.5.

Table 2.5 *Transformational behaviours: the Four 'I's*

Idealised influence	The leader wins the respect, trust and emulation of the team, by acting as a role model in the kinds of values he wishes to foster in the team: particularly in areas such as putting the needs of the team above individual self-interest.
Inspirational motivation	The leader generates a greater awareness of the value of organisational purposes and team contribution: articulates a compelling future; emphasises the challenge, meaning and value of the work; communicates high expectations, confidence and enthusiasm.
Intellectual stimulation	The leader supports learning and creative problem-solving; questions assumptions; encourages new thinking and innovation; supports people in stretching themselves.
Individualised consideration	The leader treats team members as individuals; listens to them; supports their personal growth and development; appreciates difference and diversity; creates development opportunities by delegating and acting as a coach or mentor; and avoids micro-managing performance.

6.4 Cook, Macaulay and Coldicott *(Change Management Excellence,* 2004) emphasise that successful organisational change requires leaders who are more transformational than transactional in their approach. In order to be innovative, adaptable and flexible, managers need to be able to trust their people and know how to get the best from them, by:

- Letting go and allowing others to take the initiative
- Understanding and involving people at an emotional (as well as rational) level
- Being visionary, passionate and inspiring
- Developing creativity and cooperation for the good of the whole
- Managing their own emotions and stress levels effectively
- Being more flexible in their behaviour.

6.5 They note that for transformational leadership to work, therefore, it is essential for leaders – and team members – to develop emotional intelligence and related competencies (discussed in Chapter 6, in the context of leadership development).

Inspirational leadership

6.6 Mullins notes that transformational leadership is often strongly identified with 'charismatic', 'visionary' or 'inspirational' leadership. 'Successful transformational leaders are usually identified in terms of providing a strong vision and sense of mission, arousing strong emotions in followers and a sense of identification with the leader.' When you think of great visionary and charismatic leaders, they are probably transformational. Examples might include Winston Churchill, Martin Luther King, Nelson Mandela and Richard Branson.

6.7 However, Mullins also notes that it is possible to distinguish inspirational or visionary leadership from transformational leadership, by their specific focus on the skills of motivating and inspiring people. Inspirational leadership generally includes some combination of:

- Vision articulation
- Charisma or personal 'magnetism' and power to inspire.

Leadership and vision

6.8 We noted in Chapter 1 that leadership has a 'visionary' role. Vision (or the process of 'envisioning') is defined by Johnson, Scholes and Whittington *(Exploring Corporate Strategy)* as 'strategic intent, or the desired future state of the organisation... an aspiration around which a strategist, perhaps a chief executive, might seek to focus the attention and energies of members of the organisation'.

6.9 Vision is thus to do with seeing:

- The bigger picture: emphasising the purpose and meaning of activity

- A compelling, aspirational desired future state: creating challenge, a sense of potential and high standards (supported by confidence)
- The focus of attention: taking focus off problems and mistakes (and onto learning and problem-solving); off the past and blaming (and onto the future and developing).

6.10 Strategic vision is often set out in the formal vision and mission statement of an organisation. However, the creation and articulation of vision is an attribute of effective leaders at all levels.

6.11 David Taylor *(The Naked Leader,* 2002) rates breadth of vision as a key leadership behaviour, involving:

- Putting in place a picture of a compelling future for people and departments: a picture which involves others, focuses on achievement and is constantly kept fresh and relevant
- Cultivating a wide perspective: combining strategic business knowledge with a clear view of, and involvement in, the relevant industry or market and its direction.

6.12 In order to be effective in uniting people and inspiring committed effort, a vision needs to be **compelling**: attractive and influential.

- A compelling vision is one which appeals to powerful motivating forces in its stakeholders: it is meaningful to them and becomes a guiding or driving force for their activity. The motivating forces may be the need for survival, the desire for success, association with positive values (such as integrity, quality leadership or innovation), or the possibility of injecting a heroic element into work (beating the odds in a business turnaround, meeting challenging goals, or having a positive impact on society or the environment, say).
- A compelling vision also needs to be shared (if possible, on a widespread basis). Mission statements are often regarded as rather vague or wide-ranging: however, this may be essential in order to emphasise shared aspirations and common ground between all relevant stakeholders (at least at this level: detail and specificity will be added as the vision flows down into strategies and plans).

6.13 In general, the benefits of having a clear and compelling vision (Burt Nanus, *Visionary Leadership,* 1992) include the following.

- Attracting commitment and energising people
- Giving work meaning and significance (within the greater whole)
- Establishing standards and values for excellence
- Focusing on the future.

6.14 We will examine the articulation of vision, and its role in leading change and improvement in supply chains, in Chapter 8.

Leadership and charisma

6.15 The idea of an innate 'talent' for leadership (the foundation of the old trait approach) appears to have retained currency with the persistent belief in **charismatic (or gifted) leadership**. Charisma is the ability to inspire followership on the basis of personally attractive, magnetic and inspiring qualities. It has traditionally been one of the most elusive of leadership 'qualities'.

6.16 House (1976) took some of the 'mystique' out of charisma, by arguing that it can be learned or developed as a cluster of purely behavioural competencies, including:

- **Role modelling**: setting an example, and consistently representing and demonstrating values which are positive and attractive for followers
- **Confidence building:** encouraging, giving positive feedback, communicating high expectations of followers, (eg setting challenging goals) and expressing and demonstrating confidence in their ability to meet them
- **Goal articulation:** setting out clear goals for the team, in a way that is compelling to followers: emotionally resonant, linked to core values, challenging, meaningful (in terms of contribution to the overall task) and so on

- **Motive arousal:** inspiring followers with the desire or confidence to pursue the goals, by highlighting the rewards of doing so, and the realistic expectation of being able to attain those rewards (compare the path-goal theory of motivation).

6.17 However, for many writers, inspirational leadership is also a philosophy, conviction and state of mind. Adair (*The Inspirational Leader: How to Motivate, Encourage and Achieve Success,* 2003) argues that inspirational leadership arises from a core belief in the potential for greatness in other people, and involves the drawing out, or unlocking, of the powers and capabilities of others. Jay A Conger ('Charisma and how to grow it', *Management Today,* 1999) suggests that 'passion is a big part of what drives a charismatic leader [and] what motivates and inspires those who work for the charismatic leader'.

Evaluating inspirational leadership

6.18 A number of arguments have been advanced against seeing inspirational leadership, or charisma, as a sole or sufficient approach to leadership.

6.19 Compelling 'vision casting' and charismatic leadership can become a substitute for real substance and action to make the vision a reality. Inspirational leadership has a 'feel good' factor for followers – but may not be underpinned by necessary competencies in direction, change management, delegation and follow-through. If the compelling vision is repeatedly expressed – but never achieved – disillusionment will result.

6.20 Charismatic and visionary leadership can create a 'cult of the individual', which can be dysfunctional in various ways.

- Followers may become increasingly uncritical and unquestioning of the leader (with divergent viewpoints or feedback squeezed out): this may support irresponsible, risk-taking behaviour – or simply 'wrong' directions for the team or organisation.
- Followers may become increasingly dependent on the leader for direction, motivation and validation: ceasing to use initiative and self-motivation, or to contribute their own capabilities and insights.
- Focus on the individual leader underestimates the value of consensus and collaboration, and may discourage collective responsibility and the pooling of ideas and abilities.

Chapter summary

- Trait theories of leadership take the view that leadership qualities are inherent, not developed. Unfortunately there is no agreement among researchers adopting this line as to which personality traits good leaders have in common.

- An alternative way of looking at the question of leadership is to adopt a behavioural approach, which emphasises what leaders actually do and their style of leadership. John Adair proposed an 'action-centred' (functional) approach, based on managerial activities in three key roles, which in turn are based on the meeting of three key needs: task, individual and team. The relative priority to be given to these needs is dictated by the overall situation.

- Style theories of leadership adopt a behavioural approach, which emphasises patterns of preferred, or adopted, behaviour that are more or less effective in a given leadership context.

- Two-dimensional theories focus on concern for task and concern for people, and accompanying behaviours (directive or supportive and facilitative). Blake and Mouton's managerial grid measures leaders' scores on two axes, one denoting 'concern for production' and the other 'concern for people'.

- Behavioural styles can broadly be classified as authoritative, democratic and *laissez faire*. The Ashridge Studies identified four styles – 'tells', 'sells', 'consults' and 'joins' – and found a consultative style to be most popular with team members. However, the studies also highlighted the fact that consistency is important. Tannenbaum and Schmidt emphasised that styles represent a continuum of different behaviours, not fixed extremes.

- Contingency theory asserts that there is no one 'right way' to lead that fits all situations. Leadership style has to be adapted to suit the circumstances. Hersey and Blanchard's situational model suggested that leadership style should be adapted to the team's readiness (task ability and willingness or confidence) to perform a given task.

- Transactional leadership is based on positional authority and exchange: giving followers rewards in return for their compliance. Transformational leadership is based on interpersonal influence, vision, values and inspiration, aimed at commitment and enabling change. Transformational behaviours include: Idealised influence, Inspirational motivation, Intellectual stimulation and Individualised consideration.

- Trait theory has been revisited looking at skills and values which can be modelled and learned by leaders: vision, emotional intelligence, interpersonal skills (eg in promotion, influencing and inspiration), values, integrity and authenticity.

Self-test questions

Numbers in brackets refer to the paragraphs where you can check your answers.

1 What problems are there in applying trait theory to the analysis of leadership? (1.6)

2 What are the eight leadership activities in Adair's action-centred leadership model? (2.9)

3 What are the three domains in the leadership model developed by Pedler *et al*? (2.11)

4 Distinguish between directive and facilitative leadership behaviour. (3.8–3.11)

5 Describe five key points on Blake and Mouton's leadership grid. (Table 2.2)

6 Describe the four leadership styles identified in the Ashridge studies. (Table 2.3)

7 Describe the assumptions of McGregor's Theory X and Theory Y. (3.30, 3.31)

8 What three variables in the leadership situation were identified in Fiedler's contingency model? (4.5)

9 What were the four main types of leadership behaviour identified by Robert House? (4.19)

10 Describe the four leadership styles in Hersey and Blanchard's model. (5.4)

11 Distinguish between transactional leaders and transformational leaders. (6.1)

12 What are the benefits of a compelling leadership vision? (6.13)

CHAPTER 3

Power and Influence

Assessment criteria and indicative content

3.1 Critically analyse the sources of power and how they can be used to overcome common challenges faced by procurement and supply chain managers

- Perspectives on individual power
- Processual, institutional and organisational levels of power
- Perspectives on organisational power
- The balance between order and flexibility

3.2 Evaluate the main tactics that can be used to influence stakeholders within supply chains to overcome common challenges faced by procurement and supply chain managers

- Proactive influencing tactics
- The psychological principles of influence

Section headings

1. Supply chain challenges
2. Power in organisations
3. Perspectives on power and control
4. Influencing
5. Influencing styles and tactics
6. Influencing as an interpersonal process

Introduction

Formal organisation structures attempt to define where authority lies in the organisation: that is, where formal legal (or 'legitimate') power has been conferred on an individual or group to make decisions and expect compliance from others who report to them. However, the concept of *leadership* argues that power and influence are complex concepts which cannot be viewed purely from a structural perspective.

In this chapter we look at the foundations of what it means to be a leader. First, we look at the particular **context** highlighted by the syllabus: the use of power and influence to overcome common challenges faced by procurement and supply chain managers.

We then explore where leadership influence comes from: different sources of **power** available to leaders, and how appropriate it may be to use them in a supply chain context.

Finally, we discuss the critical process of leading by **influence**: what it is, what key skills are required to exercise it, and how it can be exercised in different relationships. (We go on to develop these particular relationship contexts in more detail in Chapter 4.)

1   Supply chain challenges

1.1   The learning outcome for this section of the syllabus requires you to understand how to overcome common challenges faced by procurement and supply chain managers.

1.2   The context of this chapter on power and influence (and Chapters 4 and 5 in which we look at various internal and external stakeholders in procurement and supply) is therefore a practical one. The aim is for you to understand how power and influence can be used to overcome 'common challenges' in your professional life – and in exam case studies.

1.3   Obviously, the specific context will depend on the details of the situation or case study scenario, and the type of power or influence the individual, group or organisation has. The point is that you need to be ready to *apply* power and influence models and concepts as practical tools for resolving problems and issues in procurement and supply chain management. In this section, therefore, we will give a brief generic overview of some of the 'common challenges' to which power and influence may be applied: you can then use this to provide context and suggest examples, as you learn more about the types and sources of power and influence.

1.4   Table 3.1 shows some generic examples of 'common challenges' faced by procurement and supply chain managers, and examples of how the use of power and influence can be helpful in overcoming those challenges. Obviously, our list is not exhaustive. In your wider reading, you will be able to add case studies of your own...

Table 3.1 *The use of power and influence to overcome challenges*

CHALLENGE	USE OF POWER AND INFLUENCE
Securing co-operation for the implementation of change programmes	• Authority to require and reinforce change through underpinning systems, policies • Expertise and consultancy to educate stakeholders on the need for change • Persuasion and inspiration to secure 'buy-in' • Rewards and incentives for co-operation (We will discuss various options for influencing in change situations in Chapter 8.)
Resolving stakeholder conflicts	• Imposing a preferred or optimal solution (where authority to do so is available) • Persuasion to bring conflicting interests or viewpoints together • Negotiation to make compromise acceptable to all parties • Inspiration to motivate parties to put their differences or individual interests aside in pursuit of a compelling vision • Escalation or appeal to higher authority to legitimise a preferred or optimal solution (We will discuss various options for influencing in conflict situations in Chapter 9.)
Maintaining quality standards and driving continuous improvement	• Authority to require compliance via contracts, service level agreements, continuous improvement agreements etc • Negotiation of agreed standards and targets • Rewards and incentives for KPI attainment • Co-optation through involvement in improvement planning
Introducing cost reduction initiatives	• Authority to impose internal cost targets • Persuasion and education of business need for cost reduction • Rational argument re potential for savings (eg on the basis of open book costing) • Negotiation of cost reduction targets for suppliers, with incentives (eg gain sharing arrangements) • Demonstration of responsible, sustainable, consultative approach to cost reduction (to keep stakeholders 'on side')
Raising ethical, labour and environmental standards in the supply chain	• Authority to impose internal and supplier policies, enforce ethical codes • Persuasion and education re business case (eg on basis of reputation management) • Role modelling: setting an example for the supply chain • Rewards and incentives for standards attainment or improvement (eg preferred supplier status)

Continued . . .

CHALLENGE	USE OF POWER AND INFLUENCE
Securing internal compliance with procurement policies and disciplines (eg controlling 'maverick' buying by part-time purchasers)	• Authority to impose policies, systems contracts, approved supplier lists, e-catalogue procurement, purchasing cards etc • Demonstration of value added by procurement disciplines • Role modelling and personal influence by procurement consultants embedded in user departments, business partners • Application of performance management, education, training, development, discipline and counselling, and so on • Incentives for compliance (eg awards, recognition)
Securing supplier compliance with policies and standards	• Negotiation of robust contract terms and agreements • Clear communication of standards, expectations and KPIs • Incentives and penalties • Robust contract and supplier management • Enforcement of contract terms through escalation (involvement of higher authority) • Enforcement of contract terms through dispute resolution (with legal remedies as a last resort)
Challenging business need and user specifications to minimise wastes	• Demonstration of value-adding expertise re sourcing options (including recycling, re-use, sharing, standardisation) and supply market innovation (eg through early supplier involvement) • Persuasion via robust business case for standardisation, variety reduction, avoidance of over-specification etc
Asserting the strategic value, role and status of the procurement function in the organisation	• Demonstration of business case for procurement disciplines and effective supply chain management • Build-up of trust and credibility through interactions and contributions over time • Utilising contacts, networks and coalitions of influence: procurement marketing, procurement 'champions'
Stimulating supply market innovation	• Control over resources and rewards: signalling demand and value for innovative solutions • Creating innovation-supporting structures (eg competitive dialogue, support for SME participation, long-term co-investment with strategic innovation partners)

2 Power in organisations

2.1 Power is an aspect of any relationship – not just obvious ones such as leader-subordinate or buyer-supplier. It also applies to inter-organisational relationships, as well as interpersonal ones. Power may be defined as the ability of an individual or group to exercise influence over others.

2.2 It is important to an understanding of leadership and influence that 'power' is not the same as 'authority'. **Authority** refers to the scope and amount of discretion given to a person to make decisions by virtue of the position he holds in an organisation. It is usually conferred from the top down by delegation (although it may also be conferred from the bottom up – by election, for example). **Power** is the ability to influence – and may not be connected to formal organisational or legitimate authority.

Processual, institutional and internal levels of power

2.3 Robert Fincham ('Perspectives on power: processual, institutional and 'internal' forms of organisational power', *Journal of Management Studies,* 1992) noted that organisational power can be constituted at different levels.

- Power is **processual:** that is, it emerges out of *processes* of interaction in organisations (and supply chains): how power is gained and used in the ongoing 'game' of developing and implementing strategy. Power is a function of interpersonal and inter-group interactions, influencing and 'political' processes such as negotiating and bargaining, influencing, competing, co-opting and coalition-building among managerial interest groups or stakeholders. Power is *generated* by such groups in the course of interaction and the pursuit of divergent goals and interests.
- Power is **institutional:** radical theories of power, such as Marxist theory, insist that ultimately power is constituted in social and economic *structures* and institutions, external to the organisation. Power is

mandated (legitimised) and *devolved* (conferred) on groups from the wider structures of social class, gender, capitalism, the legal system and so on, which support the 'managerial prerogative' or 'right of managers to manage'.

- Power is **internal** or **organisational**. 'While processual and institutional views are important, explanations of power effects within organisations may be incomplete if determined by power constituted in institutions outside the organisation, or if the organisation becomes an abstracted "arena" for the interplay of group processes... Organisations also possess power capacities of their own.' Power capacities arise from legitimate, resource and expert power in the organisation, for example. Organisational hierarchies and culture confer power and reproduce power (as those in authority co-opt and select others who will sustain the existing power structure).

Forms and uses of power

2.4 Power may take various forms.

- **Overt power** is obvious, or transparent – through direct tactics such as physical or economic coercion, autocratic leadership, logical persuasion or the offering of incentives. Note that overt power need not be coercive, dominant or confrontational: it may, for example, take the form of an extremely attractive deal or persuasive argument.
- **Covert power** is subtle, hidden or implied – through indirect tactics such as withholding information or excluding someone from a negotiation or network. Conflicts of interest are not explicitly stated, and may not be apparent to observers.
- **Structural power** is built into the situation, context or relationship – as in the case of legal obligations on organisations, buyers who are dependent on suppliers (or *vice versa*), or employers who control the rewards of labour. Supply chains can be seen as having 'structural properties of power', as there are inherent balances and imbalances of power between buyers and suppliers of different sizes, in the criticality and substitutability of different materials, in the degree of 'lock in' created by relationship-specific investment and so on.

Supplier power and buyer power

2.5 Power is essentially exercised in supply chains to appropriate or claim a larger share of the value or value gains created by the process.

2.6 Porter's 'Five Forces' model (Porter, *Competitive Strategy)* suggests that buyer power and supplier power influences competition and profitability in an industry.

- **Buyer power** may be used to force down prices or obtain higher quality or improved service. The bargaining power of buyers is relatively high when: they are limited in number and/or large in size relative to supplying firms; products are undifferentiated or substitutable (so it is easy to switch brands); their spend is a high proportion of the supplying firm's revenue; or there is backward integration (ie the buyer owns or controls the supplier).
- **Supplier power** is generally used to raise prices. The bargaining power of suppliers is relatively high when: they are limited in number and/or large in size, relative to buying firms; their product is strategically important to the buyer's business, highly differentiated and not readily substituted; the volume purchased by the buyer is not important to the supplier; or there is forward integration (ie the supplier owns or controls the buying firm).

2.7 A member of the supply chain can thus seek to **increase its structural power**, most obviously by backward or forward integration, but also by manipulating any of the factors mentioned. A supplier may differentiate its product offering in an area of strategic importance to the buyer, for example, in order to increase the buyer's switching costs and dependence. A buyer may standardise its requirements so that more suppliers can compete for the business, decreasing its dependence on existing sources of supply.

Sources of power in organisations

2.8   JRP French and BH Raven ('The bases of social power' in *Studies in Social Power,* 1958) identified five different sources of power in organisational relationships.

- **Legitimate power** (or **position power**): the legal/rational, formally-conferred authority associated with a position or role in an organisation (eg a managerial role) or supply chain (eg the role of an agent). Power is also legitimised by law, contract terms and agreed standards, and any of these might be appealed to in order to reinforce an organisation's interests. The ability to exert influence is based on others' belief in the legitimacy of this authority.
- **Expert power**: the power of expertise or knowledge which is both recognised and valued by followers (as necessary for them to achieve their own goals), so that they are willing to be influenced by the expert. Examples include the influence of procurement specialists in supplier selection, for example, or (in a wider supply chain context) specialist service providers or owners of patents on processes or parts.
- **Reward power** (or 'resource power'): recognised control over resources and rewards that are scarce and/or valued by followers, so that they are willing to be influenced in return for access to those resources. This depends on how far the individual or group controls the resource, how much it is valued by others, and how scarce it is. Within a team, managers control access to rewards. In the wider supply chain, this may be the power of a buyer to offer or withhold valued business to a supplier; or the power of a supplier to control access to strategic or critical supplies.
- **Referent power** (or 'personal power'): emanating from the attractive and inspiring personality, image or charisma of the individual, and the perception by others of his or her leadership quality. This may also apply to an organisation which has a strong brand or reputation, or is a recognised leader in the industry: other organisations will seek to emulate it, or be associated with it.
- **Coercive power** (or **physical power**): the power to threaten sanctions, hand out punishments or physically intimidate others if compliance is not obtained. In the broader supply chain, it may be exercised through the aggressive use of competitive leverage by a dominant buyer or supplier (eg especially in a monopoly position).

2.9   Other researchers have added other concepts of power.

- **Connection power** (Paul Finlay, *Strategic Management*): power resulting from personal or professional access to key influencers, networks of influence and sources of information
- **Informational power** (Yukl, *Leadership in Organisations*): control over information and sources of information perceived as necessary or valuable by others (as in the old saying: 'Knowledge is power'). This may be possessed by information 'gatekeepers' at all levels of the organisation and supply chain – and in the informal communication network or 'grapevine'.
- **Negative power** (Charles Handy, *Understanding Organisations*): the power 'to stop things happening, to delay them, to distort or disrupt them' – eg by withholding or distorting information, 'working to rule', absenteeism or sabotage.

2.10   It is important to realise that an individual can operate from any or all of these bases of power, according to which one is appropriate and relevant for a particular relationship. A procurement manager may, for example, operate out of legitimate power with his subordinates; out of referent power with his manager; out of expert power in a cross-functional project meeting; and out of reward power in price negotiations with a supplier. However, French and Raven also point out that the use of one type of power (eg coercive) might undermine the leader's ability to use another (eg referent).

Using legitimate power in procurement and supply

2.11   Procurement officials have direct line authority over the members and activities of their department, section or team. With these roles, at different levels, may come the right to formulate procurement and sourcing policy, set expenditure budgets, impose approved supplier lists, direct procurement teams and so on. This supports procurement and supply chain managers in overcoming some routine challenges in regard to internal procurement performance (including the management of 'maverick' buying by non-professional buyers in user departments), since it establishes broadly enforceable guidelines for behaviour.

2.12 Legitimate power also includes legal and contractual rights, which are legitimated by common law, contract law and similar structural sources. This supports procurement and supply chain managers in overcoming some routine challenges in regard to contract compliance and performance management, since it establishes enforceable requirements on suppliers, with rights of redress or remedy in the event of non-compliance.

Using expert power in procurement and supply

2.13 Expert power is extremely important for the procurement and supply chain function, especially where buying activities have been devolved to line departments.

- **Staff authority** is the term given to the expert power of a specialist giving advice or guidance to others, even though he has no direct line authority over their activities. A procurement department, for example, may carry out buying research on behalf of line departments. Its advice may be influential, because of its knowledge and contacts in this area.
- **Functional authority** is the term used where an expert is given legitimate authority to direct the activities of others in the area of his expertise. This may be built into the structure of the organisation: for example, procurement may be given authority to carry out centralised purchasing on behalf of line departments. Alternatively, it may be expressed by authority to devise policy, procedures and rules: procurement may develop tendering procedures, approved supplier lists or call-off contracts, say, for use by budget-holders.

2.14 One of the key challenges of procurement and supply chain management in some organisations is the lack of direct functional authority. Expert power (in the sense of staff authority) will be an important tool to overcome this challenge. The credibility, status and influence of the procurement function, as an internal consultancy and business partner, depends on the demonstration of specialist, valued expertise and knowledge.

2.15 There are certain drawbacks to the use of expert power, which often affect the perception and integration of procurement and supply functions in organisations.

- Line managers may perceive that their authority is being undermined, causing political problems and possible resistance to advice and procedures.
- Expert functions may feel that they lack genuine influence, and attempt to strengthen their power base by imposing additional rules and red tape.
- Expert functions may lack appreciation of the issues facing line departments, so their advice may be inappropriate or fail to support line objectives.

2.16 The solutions to these problems are not always easy to implement in practice.

- The scope and limits of authority should be clearly defined. Any ambiguities or conflicts that emerge should be openly discussed and resolved.
- Respect for specialist expertise and knowledge should be expressed as key values in the organisation's culture (to protect the status and influence of advisory functions) – but so should the *sharing* of expertise and knowledge (to prevent the abuse of expert power). This may be expressed in multi-disciplinary teamworking and information-sharing, for example.
- Advisory departments should be educated in the strategic and operational objectives of their internal customers: information-sharing goes both ways. Their culture should emphasise their role in supporting and empowering primary value-adding activities – and this in turn will support stakeholder 'buy-in' to their programmes and initiatives (as we will see in the following chapter).

Using reward power in procurement and supply

2.17 Procurement managers exercise reward power over team members, to the extent that they control access to pay and benefits, praise, promotion prospects, development opportunities, privileges – and access to valued resources such as information, contacts, space or assistance from other team members.

2.18 Procurement professionals also exercise reward power in relation to suppliers, with the ability to award contracts, follow-on business, contract incentives and gain-sharing rewards, supplier development opportunities and other resources. This power will be particularly great if the supplier is dependent on the buying organisation for a major proportion of its income; if it would be difficult to attract other buyers (eg because of relationship-specific adaptations); and/or if the individual buyer or buying group is perceived to have control over the award of the contract (rather than it being determined by structural factors such as competitive tendering, in the public sector).

2.19 Burt, Dobler and Starling *(World Class Supply Management)* note, however, that recognition can also be a powerful motivating reward for suppliers (as for employees). The prospect of a publicised 'outstanding' rating, quality award, or inclusion on a 'best supplier' list may act as an incentive to future successful performance.

2.20 Reward power is an important tool for overcoming the key supply chain challenges of:

- Securing supply and developing quality supply chains (generally in competition with other buying organisations)
- Maintaining supplier motivation, loyalty and commitment (over and above compliance with contractual requirements).

Using referent power in procurement and supply

2.21 Procurement professionals can be inspirational role models and transformational leaders. Charismatic leadership can be used in *any* context, to support other forms of power with personal force. Boddy *(Management: An Introduction)* argues that this is more than just securing personal followership: 'Managers use their position to influence others by showing that what they propose is consistent with the accepted values and culture of the organisation. They invoke wider values in support of their proposal.' He also notes, however, that 'the effectiveness of the influence attempt depends on the other people having a similar view of the culture' – or finding the values embodied by the leader meaningful and attractive.

2.22 Referent power may be important in overcoming challenges of motivation and change management in the team or supply chain: changing procurement culture, for example, or introducing new processes, or leading the supply chain towards higher standards of sustainability, ethics or corporate social responsibility.

Using coercive power in procurement and supply

2.23 Physically coercive power, by definition, is rare in business organisations – as indeed it should be! An element of coercion, however, may operate where a manager exercises a high degree of *any* kind of power in an exploitative, degrading or intimidatory manner – including the use of aggressive or abusive language.

2.24 Reprimands, demotions and threats of dismissal may also be considered coercive (Boddy), since they are based on fear of punishment – but these are a necessary part of organisational discipline. Similarly, the threat of dropping or downgrading a supplier may be necessary as a motivator to satisfactory performance. Such measures should, however, be delivered in an impartial, fair and constructive manner, with the offer of restored relationship (as a reward for change) where possible.

2.25 The main trouble with coercive power is that at best it only secures compliance: it does not bring about attitude change and commitment. At worst, it may create resentment, retaliation – and the other negative effects of a push approach.

Sources and indicators of stakeholder power

2.26 Johnson, Scholes and Whittington helpfully classify the sources and indicators of power in the specific context of strategic management, as follows: Table 3.1. Note that power can be used to influence strategic planning and decision-making – but also implementation: a manager exercising discretion, or an outsourced service provider, may 'adjust' strategy in action.

Table 3.2 *Sources and indicators of power*

	SOURCES OF POWER	INDICATORS OF POWER
Within organisations	• Hierarchy (formal authority) • Influence (informal power: eg charismatic leadership) • Control of strategic resources (eg finance) • Possession of knowledge and skills (eg IT specialists) • Control of human environment (eg negotiating skills) • Involvement in implementation (eg exercising discretion)	• Status (eg job grade, reputation) • Claim on resources (eg budget size) • Representation (eg in powerful positions, committees) • Symbols (eg office size, titles)
For external stakeholders	• Control of strategic resources (eg materials, labour) • Involvement in implementation (eg distribution outlets, agents) • Possession of knowledge and skills (eg subcontractors, partners) • Through internal links (eg informal influence)	• Status (eg inferred by speed with which firm responds) • Resource dependence (eg dependence on supplier, size of shareholding or loans, proportion of business tied up with customer) • Negotiating arrangements • Symbols (eg level of contacts, hospitality)

3 Perspectives on power and control

Balancing order and flexibility

3.1 Many writers have highlighted the classic dilemma underlying the exercise of control in organisations, which is the need to find a balance between:

- **Order/control**: seeking to enhance the predictability of people's actions and the outputs of processes (to minimise risk and maximise quality assurance and efficiency) *and*
- **Flexibility**: improving the ability and willingness of people and processes to respond swiftly and adaptively to changing demands and situations. This is increasingly recognised as essential in dynamic and turbulent business environments.

3.2 One of the eight key attributes of excellent companies identified by Peters and Waterman *(In Search of Excellence, 1982)* was **simultaneous loose-tight properties**: that is, 'the co-existence of firm central direction and maximum individual autonomy'. Peters and Waterman argued that: 'Organisations that live by the loose-tight principle are on the one hand rigidly controlled, yet at the same time allow (indeed, insist on) autonomy, entrepreneurship and innovation from the rank and file.'

3.3 The successful solution observed by Peters and Waterman was to exercise centralised control over critical success factors through a handful of widely shared, compelling, non-negotiable **guiding values**, while allowing maximum practical autonomy and initiative to workers (especially customer-facing staff, whose flexible response to customer demands adds most value). They argued that values-based leadership offers a powerful but 'non-aversive' form of control: one which does not arouse resentment or resistance, and offers maximum flexibility in practice.

3.4   Management guru Rosemary Stewart (*Managing Today and Tomorrow*, 1991) argued for a hybrid approach to **organisational structure**, which she identified as 'tight-loose'. Some departments or areas of work may require close programming, supervision and control ('tight') while others may require greater latitude and fluidity ('loose') to encourage innovation, initiative and agility.

3.5   Stewart identified three main ways in which control can be exercised in organisations.

- **Direct control**, eg using orders and instructions, direct supervision, rules and regulations. As we saw in Chapter 2, controlling or directive leadership may be required, and may be accepted by followers, in some situations: for example, where the group is unready (lacking ability, confidence or motivation) or there is a crisis situation (since direct control achieves swift corrective results). However, this form of control may be resented and resisted where the norm is participative teamworking, or for high-maturity groups. It leaves no latitude for the exercise of initiative, discretion or innovation – other than in trying to 'get around' the controls!
- **Standardisation and specialisation** (bureaucratic control or planning systems): clear definition (or programming) of the parameters for action: task inputs, methods to be used, desired outputs and so on. Examples might include standardised quality management or environmental management systems (eg ISO 9000 or 14001) or the use of enterprise resource planning systems in the supply chain. Planning systems ensure that critical success factors are standardised across the organisation, while flexibility may be allowed within the defined parameters.
- **Influencing**: shaping the way that people think about what they should do, and bringing their values into line with those of the organisation. Johnson, Scholes and Whittington identify this as **social and cultural control**: the way norms and expectations of behaviour become standardised in a group or organisation, and the way in which processes of socialisation and social influence encourage individuals to conform. Culture-influencing processes include vision creation, education and training, consultation and involvement, rewards and reinforcements. This is an indirect form of control, based on stakeholder 'buy-in' and internalisation of goals and values: it is particularly important in dynamic environments, because it supports change. As Peters and Waterman's findings suggested, this is often the most effective and non-aversive way of exercising control.

3.6   Johnson, Scholes and Whittington add a number of other control mechanisms.

- **Performance targets and KPIs.** The performance of the organisation (or SBU or function) is evaluated according to its ability to meet defined targets (control) – allowing it discretion on how resources can be allocated to achieve them (flexibility).
- **Self control**. Personal motivation is used to influence the quality of employee input and conduct (control), without direct intervention (flexibility). This requires clear goals and objectives; information and performance feedback; mechanisms for knowledge sharing and integration; and supportive, credible, role-modelling leadership. People behave in desired ways because they understand the need to do so, and are willing to commit themselves to the good of the team.

3.7   Charles Handy *(Understanding Organisations,* 1993*)* focused on the **trust-control dilemma** inherent in the leader-subordinate relationship. Handy expressed this as a simple equation:

$$T + C = Y$$

T is the trust the leader has in team members, and the trust which they *perceive* the leader has in them. C is the degree of control exercised by the leader over the team. And Y is a constant, unchanging value. In other words, as trust increases, control decreases – and *vice versa*. The less a leader feels able to trust a team member to carry out a task effectively, the more control he will exercise. The more control is exercised, the less trusted the team will feel.

3.8 Mullins, however, notes that some individuals have a motivational need or drive for power or control: 'some managers positively strive for and enjoy the exercise of power over other people. They seek to maintain absolute control over subordinates and the activities of their department or section, and welcome the feeling of being indispensable.' Such individuals can become 'control freaks' or micro-managers. They can be personally highly effective – but cause de-motivation, resentment, resistance and waste of talent and potential in a team.

Balancing authority and collaboration

3.9 A similar issue concerns the balance between:

- **Authority** (the leader takes swift, decisive, directive and unilateral action, where required) and
- **Collaboration** (the leader is aware that he does not have all the answers, or the best answers, and has the flexibility to put time and effort into consultation and delegation, in order to get the best wisdom and commitment from the team).

3.10 Turbulent and uncertain business environments create expectations for clear, authoritative leadership – but the desire to 'take control' and 'be decisive' can be counterproductive, if its effect is to lead to lower-quality, less acceptable or motivating decisions.

3.11 Mullins argues that successful leaders use authority 'without arrogance'. He cites the work of Richard Reeves and John Knell ('Your mini MBA', in *Management Today*, 2009) to suggest that successful leaders:

- Build a 'culture of discipline' focused on marshalling resources, getting things done, and controlling costs
- Keep in touch with how people are feeling, in order to gauge morale and *esprit de corps*
- Know where they are strong – but also know their weaknesses and are willing to seek information and help when required
- Have a clear sense of where the organisation is going – but recognise that this is the result of collective decision-making by a talented team.

Power and dependency issues in supply chains

3.12 Stephen P Robbins and Timothy A Judge *(Organisational Behaviour,* 2009) suggest that 'a person can have power over you only if he or she *controls something you desire'.* We have already seen that expert and reward power largely depend on the extent to which followers desire or value the expertise or rewards. However, this also raises a key aspect of power: dependency.

3.13 Andrew Cox *et al* ('Supplier Relationship Management: A Framework for Understanding Managerial Capacity and Constraints' in *European Business Journal,* 2003) depict the key issues of power and dependency in supply chains in a simple matrix: Figure 3.1.

Figure 3.1 *The power/dependency matrix*

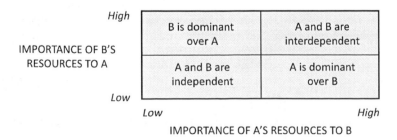

3.14 Where B is important to A, but A is not important to B, then B is the dominant partner in the relationship. A major supermarket would be a dominant buyer to produce suppliers, for example, while a major pharmaceutical company might be a dominant supplier of a pharmacy chain. Independence (neither party needs the relationship) and interdependence (both parties need the relationship) create a more equal balance of power. Broadly speaking, each party will wish to avoid a situation where the other party is dominant.

3.15 For buyers, the dangers of over-dependency on suppliers are obvious enough (what happens if our strategic supplier seeks more lucrative business elsewhere, or engages in opportunistic adversarial behaviour?). However, responsible purchasing emphasises that there are also dangers in an over-dominant position.

3.16 Responsible buyers may be reluctant to take too much of a supplier's turnover, or to insist on relationship-specific adaptations – even though the supplier might be keen to get more business. This is a responsibility and sustainability issue: protecting the supplier from risk, if the buyer, for whatever reason, terminates the relationship. Buyers may also benefit from suppliers' having a good range of customers: being more attuned to the market, and supported by multiple customer resources for supplier development. This is an issue that should form part of regular communication between buyer and seller.

Ethical and responsibility issues of power in supply chains

3.17 The Responsible Purchasing Initiative makes it a key principle of responsible purchasing that: 'Good procurement professionals are aware of the power they exercise and use it responsibly to avoid abuses in the supply chain.'

3.18 Resource power and coercive power are clearly open to abuse in power-imbalanced or structurally 'asymmetric' supply chain relationships: that is, relationships which are essentially *unequal* in terms of power, influence, 'voice', scale, or dominance of a market or sector. As part of the sustainability risk management process, buyers should seek to identify areas of the supply chain, and sustainability issues, which are vulnerable to the abuse – or unhelpful use – of power.

3.19 The use and leverage of power is a widely used technique, underpinning many buying strategies. The buying power of large global purchasers gives them the ability to bargain hard with suppliers – and in the case of small, less powerful suppliers, to dictate and enforce prices and terms of trade to suit their own interests. This may, as we have seen, have the effect of:

- Disempowering suppliers, especially at lower levels of the supply chain, creating vullnerability and the risk of exploitation (which in turn can have social, economic and environmental consequences)
- Squeezing suppliers' profit margins so that they are unable to pay living wages or invest in improved labour conditions, quality and business development
- Forcing suppliers to pursue unsustainable practices (such as enforced overtime, forced working and corner-cutting on health and safety and quality)
- Passing 'top-down' pressures down the supply chain, creating knock-on effects of poverty and disempowerment to progressively more vulnerable suppliers, producers and workers
- Robbing the buying organisation of the potential benefits of supply chain input (for decision making and innovation), feedback (for learning) and commitment
- Stimulating scrutiny from regulatory bodies, media and pressure groups, owing to the recognised unfairness and unsustainability of such relationships.

3.20 Coercive, arbitrary, unfair or abusive exercise of power in supply chains (as in interpersonal relations) is generally discouraged, on several grounds.

- Firstly, it may be unlawful or unethical. Key examples include: abuse of a monopoly position under competition or 'anti-trust' laws; unfair treatment of suppliers in a public sector tender situation, under

EU public procurement directives; or abuse of a position of influence for personal gain, under relevant codes of professional ethics (such as that of CIPS).

- Secondly, it is generally counter-productive: aversive forms of power may secure short-term compliance, but they generally cause resentment, resistance (from 'work to rules' to active sabotage), and loss of potential for long-term relationships and synergy. This is why adversarial relationships, based on overt competitive leverage, are not considered suitable for all supply situations. They are rarely likely to achieve long-term best value for money, or potential for mutually satisfying partnerships.

3.21 Even in relatively dominant relationships with suppliers or outsourced-service providers, power may be exercised constructively in the form of:

- Mutual obligations, expressed through negotiated supply contracts and service level agreements
- The offer of approved or preferred supplier status or public acknowledgement for performance and/or improvement
- Fair competitive pressures to meet price and non-price criteria (eg through fair and transparent competitive tendering)
- The potential for ongoing, stable, mutually beneficial business relationship, as an incentive for compliance and continuous improvement.

3.22 Here are some measures that may be taken to improve the responsible use of power by buyers.

- Training buyers to be aware of the power they exercise; how power and influence are used; and their potential sustainability impacts on supply chains
- Developing an understanding of the end-to-end supply chain, and points of vulnerability (eg through supply chain mapping) – as part of an emphasis on robust risk management
- Establishing effective oversight and governance of sourcing strategies and supply chains: eg through independent review of sourcing strategies, accountability structures and sustainability reporting mechanisms
- Effective mechanisms for supply chain control, audit and feedback gathering, so that the impact of buying decisions and practices can be assessed
- Capture and dissemination of learning from critical incidents and supplier feedback, in order to solve problems and initiate changes in purchasing practice

3.23 It should also be noted that power can be intentionally used to positive effect in supply chains and supplier relationships.

- Expert power may be used to develop and empower suppliers and supply chains, eg through technology transfer and support for business development.
- Referent power may be used to share and benchmark best practice standards, and to secure supply chain emulation of the buyer's sustainability standards, through sustainability leadership and role modelling.
- Reward power may be used to exercise responsible influence over the supply chain, to secure compliance with desired sustainability standards: eg through the use of sustainability criteria for access to contracts, supplier awards, and financial incentives for the achievement of improvement targets.
- Reward power may be used to develop required capabilities and sustainability standards in the supply chain, through investment in supplier training and development.
- Reward power may be exercised responsibly by the buying organisation through fair and sustainable pricing, rather than price leverage.

4 Influencing

What is influencing?

4.1 Influencing is the process of applying some form of pressure in order to change other people's attitudes or behaviours: to secure their compliance (with requests), obedience (to orders), conformity (to norms or expectations) or commitment (to a shared vision).

4.2 We will look in detail at influencing methods and tactics later, but from your own experience, you may be aware that there are many forms of pressure that can be used to change people's minds or gain their co-operation, including: persuasive arguments, powerful information or ideas (as when we talk about 'influential' books or movies); the desire to emulate a role model; or the desire to be part of a group (and therefore to conform to its ideas and behaviours).

4.3 Power can also be applied to direct people's behaviour in various ways, because (as we have seen) it implies the right to do so (as in the case of organisational authority), or the ability to offer (or withhold) something that individuals value enough that they are willing to comply.

Influencing and negotiation

4.4 Negotiation is a process through which two parties come together intentionally to confer with a view to concluding a jointly acceptable agreement. John Gennard & Graham Judge *(Employee Relations)* define negotiation as a process involving both purposeful persuasion (where each party presents its case or viewpoint, with the aim of getting the other party to agree) and constructive compromise (where both parties accept the need to move closer towards each other's position).

4.5 Influencing is thus different from negotiation in several key respects.

- Influencing is not a single event or series of events: it is a continual process.
- Influencing need not be an intentional (or even conscious) process for either or both parties: you can influence someone without knowing it, and you can influence someone without *their* knowing it.
- Influencing need not involve conferring, or two-way presentation of arguments: it can simply be applied from one party to another.
- Influencing need not end with an explicit joint agreement.
- Influencing need not involve compromise or movement by both parties to reach middle ground: its aim is to draw the influencee over to the influencer's position.

4.6 In some ways, though, the processes are linked. Techniques and tactics of influence and persuasion are, by definition, used by both parties in a negotiation. And the aims of *ethical* influencing are not dissimilar to a negotiated approach: the aim is to allow both parties to have their views and needs taken into account, and to integrate their goals and interests so that the outcome is perceived as a win-win.

Influencing and manipulation

4.7 Most modern writers on influencing recognise that influencing skills are 'dangerous', in that they allow people to manipulate or control others: coercing or tricking them into doing something they don't want to do. Gillen *(Agreed: improve your powers of influence, 1999)* distinguishes clearly between what he calls 'manipulative' influencing and 'positive' (or ethical) influencing.

- **Manipulative influencing** uses tactics based on dishonest logic or negative emotion (such as fear or guilt). Such an approach seeks to dismiss or override the influencee's beliefs or interests, using tactics such as bullying, false logic, cajoling, bribing and emotional blackmail.
- **Positive influencing** is defined as 'non-manipulative, persuading behaviours that demonstrate that you are treating people openly, honestly and respectfully' – as befits a leader. A positive influencer

seeks to understand the influencee's point of view (through questioning and active listening); allows the influencee to feel heard (through empathy); *then* seeks to help the other person to understand the alternative point of view (through clear, assertive communication); and finally invites or leads the influencee to agree (through rapport-building and persuasion).

4.8 Manipulative influencing can be effective in gaining agreement or compliance – in the short term. However, it tends to have negative side-effects such as resentment, unhelpfulness, and lack of ownership of what has been agreed.

4.9 In contrast, positive influencing 'uses openness and honesty which show respect to the other person, and makes it easy for them to appreciate your point of view. If they accept your invitation to agree with you, their commitment is likely to be sustained into the future' (Gillen). This is important for the development and maintenance of constructive, collaborative, potentially long-term and increasingly trust-based supply chain relationships.

Objectives and outcomes of influencing attempts

4.10 Different influencing styles or approaches have different effects on the influencee – and influencees can respond to attempts to influence them in different ways. We have already suggested, for example, that the use of positional authority or coercive power (and win-lose negotiation) may gain compliance, but may also create underlying resentment and resistance – while the use of expert and reward power (and win-win negotiation) can secure buy-in or ownership of the agreed course of action.

4.11 The literature on leadership and influencing suggests that people's responses to influence attempts take three basic forms: resistance, compliance and internalisation.

4.12 **Resistance** means that intended influencees position themselves against the request, and actively attempt to avoid having to comply with it. This may take the form of outright refusal (if the influencer lacks power); apathy or excuses (in order to avoid involvement); requests for changes or clarifications (to delay the issue); or objections (to dissuade the influencer from persisting with the plan). There may also be attempts to undermine the influencer or the plan, by foot-dragging (delay), sabotage, criticism (to others), creating an opposing coalition, or appealing to higher authority.

4.13 Boddy notes that: 'Resistant staff will have no commitment to the work. They do what is required grudgingly, and without enthusiasm or imagination. While it may be possible to overcome resistance by using threats or coercion, this may not be the most useful reaction in the longer term.'

4.14 Note that these tactics may apply to supply chains, as well as to individual team members. You should be able to come up with examples such as: quality or service levels that are on the borderline of acceptability; delays and excuses; requests for changes to delivery or contract terms; withholding delivery or payment and so on.

4.15 **Compliance** means that intended influencees are willing to do what is requested of them, but no more. They make the minimal effort necessary to satisfy the terms of the legal and psychological contract they have agreed to – but no more. (This is sometimes called *'satisficing' behaviour*.) Compliance is at best unenthusiastic and at worst grudging to the point of sabotage. Underlying attitudes have not been altered by the influence attempt.

4.16 Compliance may be sufficient in some contexts: where the work is highly programmed or automated, for example. However, the modern business environment is increasingly characterised by complex and flexible work processes, a growing service and knowledge-based sector, and a focus on competitive advantage through customer and supplier relationship management, quality and innovation. In such an environment, organisations need their people to work with commitment, imagination, initiative and flexibility; buyers need their suppliers to work proactively with them towards innovation, flexibility, improvement and value-adding goals. Managers may be satisfied with compliance: leaders will attempt to use their influence to achieve more.

4.17 In one sense, however, you should be aware that 'compliance' is a key value in the leadership of purchasing: the need to comply with relevant legislation and regulation (on health and safety, equal opportunities, consumer protection, contract law and so on). Even then, there is a growing recognition that 'the law is a floor': it defines minimal standards of acceptable conduct – not good or best practice. Many socially responsible organisations are replacing a 'compliance-based' approach to ethics with an 'integrity-based' approach, based on internalisation and commitment.

4.18 **Internalisation** means that intended influencees are brought to agree internally with the request, decision or viewpoint of the influencer: it is aligned with their own goals, beliefs and interests, so that they are able to buy into it in a personally-committed way. They are therefore likely to be willing to put forth extra effort and energy on its behalf: not just complying with the requirements or expectations of others, but doing their best to support success. Signs of internalisation may include: staff or supply chain partners giving proactive input and suggestions for innovation or improvement; willingness to collaborate to resolve conflicts and problems; the communication or teaching of new values and ideas to others; and so on.

4.19 Gary Yukl, RH Guest and other writers use the term 'commitment' in place of internalisation, as the most effective outcome of leadership influence. It is founded on mutually-beneficial, long-term relationships and exchanges (whether with employers or with supply chain partners) and shared values.

5 Influencing styles and tactics

Push and pull influencing behaviours

5.1 Some methods of influencing are more directive (power-based) than others. There are two broad approaches to influencing: Table 3.3.

Table 3.3 *Push influencing and pull influencing*

A PUSH APPROACH	A PULL APPROACH
• Exerting power or authority • Influencees are fully aware of the process • Aimed at securing compliance, often against the resistance of influencees	• Persuasion or interpersonal influence • If performed effectively, influencees may not be consciously aware of the process • Can secure commitment, if influencees own the need for action or change as fitting their own goals and interests

5.2 While push approaches may secure compliance, they reflect a power imbalance and the pursuit of one party's goals at the expense of the other's. This can create resentment and barriers to a fully collaborative relationship.

5.3 Pull approaches tend to foster positive and trusting relationships, with the potential for true collaboration, as they integrate the goals and interests of both parties. The influencee complies or co-operates because he wants to: it's perceived as a win-win outcome.

Persuasion

5.4 Persuasion may be defined as: 'a means of exerting influence over people by means *other than using authority or power*.' It is the basis of a pull approach to influencing: pulling or leading people to change by bringing their beliefs and goals into alignment with those of the influencer.

5.5 A persuasive negotiation strategy is one which, essentially, seeks to appeal to the needs, goals and interests of the other party. Persuasion is a form of *motivation*: if you can make it look as if aligning themselves with your viewpoint or plans will offer others something of benefit to them, they will be more amenable to persuasion. This may take the form of positive reinforcement (offering satisfaction of a need or desire, or the solution to a problem) or negative reinforcement (confronting people with the potential negative outcomes of *not* agreeing or changing).

5.6 Another key approach to persuasion is **logical argument**, usually supported by relevant and verifiable factual evidence. The demonstration of objectivity or fairness to both sides of an argument or question may also be used to enhance your credibility or 'believability' – since it takes the other party's objections into account.

5.7 Logical argument is essentially a facilitative approach, whereby each step of the argument is clearly explained and linked. 'For someone to be convinced of something, the "penny has to drop" in their mind. That is, it has to make sense to *them*. No matter how obvious something is to you, if you want someone's help, co-operation or agreement, it has to be obvious to them' (Gillen, *Agreed: Improve your Powers of Influence).*

5.8 Here are some examples of facilitative communication skills (often identified with 'active listening').

- The use of questions and answers, to support information exchange
- Presenting complex arguments in manageable segments
- Summarising each section of a discussion or argument, to reinforce understanding
- Asking for feedback, to check understanding
- Sensitivity and flexibility to respond to verbal and non-verbal signals of where the other party is 'up to': resistance, perplexity, readiness to move forward – and so on.

5.9 Lewicki, Barry and Saunders *(Essentials of Negotiation)* emphasise that the effectiveness of persuasion depends on the effectiveness of communication. The key question is whether the targets of persuasion are (a) motivated and (b) able to carefully process the communication 'message' we are sending.

- If they are, we enjoy a **central route to influence**, which can lead to enduring commitment and attitude change – because the recipients of our message are able to internalise it.
- If they are *not*, we enjoy at best a **peripheral route to influence,** because our persuasive message is not getting across clearly. Failure to 'hit home' with our message can lead to short-term compliance, but not internalisation or commitment – especially since the other party will be open to counter-influences which may undermine our message.

5.10 A persuasive communication style therefore uses techniques such as: the building of rapport; open or positive body language; pacing and leading (showing that you hear and understand the other person's viewpoint *before* you attempt to re-frame it); and speaking with appropriate emphasis, appeal and interest.

Influencing methods

5.11 Yukl *(Leadership in Organisations,* 1998) identified three basic types of influence which could be used depending on one's intended purpose.

- **Impression (or image) management** is designed to create or enhance one's credibility and congeniality in the eyes of other people.
- **Political influence** is designed to gain and apply various forms of power, in order to influence decisions in favour of one's own (or group) interests.
- **Proactive (or ecological) influence** is designed to set up conditions in which one is more likely to get the help, support or resources one needs: establishing rapport and trust, building networks and relationships and so on.

Proactive influencing tactics

5.12 There are many more specific classifications of influencing strategies, tactics and styles, and you may encounter favourites of your own during your studies.

5.13 Yukl and CM Falbe ('Influence tactics in upward, downward and lateral influence attempts', in *Journal of Applied Psychology,* 1990) studied management behaviour in different directions to derive nine basic tactics: Table 3.4.

Table 3.4 *Influencing tactics*

TACTIC	APPROACH	ADVANTAGES	DISADVANTAGES
Rational persuasion	Logical argument and evidence, designed to demonstrate credibly that the request or plan is desirable and feasible	• Fosters agreement and commitment, rather than mere compliance • Bolsters low position power with expert power and perceived objectivity	• May be difficult or ineffective if the argument is weak, or up against genuine conflicts of interest or ideology
Inspirational appeal	Appeal to the influencee's ideals, values and aspirations, and/or statements of belief and encouragement, arousing confidence and enthusiasm	• Addresses powerful and positive motivating factors • Suits values-based culture, transformational leader	• Can be perceived as shallow and manipulative, especially if promised rewards do not accrue.
Consultation	Asking the influencee to participate in planning an activity or programme, or demonstrating willingness to take the influencee's ideas and concerns into account	• Input may enhance a decision; ownership, implementation • Fosters communication and co-ordination • Compliance issue (eg with employees)	• Takes time • Allows divergent interests and conflict to emerge. (NB may be seen as useful feedback, aid to genuine consensus)
Ingratiation	Getting the influencee to think well of you, or to be in a co-operative frame of mind, before a request is made (sometimes known as 'buttering up'!)	• Repays investment in trust, rapport and relationship-building • Helps to condition responses.	• Can be transparent, perceived as manipulative and treated with suspicion. ('What does he want?')
Exchange	Offering a reciprocal exchange of favours ('Do this and I'll owe you one') or promising a share of the benefits or added value accruing from the plan	• Recognises divergent interests or goals • Perceived as fair: neither party gains a hold over the other • Exploring 'currencies' can create win-win	• Less effective in power-imbalanced relationships: what can the weaker party meaningfully offer in return?
Personal appeal	Appealing to personal friendship and loyalty between the influencer and influencee	• Repays investment in rapport, trust and relationship-building	• Can be perceived as (or lead to) unethical lack of objectivity Ineffective where no trust or rapport exist
Coalition	Seeking the help of others to persuade the influencee, or using the fact of their support as a reason for the influencee to agree as well	• Enhances influence, without creating personal threat • Helps to disseminate influence and information	• Can be perceived as political • Can create resentment
Legitimating	Establishing the objective legitimacy of a request (eg on the basis of authority, rules, policies, custom, contract terms)	• Depersonalises conflict by appealing to shared and objective imperatives	• May be resented as a threat of escalation, or way to avoid addressing influencee's concerns
Pressure	Threatening sanctions, or using assertiveness bordering on aggression, to demand compliance	• Can secure swift compliance • Can wear down resistance	• Compliance rather than commitment • Can foster apathy, resentment, resistance, conflict

5.14 Different tactics are typically used depending on the 'direction' of the influence: for example, managing upwards (influencing people in more senior positions in the organisation), managing across (influencing peers, colleagues and supply chain partners) and managing downwards (influencing direct reports or 'subordinates', and teams in which you have a direct leadership role). We will look at which influencing tactics are most appropriate (and most often used) in each context, in Chapter 4.

5.15 In general, however, the choice of influencing tactic will depend on: the leader's power or resources to make the tactic work; the likely response of the other person (and whether this suits your goals for the outcome and the relationship between you); the potential costs of the strategy (in terms of reciprocal obligations, broken relationship or loss of credibility, say); how ethical the strategy is (in its effect on others); and the prevailing culture of the organisation (which may make some tactics more acceptable than others).

Psychological principles of influence

5.16 Another perspective on the tactics of influencing comes from the research of Robert Cialdini. (*Influence: The Psychology of Persuasion,* 2001). Cialdini identified six basic social and psychological principles that form the foundation for successful strategies used to achieve influence.

- **Reciprocation**. An individual is usually highly motivated to reciprocate in response to the behaviour of another individual. This means that a leader can give benefits to someone he wants to influence in the future, confident that the recipient will be motivated to respond to his influence when the time comes.
- **Commitment/consistency**. Individuals have a strong desire to behave consistently. They are typically uncomfortable in taking a stance that contradicts something they have said or done earlier. Effective leaders are adept at inducing individuals to take an initial position consistent with a behaviour that they intend to request later.
- **Authority**. People are more willing to follow the directions or recommendations of someone to whom they attribute relevant authority or expertise. By his actions, an effective leader will convince others of his authority and right to expect compliance.
- **Social validation**. Individuals are inclined to see the actions of others – especially others similar to themselves – as providing guidance for their own decisions. Effective leaders are skilful in arguing that others have adopted the course of action now recommended by themselves.
- **Scarcity**. If people can be persuaded that objects or opportunities are scarce, they are more likely to desire them. Cialdini cites the example of a beef importer who told his customers, on good authority, that there was about to be a shortage of a particular product. Sales orders increased dramatically overnight.
- **Liking/friendship**. People prefer to say yes to individuals they know and like. Many effective leaders are charismatic: they have the ability to attract liking and friendship. This makes it more likely that their influence will lead to the desired objectives.

6 Influencing as an interpersonal process

6.1 In this section, we will look at some of the key interpersonal skills for influencing.

Interpersonal sensitivity

6.2 It is worth remembering that business people are people. This may seem obvious, but it is all too possible to approach dealings with key stakeholders as if they were 'resources' or 'elements in the value chain' or 'problems' – without remembering that they are also human beings.

6.3 The core leadership quality of emotional intelligence includes being aware of, or sensitive to, the needs and emotions of other people – and being able to respond flexibly to those needs and emotions in such a way as to build relationships and get the best out of people. James Borg (*Persuasion*, 2004) argues that this is also the key to a leader's ability to influence: persuasive power depends on empathy (the ability to identify and understand the other person's feelings, ideas and situation) and sincerity (conveying genuineness and trustworthiness).

Rapport

6.4   Rapport may be defined, most simply, as the sense of relationship or connection we have when we relate to another person.

6.5   We have 'positive rapport' with people we find warm, attentive and easy to talk to: we are inclined to feel comfortable and relaxed with them, or attracted to them. We all know from experience that some people are easier to relate to than others. Some individuals seem distant or uninterested in us, or we feel less comfortable around them: we would call this low or negative rapport. (Fortunately for leaders, this is not a matter of personality, but of behaviour: establishing positive rapport is a skill which can be learned.)

6.6   Rapport is a core skill for influencing, in simple terms, because: 'influencing is easier if the other person feels comfortable with you; if they feel they trust you; if they feel you understand them' (Gillen, *Agreed*). In more detail, rapport:

(a)   Helps to establish trust and a belief in the common ground between you and the other person: your viewpoint is then more likely to be received openly, rather than defensively.

(b)   Is the basis of the positive influencing approach, sometimes called **pacing and leading**. First you 'pace' the other party (listening to, empathising with and reflecting back their views, feelings and needs). This earns trust and rapport from which you can 'lead' (influence) the other person (eg by reframing the problem or changing the emotional tone of the discussion).

(c)   Creates a reason for people to agree with you, or do what you want them to do, because they like you! (A powerful motivator, even in business contexts...)

(d)   Overcomes some of the barriers created by power imbalances and differences or conflicts of interest, reducing the tendency towards adversarial or defensive attitudes.

6.7   Key **rapport-building techniques** are based on the idea that it is easier to relate to someone who is (or appears to be) *like* us in some way; with whom we share some beliefs, values, interests or characteristics; and who treats us as a valued and interesting person. Some useful techniques therefore include:

- Subtly matching or 'mirroring' the other person's posture, body language and/or volume, speed and tone of voice. (This also reflects their mood and helps them to feel understood.)
- Picking up on the other person's use of technical words, colloquialisms and metaphors – and using them too (if you can do so with understanding and integrity) or incorporating them in comments and discussion summaries.
- Picking up on the other person's dominant way of experiencing and expressing things, which tend to be based on sight, sound or feeling ('I see what you mean', 'I hear what you're saying', 'That just hit me') and using similar modes of expression ('Do you see?', 'How does that sound to you?', 'What's your feeling about that?')
- Listening attentively and actively to what the other person is saying; demonstrating this with encouraging gestures, eye contact (where culturally appropriate) and so on; and asking supportive questions or summarising, in order to show that you are interested and want to understand. (This is the skill of **empathy**.)
- Finding topics of common interest, and emphasising areas of agreement or common ground where possible
- Remembering and using people's names.

Communication skills for influencing

6.8 Influencers require a broad repertoire of communication skills. Gillen, for example, includes among his list of influencing skills: probing (using questions); active listening; expressing empathy with another person's viewpoint and feelings; communicating assertively; building and maintaining rapport; focusing on interpersonal processes (rather than merely the content of what is being said); and using and interpreting body language.

6.9 Borg offers a similar list, adding an important situational element: the need to be aware of the context in which your attempts at influencing are being experienced by the other person. Examples include being aware when your visit or telephone call 'comes at a bad time' for someone, or being aware that the person is distracted and rapport has been broken. Rather than fighting these barriers to influence, it may be better to empathise – and offer an alternative time to raise the issue.

Behavioural technologies

6.10 Perhaps the best known of the behavioural technologies used to train people in influencing and negotiation is **neuro-linguistic programming** (NLP), which seeks to help people to:

- Understand how sensory perception and language influence behaviour
- Utilise techniques based on the ability of thoughts, language and sensory cues to change or reinforce behaviour
- Act more intentionally to produce the results they want in their own behaviours and in their interactions with other people.

6.11 Some of the mainstream technologies established by the developers of NLP, for use in negotiation and influencing, include the following.

- **Preferred information-processing channels**: determining how people best process information, whether visually, by hearing or by touch, and using this:
  - In establishing rapport: reflecting the other person's dominant channel ('I see what you mean', 'I hear you', 'That just hit me') so that they feel you are like them and they relate to you
  - In persuading and influencing: visual people may need to see evidence or have information in writing ; audio people may need to be told; kinetic people may need to handle samples, or experience something in action.
- **Mirroring**: picking up aspects of another person's body language, vocal tone, vocabulary and dominant information-processing channel – without obviously 'mimicking' – in order to establish rapport
- **Pacing and leading**: 'walking alongside' the other person by establishing rapport and empathy (reflecting back their views, summarising their feelings, mirroring their body language and expression) – and *then* changing the tone, pace or body language, re-framing the issue and so on. Having first got the person in tune with you, you are better positioned to take them with you when you move forward or make a change.
- **Anchoring:** using conditioning techniques to evoke resourceful states for negotiation (confidence, assertiveness or calm) when needed. This is done by accessing that state (from past memories or imagination) and then 'anchoring' it to a physical sensation (such as pressing the back of the hand): the desired state should then be able to be triggered simply by duplicating the physical sensation.
- **Mental rehearsal**: visualising, as fully as possible, the negotiation process or outcome. This is a way of mentally rehearsing and scripting events, but it can also be combined with anchoring to associate calm, confident states with the negotiation process.
- **Framing and re-framing**: putting things in different contexts to shift assumptions and generate options
- **Positioning**: shifting the issue upward (to higher outcomes or criteria), downward (to details), sideways (to alternative options) or outwards (to other viewpoints) to help shift 'positions' into different perspectives

- **Intentional use of language** to shift thought and behaviour patterns. One simple example is using 'and' instead of 'but', to convey co-operation and avoid shutting down options. Other examples, highlighted by the Senior Assessor for the old *Effective Negotiation* module *(Supply Management,* 7 June 2007) include:
  — 'Tag questions': eg 'We'll agree on that, won't we?' The first part is effectively an instruction (since the hearer's brain processes the active key words and ignores the rest), but it is disguised by being turned into a question. Tags can be reinforced by body language such as eye contact and nodding.
  — 'Double binds': eg 'You'll be signing the contract today or tomorrow?' Again, there's a disguised instruction, made acceptable by apparent freedom of choice – while limiting the options to an either/or (both favourable to the influencer: note that there is no 'not signing' option as a direct answer to this question).

3

Chapter summary

- There are different sources of power in organisational relationships (French and Raven): legitimate power (authority); expert power; reward power; referent power and coercion. Each type may be used in purchasing relationships in different contexts.
- Influencing is the process of applying pressure in order to change other people's attitudes or behaviours: to secure their compliance (with requests), obedience (to orders), conformity (to norms or expectations) or commitment (to a shared vision).
- Influencing can be distinguished from negotiation (although influencing techniques may be used as part of the negotiation process) and from manipulation (although manipulative influencing tactics may be used).
- Key interpersonal skills for influencing include: interpersonal sensitivity; rapport building; empathy; pacing and leading; establishing trust; and communication.
- There are two broad approaches to influencing: push (power-based) and pull (persuasion and inspiration based). Persuasion is a means of exerting influence *other* than by using authority or power: it aims to bring other people's beliefs and goals into alignment with those of the influencer, using logical argument, facilitative techniques and a persuasive communication style.
- There are three basic outcomes of influencing attempts: resistance (overt or covert); compliance (doing just enough but no more); and internalisation or commitment (agreement, ownership and proactive support).
- Yukl and Falbe classify nine influencing tactics: rational persuasion; inspirational appeal; consultation; ingratiation; exchange; personal appeal; coalition; legitimating; and pressure.

Self-test questions

Numbers in brackets refer to the paragraphs where you can check your answers.

1   List challenges faced by leaders in supply chains. (Table 3.1)

2   Define power in an organisational context. (2.1)

3   Describe the sources of power in organisational relationships, as identified by French and Raven. (2.8)

4   Distinguish between staff authority and functional authority. (2.13)

5   Describe three ways in which control can be exercised in organisations (Rosemary Stewart). (3.5)

6   Sketch the power/dependency matrix developed by Andrew Cox *et al.* (Figure 3.1)

7   Define 'influencing'. (4.1)

8   In what ways does influencing differ from negotiation? (4.5)

9   Distinguish between push and pull approaches to influencing. (Table 3.3)

10   List the nine influencing tactics identified by Yukl and Falbe. (Table 3.4)

11   Define 'rapport'. (6.4)

CHAPTER 4

Leadership Contexts

Assessment criteria and indicative content

2.1 Evaluate the main influencing styles that can be used in the effective leadership of a supply chain

- Implementing a vision of improved procurement and supply chain management
- Models for managing in four different directions
- The relevance of managing upwards and across to achieve desired results for improved supply chain management
- The merits of escalation as a means of influencing
- A range of influencing styles for cross-functional leadership both within and outside the bounds of formal teams

Section headings

1   Leading in four directions
2   Managing upwards
3   Managing across
4   Managing direct reports and teams

Introduction

In this chapter we explore some of the structural contexts in which leadership takes place.

We examine each of the four 'directions' in which a procurement and supply chain manager may be required to exercise effective leadership: upwards (leading our bosses), downwards (direct reports and teams), sideways (across functions eg in procurement teams and projects) and outwards (external stakeholders in the supply chain). The management and influencing of external stakeholders will be considered separately, in more detail, in Chapter 5.

The syllabus emphasises that leadership in these contexts relies heavily on the use of 'influencing' – since, other than the case of managing downwards, the manager may well lack formal authority to 'command and control' the other parties in the relationship. Our discussion here builds on our coverage of power and influencing in Chapter 3, and applies Yukl and Falbe's model of 'influencing tactics' (among others) to the consideration of multi-directional leadership.

1 Leading in four directions

Driving improvement in procurement and supply chain management

1.1 It is worth noting here, as in Chapter 3, that the context envisaged by the syllabus for evaluating effective upward, downward and lateral influencing styles in the supply chain is 'implementing a vision of improved procurement and supply chain management'. We discuss the articulation and communication of vision in Chapter 8 on change management. The main thing here is to highlight the *purpose* of effective four-directional leadership in supply chains – which is to add value, enhance competitiveness and secure continual improvement in processes, conduct and performance.

Leading in four directions

1.2 The discussion so far in this Course Book has generally envisaged leadership as a top-down process, as typified by the perception that 'leaders have followers'. However, the concept of informal leadership emphasises that the exercise of leadership and influence does not necessarily occur within a formal, top-down hierarchy or 'chain of command'.

1.3 David Buchanan and David Boddy *(Take the Lead: Interpersonal Skills for Project Managers,* 1992) argue that management and leadership are potentially exercised in four different directions: Figure 4.1

Figure 4.1 *Leading and influencing in four directions*

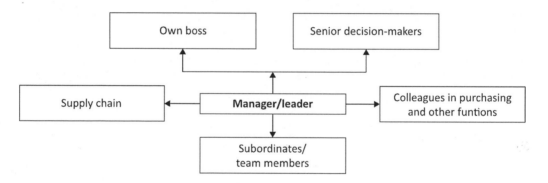

1.4 We will now look in detail at the influencing styles and leadership techniques that can be used in managing upward, across and downward. The management of external stakeholders in the supply chain will be considered separately in Chapter 5.

2 Managing upwards

The relevance of managing upwards

2.1 Upward management is an important process in achieving desired results for improved supply chain management:

- For lower levels of management to gain access to the decision-making authority, information and resources only available at higher levels
- For people to gain the support (or at least authorisation) required to put their plans into action
- For procurement managers to secure executive sponsorship for procurement projects and key supplier relationships
- To manage the expectations of more senior managers, ensuring that deadlines and success measures are realistic, job relevant and adequately resourced
- To keep superiors informed, and to habituate them to reporting by exception, in order to avoid micro-management (or 'management by interference')

- To promote the achievements of individuals or teams to superiors, so that their ability and potential will be noticed. (This may be an important part of procurement marketing in an organisation, for example, in order to enhance the credibility and status of the procurement function – with the aim of securing a more strategic role in relation to issues such as make/do or buy decisions, sourcing strategies and supply chain development.)

How to manage upwards

2.2 The main issue for influencing upwards is that you lack positional authority to impose what you want – or even perhaps (in the case of significantly higher managers) to get a hearing. Managing upwards requires assertiveness (the ability to state clearly, calmly, positively and persistently what you want) and subtlety.

2.3 Research shows that, when influencing up, managers use tactics in the following order of preference.

- Rational persuasion: particularly effective because it is appreciated by the superiors themselves as a positive contribution to business objectives.
- Coalition: bolsters the individual's position without direct threat, as it makes the influence collective rather than personal
- Ingratiation or personal appeal: where trust and rapport exist, this can be utilised.

2.4 Exchange is less popular in this context, since the power imbalance may undermine reciprocity: what can the subordinate meaningfully offer in return?

2.5 A mix of rational persuasion and coalition may be particularly effective in leading upwards. Upward reporting can be used to gain support and sponsorship for ideas, initiatives and plans: using logical argument to sell your ideas; gathering support from people involved in the decision-making process; and/or getting key influencers to become sponsors or champions of your ideas, who can get them on the agenda and push for them within the decision-making group. It also demonstrates your political awareness and influencing skills.

2.6 **Persuasive communication** to one's superiors (particularly senior decision-makers) should:

- Use appropriate channels and methods of communication
- Be concise, relevant (to the superior's concerns and goals), professional and timely: not alienating recipients by wasting their time
- Present logical argument, leading to a firmly supported conclusion or recommendation. Supporting evidence need not be supplied in detail, but it should be clear that such evidence is available
- Present a business case for any proposals, plans or recommendations being put forward. This is a basic point of influencing and motivation in this context: senior managers, in particular, will only engage if it will further the strategic objectives of the business. In addition, it demonstrates the subordinate's ability to take a big picture view of priorities (sometimes called **helicopter ability**): a useful part of impressions management.

2.7 Effective upward management supports supply chain management in the following ways.

- Helping emergent ideas to find shape and direction through the process of communication, evaluation and lobbying for support
- Helping secure support and resources, when needed, in order to achieve results
- Maximising follow-through on promises of support and resources
- Raising the organisational profile and status of a project or department
- Minimising managerial interference (by demonstrating competence and/or assertively resisting micro-management)
- Modelling upward communication flow (which may encourage suggestions, ideas and feedback from your own subordinates)

2.8 Consider how the opposite effects would show the symptoms of poor upward management (in an exam scenario, say)...

3 Managing across

Cross-functional leadership contexts

3.1 A purchasing manager may exercise lateral influence within the organisation in:

- **Cross-functional teams:** for example, a project team which includes a procurement officer or adviser, or
- **Cross-functional networks:** formal and informal communication, for the purposes of information-sharing and co-ordination, between colleagues in different functions (as, for example, when a procurement manager sets buying protocols for user-department buyers, or seeks to have input to new product design or operations management processes).

3.2 Tom Peters *(Liberation Management)* used the term **horizontal structures** for organisational forms which allow work and information to flow freely across functional boundaries, without the vertical barriers created by specialisation, departmental job demarcations and formal communication channels.

3.3 Cross-functional teams are a key tool for co-ordination across organisational boundaries, since they typically involve representatives of different functional departments or units. This increases the flow of communication, informal (network) relationships and co-operation. It is an important element in aligning business processes, so that the flow of added value towards customers (and customers' experience of the organisation) is not impeded by vertical barriers.

3.4 Product development, supply, customer service, innovation and learning are all essentially horizontal activities, requiring the free exchange of information and work flows across functional boundaries as value flows towards the customer. Cross-functional teams contribute significantly to the flexibility and responsiveness of organisations (and supply chains) in competitive and fast-changing environments. They support innovation through the pooling of different expertise and knowledge, and they enable swift decision-making by avoiding lengthy vertical channels of communication and authorisation.

Cross-functional leadership roles

3.5 Cross-functional working often requires different leadership roles.

- There may be a designated **team leader or project manager**, who has primary responsibility for building and managing the team and for delivering unit or project outcomes on time and within budget.
- There is likely to be a **team or project sponsor**: a key stakeholder who has primary responsibility for the achievement of the team or project's business objectives, and who provides and is accountable for the resources invested into the project. For permanent cross-functional co-ordination, the sponsor role may simply reflect the nearest point in the organisation structure at which all team members report to the same manager (who has responsibility for a range of functions). For projects, however, there is usually a defined individual or group who initiates the project, and ensures that the human and other resources are available to support its objectives. The sponsor's role is to act as an integrator and facilitator of the team's efforts.
- The team may effectively be **autonomous or self-managing**. Self-managed teams contract with management to assume various degrees of managerial responsibility for the team's task activity (day-to-day planning and control) and internal people management functions (selection, coaching, development and so on). Team members learn and share management tasks: no immediate manager is visible, although the team may report to a sponsor.

Leadership challenges of cross-functional working

3.6 Despite the benefits and popularity of cross-functional teamworking, there are a number of management and leadership challenges associated with it.

- While representing different viewpoints and interests can enhance decisions (and their acceptability), it also adds potential for time-consuming complexity, conflict and consensus-seeking.
- Horizontal structures may lack clear authority structures: team members may need to exert informal influence through persuasion, politics, negotiation or personal leadership in order to have their functional perspective heard.
- All teams take time to develop before they perform effectively: to overcome conflict, build trust, allocate roles and determine a shared working style. The leader will need to facilitate or work around these processes in order to support the team in getting to the 'performing' stage of development.
- There may be difficulties of dual authority structures and conflicting demands, if cross-functional team members also report to their individual departments. Leaders may need to negotiate resources and priorities with departmental managers. They may also have to support team members through the stress of conflicting demands and dual reporting.
- There may be practical difficulties of organising meetings and information flows, given different functional work patterns, locations and so on. (ICT links may be used to support 'virtual' teamworking, meetings, data-sharing and so on.)

Influencing styles for cross-functional leadership

3.7 The key issue for lateral influence is that, like upward influence, it may not be supported by legitimate positional power. The procurement manager may have expert power in these situations, but additional influencing tactics may be required if the expert power is not recognised or valued by others (as may well be the case).

3.8 When 'influencing across', Yukl and Falbe found that managers use influencing tactics in the following order of preference.

- Personal appeal or ingratiation: reflects the balance of power between the two parties – and investment in networking and relationship-building
- Rational persuasion and consultation: capitalises on the potential for expert power, and fosters trust, information-sharing, co-operation and integration
- Exchange: the equality of power and interdependency gives particular value to the concept of reciprocity in this case. The parties may be able to trade relatively equal benefits or favours, to mutual advantage – and without one party gaining a hold over the other.
- Legitimating. In the absence of positional authority, this might involve appeals to organisational policies, procedures and interests.

The merits of escalation as a means of influencing

3.9 Escalation is used in various senses, to describe a raising of the intensity of one's response to situations. A conflict may be said to escalate if the level of adversarialism, and the intensity of the pressures applied in the attempt to influence the outcome, are raised. So, for example, the order of the influencing tactics in Table 3.4 may be seen as a progressive escalation, moving away from pull approaches towards push approaches.

3.10 On the one hand, such escalation gives a clear message that the influencer is serious about the issue, and intends to use all ethical means to pursue his or her objectives. This may have the effect of wearing down resistance and minimising frivolous objections. On the other hand, there are costs to escalation, in terms of the potential for hardened resistance, resentment, the owing of reciprocal favours and so on: we noted some of the effects of push influencing tactics earlier.

3.11 A conflict may also be said to escalate if it involves appeals to higher authority, involving more serious consequences. Another influencing tactics model, by David Kipnis *et al* ('Intra-organisational influence tactics: explorations in getting one's way' in *Journal of Applied Psychology,* 1980) includes appeal (or threatening to appeal) to higher authority in the organisation (or external powers such as regulators or key stakeholders) to gain agreement or compliance: ie 'going over the head' of the intended influencee.

3.12 Again, this may be effective where an issue is serious, and may be a method of de-personalising potential conflict (because it allows third party arbitration or sets up objective external standards by which a decision can be made). However, it may also be seen as an aggressive political move which causes resentment. It is often considered more constructive to resolve issues on a 'peer' basis.

Networking

3.13 A key source of cross-functional (and cross-organisational) influence is networking: making and cultivating interpersonal contacts. This is what makes consultation, friendliness, coalition and other forms of influencing – which depend on knowing and developing relationships with people – possible.

3.14 Networking is identified by Pedler, Burgoyne and Boydell *(A Manager's Guide to Leadership,* 2004) as one of the core practices of leadership. They argue that 'networks are the key to **connection power** – one of the most underrated forms of power and one that has grown in importance in the information age. Developing connection power means building personal networks that also help create power for the others in these relationships. They make it easy to contact and access relevant people when we need help to accomplish tasks. A wide network provides the wherewithal to cross departmental boundaries and other disputed territories, including even hierarchies, to get things done. Through connecting as peers we can access people in authority structures, both more and less powerful than ourselves.'

Interdepartmental relations

3.15 Taylor *(The Naked Leader,* 2002) stresses the need for leaders to promote their departments and teams, in order to raise their profile, and manage perceptions of them in the organisation. 'People, and what they think of us, are the key. The active promotion of your team's services, and results, is a growing priority on business leaders' agendas... That will buy us time, and support, to carry out our roles and achieve more... Make sure you are communicating with [other functions and superiors] when things are going well, and not just in response to complaints...' (This works with external customers too...)

3.16 **Procurement marketing** is, simply, the way the procurement function 'markets' itself in the organisation. In the same way as the organisation (through its marketing function) promotes itself and its brands, products and services to potential customers in the external market, so the procurement or purchasing function needs to promote itself and its services to its internal customers. This is particularly important if internal customers have the option of obtaining services elsewhere (eg from a procurement consultancy or outsourced service provider, or by carrying out purchasing activity themselves).

3.17 Like product marketing, procurement marketing is effectively an exercise in both (a) market and customer research and (b) customer communication (or promotion). Some of the questions that may form a basis for procurement marketing planning include the following.

- Who are the key customers of procurement?
- What are these customers' key needs, wants and expectations in the area of procurement?
- How effectively is procurement fulfilling these needs, wants and expectations?
- What (if any) are customers' perceptions of the status, credibility and value contribution of procurement; the services it offers; and the level and cost of the service it provides?
- Who are the key competitors of procurement in providing service to internal customers?
- What unique competencies, strengths and weaknesses does procurement have in comparison to its

competitors (ie what are its current and potential sources of competitive advantage?)

- What are procurement's key promotional messages or 'selling points' to internal customers? What 'track record' can be demonstrated – or what 'success stories' can be promoted? What is the 'business case' for procurement?
- How effectively does procurement gather information, on an ongoing basis, about customers, their needs and their level of satisfaction with the service provided?
- How effectively is ongoing contact and communication with customers managed? (In other words, how good is procurement's customer relationship management?)
- How committed is procurement to the continuous improvement of its services, in order to maintain customer satisfaction and loyalty?
- What performance measures will procurement use to evaluate its customer service and marketing effectiveness?

4　Managing direct reports and teams

Influencing styles for 'managing down'

4.1　Leading direct reports is in some ways the most straightforward context of influencing, because managers have formally delegated positional power or authority over subordinates (or teams of which they are the designated or elected leader). There is a legitimate expectation that requests and instructions will be complied with, and this can be backed up by a disciplinary framework of rewards and punishments. Influence and leadership are therefore applied in order to gain commitment over and above mere compliance.

4.2　When **influencing down**, Yukl and Falbe found that managers use influencing tactics in the following order of preference.

- Inspirational appeal (by transformational or democratic leaders)
- Rational persuasion: effective because it explains the reason and significance of the request, allowing subordinates to 'buy into' it rather than simply complying without question
- Pressure (by autocratic leaders).

4.3　In the broader employee relations context, consultation is also becoming highly valued as a strategy (supported by UK and EU law) for securing employee commitment to organisational objectives: employees' input is now being actively sought at all levels, on decisions to which they can contribute and on matters of concern to them.

4.4　We have already looked at the main models and concepts for leading subordinates and teams, in Chapters 1 and 2 – as the most common context of management and leadership.

4.5　Applying Yukl and Falbe's influencing tactics to leadership style models:

- An autocratic (tells) style of leadership obviously tends to rely on positional authority (in the form of legitimating) or pressure.
- A sells style relies on persuasive influencing techniques such as inspirational appeal, coalition, personal appeal, and exchange.
- The more democratic the leader's style, the more he will need to use more subtle forms of influence, including rational persuasion and consultation, so that the team's views and goals come into alignment with his own.

4.6　Remember that, according to modern contingency theories, there is no one best strategy for using leadership influence: it depends on the readiness of the followers (in Hersey and Blanchard's situational model), among other factors.

Leading to develop individual performance

4.7 Many different models may be used to describe the factors in individual performance at work. We have developed our own easy-to-remember framework for this discussion, in the form of three Cs. You might use this framework as a checklist of factors to be considered if, as a leader, you encounter a poor-performing team (at work or in an exam scenario).

- Commitment: how willingly and energetically people approach their work
- Contribution: the conditions required to support effective working and task fulfilment
- Capability: the aptitudes, skills and competencies people bring to the work – and how they can be developed

4.8 **Commitment** is an elusive concept, but Mowdray, Porter and Steers describe it as: 'the relative strength of an individual's identification with and involvement in a particular organisation. It is characterised by at least three factors: a strong belief in and acceptance of an organisation's goals and values; a willingness to exert considerable effort on behalf of the organisation; and a strong desire to maintain membership of the organisation.'

4.9 Employee commitment correlates strongly with effective leadership – which, by definition, involves the use of vision articulation, motivation, role modelling and other techniques to foster willing and above-compliance levels of effort.

4.10 Individual and team **contribution** must be enabled and supported by organisational conditions (including leadership). Contribution must be:

- *Commissioned:* by clear task objectives and delegation of sufficient authority to perform them. People need to know what the organisation expects and backs them to do.
- *Controlled:* by clear values, policies, procedures (if necessary), targets and success criteria – and the feedback to adjust performance accordingly. People need to know where they stand, and where they're 'up to' in pursuing their objectives.
- *Championed:* by leadership support, acknowledgement and inspiration. People need their leaders to value their contribution, mobilise resources on their behalf, and model what is required.
- *Co-operative:* via mechanisms for co-ordination, information-sharing and teamworking. Organisations are formed because there are limits to what individuals can accomplish alone – but integration is required if they are to achieve positive synergy, where the whole achieves more than the sum of its parts (2 + 2 = 5).

4.11 This idea of supporting and enabling people in giving their best underpins the concept of empowerment. It turns the organisational pyramid on its head, and argues that rather than workers supporting leaders in achieving their objectives, the role of leaders is to support workers in achieving *their* value-adding objectives. This is discussed further in Chapter 10.

4.12 Individual and team contribution also depends on **capability:** what people are 'able' to do.

- *Capacity:* what people are capable of, or able to learn: their qualities and aptitudes (things they are naturally good at or suited to)
- *Competence:* what people are able (or can learn) to do. This includes knowledge, skills (learned effective behaviours) and competencies (ability to perform specific tasks to a required standard).
- *Creativity:* the ability to do *new* things and formulate new ideas or combinations of ideas. This is a highly valued element in work performance in the modern environment.

4.13 One of the key tasks of leaders is to source and develop high-quality, flexible (and, if possible, distinctive) capabilities in their workforces and teams.

Leadership roles in teams

4.14 A team has been defined as 'a small group of people with complementary skills who are committed to a common purpose, performance goals and approaches for which they hold themselves basically jointly accountable' (Jon R Katzenbach & Douglas K Smith, *The Wisdom of Teams,* 1993).

4.15 As we saw in Chapter 1, the leadership role may be taken by a designated individual, or the functions of leadership may be rotated or distributed among team members. In Belbin's model of the ideal mix and balance of roles in a work team (Belbin, *Team Roles at Work,* 1993), leadership is represented by a cluster of different roles.

- The Plant (creative, imaginative, unorthodox) may exercise the role of visionary: creating and articulating ideas and solutions to difficult problems
- The Resource Investigator (extrovert, enthusiastic, communicative) exercises a leader's entrepreneurial and liaison functions: exploring opportunities and developing contracts
- The Shaper (challenging, dynamic, thriving on pressure) exercises charismatic interpersonal leadership, to inspire and influence the team, especially in the face of challenges and obstacles
- The Co-ordinator (mature, confident, a good chairperson) exercises task leadership, as organiser and co-ordinator.

4.16 Belbin also distinguishes between two contrasting styles of leadership in teams.

- The **solo leader** is autocratic and directive in approach, using a combination of modelling (expecting others to follow) and direction (expecting others to comply). A talented solo leader can be effective in contexts where crisis or urgency has arisen, or where there are existing problems within the team or department: decisions can be taken and implemented quickly, and barriers to communication and co-operation by-passed. However, solo leadership can also reflect Theory X assumptions, resulting in micro-management, interference, insistence on conformity and a cult of authority.
- The **team leader** deliberately limits his or her role, exercising a more democratic style of leadership: creating a sense of mission and purpose; respecting the diversity, skill and knowledge of the team (in Blanchard's words: 'no one of us is as smart as all of us'); and expressing respect and trust through participation and delegation.

4.17 In **self-managed teams**, team members collaboratively share decision-making on all the major issues affecting their work and internal processes. Leadership roles may be shared or rotated, as appropriate. Weekly team meetings are typically used to identify, analyse and solve problems: reviewing teamworking and progress; getting team members to research and present issues and so on. Any external leadership, once goals have been set for the group, is primarily supportive and facilitative (and only when needed): essentially, however, the leader uses a 'delegating' style (in Hersey and Blanchard's situational leadership model).

4.18 Self-managed teamworking requires a high level of competence on the part of team members – and a high degree of trust on the part of managers (to give the team discretion in planning, implementing and controlling tasks). There must also be clear objectives, role definitions and review milestones and measures, as a framework for team discretion. Communication and reporting mechanisms must be in place for co-ordination and control.

Leading virtual teams

4.19 The globalisation of business has increasingly led to the formation of 'virtual' organisations and teams: geographically dispersed, with communication and collaboration supported by ICT tools. This presents various challenges for team leadership.

- **Team building and co-ordination.** Virtual teams imply that team members are working in remote or dispersed locations – potentially worldwide. This limits many opportunities for team cohesion-building and interpersonal interactions, which must be replaced by management. This may involve: creating opportunities for personal interactions where possible (eg annual conferences); regular virtual meetings and briefings; data sharing (eg using email or extranet or intranet facilities); opportunities for informal networking (eg using social media); and strong expressions of team and corporate identity and solidarity.

- **Team communication**. In addition to ICT-enabled communication systems and mechanisms for regular communication, the organisation may have to give attention to the training of remote team members, and their leaders, in communication skills: rapport building (over audio and/or audio-visual links); facilitative communication styles and so on. Remote communication lacks the richness of face-to-face interaction (even when audio-visual): careful attention will have to be given to the accuracy of communication; checking understanding; and avoiding misunderstanding due to lack of visual cues and/or the distancing effect of technology (eg the tendency to sound more abrupt in emails).

- **Leadership and supervision**. 'Position power' may have little meaning in virtual or remote working, and virtual teams are by their nature more or less self-managing. Team leaders or co-ordinators will have to develop management styles appropriate to this situation: developing mutual trust; delegating effectively (while maintaining availability for guidance where required); and adopting the role and style of a facilitative coach and resource mobiliser. It may be difficult to 'supervise' work in any conventional sense: the leader will have to focus on monitoring and measuring outcomes and results – rather than attempting to control work patterns or time management.

- **Cultural diversity.** Team members may live and work in widely different geographical regions and countries, giving rise to challenges of cultural diversity. Anne Marie Francesco and Barry A Gold (*International Organisational Behaviour*) argue that: 'Cultural diversity, which will be increasingly common, adds to the complexity of managing virtual teams because different values, customs and traditions require leadership – under conditions that reduce the ability to use direct leadership.'

- **Infrastructure and logistical issues**. In addition, globalised virtual teamworking creates a range of challenges in regard to: different time zones and office hours; different availability of infrastructure (eg access to broadband internet or mobile telecommunications networks); different legal regimes and jurisdictions (as the context for employment contracts, as well as supply and business contracts); and so on.

Team building

4.20 There are many different techniques of team building (creating cohesive groups), but they are generally based on fostering the following elements.

- **Team identity:** the sense of being a team (sometimes called *esprit de corps* or 'team spirit'). This may be done by naming the group; expressing the team's identity in slogans and mottos; building a team history in stories and jokes (especially heroic successes and failures); or giving the team distinctive 'badges' or symbols.

- **Team solidarity:** loyalty to the group, so that team members put in extra effort for the group and in support of its norms and values. This may be done by expressing solidarity ('one for all and all for one'); encouraging interpersonal relationships within the team; controlling intra-group conflict and competition in positive, affirming ways; and celebrating group (rather than individual) successes.

- **Commitment to shared goals:** cooperation in the interests of team objectives. These may initially be team maintenance goals, but if they can be integrated with task goals (by offering the team the satisfaction of achievement, recognition or reward) the cooperative drive can be turned to the organisation's advantage.

- **Competition, crisis or emergency:** members of a group will act in unison if the group's existence or patterns of behaviour are threatened from outside. Competition within groups erodes cohesion – but competition with other groups enhances it.

4.21 Team-building strategies encourage commitment to shared work objectives and to the cooperative working required to achieve them. This is likely to be a key tool for building virtual or multi-organisational supply chain teams, as well as conventional in-house teams. It will involve the following activities.

- Clear articulation of the team's task objectives and their place in the organisation's (or supply chain's) activity as a whole
- Involving the team in setting specific targets and standards and agreeing methods of organising work. (This may also include a broader consensus on how the team wishes to work together: members' expectations of each other; and ground rules for group processes such as role allocation, information-sharing, decision-making, leadership and so on.)
- Ensuring that, as far as possible, all interests and perspectives have been heard and acknowledged, so that consensus is genuine (rather than false, because a 'group' decision has been imposed)
- Providing the resources the team requires to fulfil its objectives
- Giving regular feedback on progress and results via team briefings
- Continually inviting input, feedback and suggestions from team members (depending on leadership and operating style), so that they can influence work methods and drive improvements
- Positively reinforcing behaviour that demonstrates commitment to the task (through rewards, recognition and celebration)

Key values in positive team relationships

4.22 The leader has a key role in modelling and promoting the cultural values that build co-operative and mutually enriching relationships within a team. Key values underpinning such relationships include the following.

- **Consideration, respect and dignity** for individuals: validating people's sense of self-worth and contribution; encouraging respect for individual differences (without harassment, prejudice or discrimination) and courtesy and respect in all interpersonal dealings, particularly in disagreement or conflict
- **Trust:** encouraging open communication and information-sharing (particularly, owning up to problems and difficulties); and allowing every member to focus on their part of the task, knowing that the others will perform theirs
- **Fair and equitable treatment:** ensuring that decisions which affect team members (such as the allocation of tasks and resources, arbitration of disputes and investigation of grievances) are made equitably and objectively; that discipline and rewards are applied consistently and without partiality; and so on
- **Recognition and credit**: giving acknowledgement, credit, thanks and praise (positive feedback and celebration) where it is due – a powerful, low-cost motivator
- **Equal opportunity:** ensuring equal access to opportunities for training, promotion and rewards – regardless of gender, race, age, disability or other criteria
- **Diversity:** supporting diverse cultures (eg encouraging discussion of represented cultures' values and norms); abilities (eg being aware of language issues in cross-cultural teams); lifestyles (eg by offering flexible working hours); and personality types (eg appreciating the contribution of different personality types, using models such as the Myers Briggs Type Inventory®)
- **Ethical conduct:** practising and encouraging personal integrity, honesty, confidentiality of information, professional courtesy, support for colleagues – and whatever other ethical values (eg in regard to suppliers and customers, the environment or the community) the team collectively adopts.

The team leader as motivator

4.23 Reward and motivation systems such as pay, benefits, promotion and job design may be determined at a department-wide or organisation-wide level. Motivation theories are not mentioned in the syllabus – having been covered in detail in *Management in Procurement and Supply* at Advanced Diploma Level.

However, it is worth noting that they suggest several behaviour-focused ways in which a team leader can contribute to the motivation of his team.

- Clear **goals and objectives** are essential in order for individuals to calculate how much effort a task will require (and whether it is worth it, given the rewards on offer). They also provide yardsticks by which individuals can measure and feel good about their progress.
- **Participation and involvement** are powerful motivators – as well as potentially improving the quality of decision-making. If team members can be involved in setting goals, and articulating values, they are more likely to own and pursue them in a committed way. A team charter or contract may even be drawn up to clarify the team's commitment to each other: what the team wants to accomplish, why it is important, and how the team will work together to achieve results.
- **Ongoing** formal and informal **feedback on progress** and results is essential for individuals to calculate what further effort is required; to build confidence and shared accountability; and to enable milestones to be celebrated.
- **Praise and recognition** should not be underestimated as a reward and incentive to further effort: they are highly valued by employees – and yet they cost the manager nothing to give.

4.24 Teamworking gurus like Ken Blanchard advocate 'Keeping the accent on the positive'.

- Looking for (and rewarding) positive behaviours that reflect the purpose and values of the team
- 'Catching people doing things right' instead of wrong
- Redirecting people towards the goal, when they get things wrong, instead of punishing them
- Linking all recognition and rewards back to the team's purpose and goals.

Leadership for effective teamworking

4.25 There are many different models of the factors required for effective teamworking. Mike Woodcock *(Team Development Manual,* 1989) lists ten 'building blocks' for teams.

- Leadership: adopting a leadership style that fits the task, team and situation (if there is a designated leader) or ensuring that leadership roles and functions are fairly distributed or rotated to those best able to exercise them (and to develop others)
- Membership: ensuring a suitable mix of competencies and member roles
- Climate or culture: creating a cooperative atmosphere and style, based on trust
- Objectives: clarifying and articulating specific, meaningful and achievable goals which can be shared by the whole team
- Achievement: creating opportunities to learn and celebrating improvement
- Work methods: developing workable procedures for task and group functioning
- Communication: facilitating openness and honesty, information sharing, ideas generation and constructive feedback, often via team briefings
- Interpersonal relations: controlling conflict and facilitating trust and co-operation
- Individual development needs: giving team members opportunities to grow and develop within the team
- Review and control: regularly evaluating and feeding back on team performance and improvement needs

4.26 The opposite of these building blocks (inappropriate leadership style, inadequate mix of competencies, poor communication etc) are referred to in Woodcock's model as 'blockages'. You should be able to work out what the ineffective version of each building block is – and the effect they would have on team functioning.

4.27 Perhaps the most significant potential for conflicts and impaired performance within a team arises from power issues. The leader may lack power within the team to draw it together and focus its efforts: this may create a power vacuum, within which other members compete for influence. Individual team members (or the team as a whole) may not be sufficiently empowered to meet expectations or objectives. There may be an unequal distribution of power, which stifles contribution from some members and creates false consensus.

4.28 A further danger of power imbalances is that they tend to foster politics and 'game' playing (Mintzberg, *Power In and Around Organisations,* 1983): enhancing one's own power base, and undermining those of others, by manipulating or withholding information, forming coalitions, destroying others' credibility and so on. Such behaviours disintegrate the team – and take up a lot of its time and energy, that could more constructively be focused on the task. We will return to the topic of conflict management in teams and supply chains in Chapter 9.

Leaderless teams

4.29 Some uses of teams deliberately remove the direct leadership role, in order to explore un-directed group processes between members. One use of the leaderless team, for example, is in group training.

4.30 T-groups (training groups) are a tool of sensitivity training, in which members of a group focus their attention on understanding their own behaviours, how they impact on others, and how they are perceived by others. A T-group typically involves between 8 and 12 people in a leaderless (power-balanced), unstructured (no agenda or planned activities), face-to-face meeting, which is facilitated (but not actively directed) by a trainer. The only agenda is the observation and feeding back of the group's process and group members' behaviours. Similar group exercises are used as part of assessment centres (group selection activities, often used for management selection).

4.31 The benefit of leaderless groups is that, faced with confusion and lack of agenda, people will fall back on habitual or characteristic coping behaviours. This gives the opportunity for these behaviours to be observed and discussed by the group, to analyse: what drives the behaviours; how effective they are in getting the individual's needs met; how they are perceived and experienced by others in the group and so on. Individuals are thus encouraged to become more self-aware, by examining their own self-image and behaviours, and more sensitive or receptive to the feelings and perceptions of others. In other words, the process helps to develop emotional intelligence which may be of use in future group functioning.

4.32 The use of feedback in leaderless groups also gives members a useful tool for future learning and self-development (eg through coaching or mentoring). The process can be used to support change, since the intense experience of discomfort can be a powerful spur to consideration of new perspectives, values, attitudes and behaviours. (Group sessions may also be supported by information content, case studies and so on.)

> ## Chapter summary
>
> - Upward management is most often based on rational persuasion, coalition and personal appeal. There is a particular need for exception reporting and business case presentation in persuasive communication to senior managers.
> - Leading direct reports and teams depends on the leader's style: inspirational appeal is suited to a transformational leader, rational persuasion and consultation to a democratic leader, and pressure and legitimating to an autocratic leader.
> - Individual effectiveness at work depends on many factors, which can broadly be classified as commitment (motivation and willingness); contribution (organisational conditions enabling performance, including goals, controls, leadership support and co-operative structures); and capability development.
> - Leading in cross-functional teams, networks and interdepartmental relations depends on personal appeal, rational persuasion and consultation, and exchange. Networking is a key skill for managers, in order to develop connection power.

 ## Self-test questions

Numbers in brackets refer to the paragraphs where you can check your answers.

1   What are the four different directions in which leadership may be exercised, according to Buchanan and Boddy? (Figure 4.1)

2   List reasons why upward management is an important process in supply chain management. (2.1)

3   In what ways does effective upward management support supply chain management? (2.7)

4   Describe the leadership roles that may be required in cross-functional leadership. (3.5)

5   What tactics are preferred by leaders when influencing laterally? (3.8)

6   What is meant by 'connection power'? (3.14)

7   What tactics are preferred by leaders when influencing downwards? (4.2)

8   What are the three Cs in relation to individual performance at work? (4.7)

9   Distinguish between solo leaders and team leaders (Belbin). (4.16)

10   List Mike Woodcock's ten 'building blocks' for effective teamworking. (4.25)

CHAPTER 5

Stakeholder Communication and Engagement

Assessment criteria and indicative content

 2.3 Create a communication plan to influence personnel in the supply chain that: provides an analysis of stakeholders; indicates how stakeholder mapping influences the communication plan; details appropriate leadership/influencing styles to obtain stakeholder buy-in; and indicates how electronic systems can be used to support stakeholder communication

- Stakeholder analysis, including primary, secondary and key stakeholders
- How to obtain buy-in to supply chain strategies from stakeholders
- Perspectives on stakeholder mapping
- How to use intranet and internet websites for publishing information

Section headings

1 Stakeholder analysis and management
2 Stakeholder mapping
3 Stakeholder influencing
4 Stakeholder communication and engagement
5 ICT tools for stakeholder communication
6 The communication plan

Introduction

In this chapter we pursue our discussion of 'managing across' from Chapter 4, by exploring in more detail the processes by which procurement and supply chain managers can lead and influence stakeholders in the internal and external supply chains.

We start with an overview of the various stakeholders in the supply chain. We then go on to develop a stakeholder analysis and management process, including the identification, mapping, categorisation and prioritisation of stakeholder groups; the engagement of stakeholders to secure 'buy-in' to supply chain strategies and initiatives; and the planning and implementation of communication strategies for stakeholder management.

The syllabus frames these topics within the requirement to develop a communication plan, containing all of these elements. This practical focus strongly suggests that such a task may be set in relation to a particular stakeholder environment, as part of an exam case study question. In the final section of this chapter we will suggest a generic template for such an exercise.

1 Stakeholder analysis and management

1.1 Stakeholders are individuals and groups who have a legitimate interest or 'stake' in an organisation, process, project or decision. They may have invested money in it, or contributed to it, or they may be affected by its activities and outcomes.

1.2 Stakeholders are *affected by* the organisation's activities in different ways and to different degrees. Any given stakeholder group will have a bundle of needs, wants, expectations and concerns in regard to the organisation: 'interests' which the group will seek to protect or promote in their relationship with the organisation. So, for example, suppliers will have an interest in efficient information flows, payment as agreed, fair treatment of tenders, and mutually beneficial ongoing business. Customers will have an interest in safe and satisfying products and services, value for money, ethical business dealings and so on.

1.3 Stakeholders also have power to *affect* the organisation's activities in different ways and to different degrees. Financiers have the power to withhold resources if their needs are not met. Customers can similarly withhold their custom and support. Suppliers influence the quality, cost and timely availability of products and services, and therefore the organisation's competitive advantage. And so on.

1.4 All these influences may impact on the structure, systems, policies and values of the organisation – and individual functions such as purchasing and supply. The more influence a stakeholder has, the more likely it is that managers will have to take that stakeholder's needs and wants into account.

Internal and external stakeholder analysis

1.5 One generic method of classifying stakeholders is to identify them as internal, connected and external groups, whose interest in the organisation can be summarised as follows.

- **Internal stakeholders** are members of the organisation: the directors, managers and employees who operate within the organisation's boundaries. They have a key stake in the organisation's survival and growth (for continued employment and prosperity); the fulfilment of task goals (as a measure of their competence and success); and the fulfilment of their personal goals (for income, security, career, status and so on).
- **Connected stakeholders** are external stakeholders who have direct legal, contractual or commercial dealings with the organisation. These include shareholders, who have a key stake, as owners, in the financial performance of the organisation. They also include:
  — Financiers, such as banks (*interest:* security of loans, return on investment).
  — Customers and consumers (*interest:* satisfaction of complex expectations and motives for purchasing a product or service; ethical business dealings; helpful service and support; accurate information).
  — Suppliers (*interest:* efficient information flow; payment as agreed; mutually beneficial long-term relationship; feedback and support to enhance service).
  — Distributors (*interest:* reliable supply; quality and added value; marketing support; earnings through discount margins or commissions; mutually beneficial long-term relationship).
- **External or secondary stakeholders** do not have direct contractual or commercial dealings with the organisation, but have an interest in, or are affected by, its activities. They include:
  — Government and regulatory bodies (*interest:* economic activity; tax revenue; compliance; reports and returns; social responsibility).
  — Pressure groups and interest groups (*interest:* awareness of a particular cause or issue, eg environmental impacts; protection of the rights and interests of the group, eg disabled workers).
  — Professional bodies and trade unions (*interest:* protecting the interests of members; promoting professional standards and ethics).
  — The local community (*interest:* employment; provision of goods and services; social responsibility and involvement).

Primary and secondary stakeholder analysis

1.6 Another generic perspective on stakeholders classifies them as primary, secondary and key.

- **Primary (or market) stakeholders:** internal and connected stakeholders, who engage directly in economic transactions with the business. Examples include shareholders, financers, customers, suppliers and employees.
- **Secondary (or non-market) stakeholders**: external stakeholders who do not engage in direct economic exchange with the business, but still affect and/or are affected by its activities. Examples include the general public, communities, the media, government and its agencies, and pressure groups and interest groups.
- **Key stakeholders:** primary or secondary stakeholders who are identified as a priority in a given situation or context, because of the opportunity or risk they present to the organisation and its plans. Stakeholders may be identified as 'key' on the basis of their power or influence, the importance of their participation or co-operation in an activity, their potential to support or disrupt a plan, or the importance of their 'stake' in an issue (ie the extent to which their interests are affected by the plan or activity). We will discuss this further when we explore stakeholder analysis and mapping.

1.7 If asked in the exam about external stakeholders who impact on, or are impacted by, procurement and supply chain activity, don't neglect the secondary stakeholders. The view of what constitutes a legitimate stakeholder has broadened from a focus on groups involved directly with the organisation, function or project to a wider range of groups who are less directly affected by its activities and their results.

1.8 The widening of an organisation's responsibilities to these less directly connected groups is a major trend in modern business, under the umbrella term of **corporate social responsibility** (CSR) — and CIPS takes it very seriously. Businesses have, in particular, become increasingly aware of the need to maintain a positive reputation in the marketplace, and this may require a more inclusive approach to stakeholder management, which recognises the legitimate needs and concerns of wider, secondary or 'indirect' stakeholders.

Stakeholders in procurement and supply chain activity

1.9 In addition to organisational stakeholders in general, each function, unit and project of an organisation may be said to have stakeholders, whose needs and influence must be taken into account. For any given procurement activity, decision or project, it should be possible to identify stakeholders with similar interests and influence to those listed above.

- The owner or sponsor of the project or activity, who puts authority behind it, initiates it, and sets its objectives
- Customers and users of the activity or its outputs: departments who receive purchasing advice and assistance, or end users of the purchased resources and services
- Participating staff, who may be drawn from the procurement department or from other functions, whether through cross-functional work-flow and information-flow, or in dedicated cross-functional project teams (depending on the activity and its organisation)
- Suppliers, who have a key stake in any procurement and supply activity or project, and are the subject of procurement professionals' key social responsibilities (Lysons and Farrington, *Purchasing & Supply Chain Management)*
- External collaborators, such as outsourced-service providers (project management, logistics etc), research consultants, legal advisers and so on
- Secondary stakeholders not commercially connected to, but impacted by, the project: for example, the communities from which supplier labour is drawn; those affected by environmental and economic impacts of the project; interest groups concerned with the environment, trading practices, consumer rights and so on.

Stakeholder management

1.10 Stakeholder management recognises the need to take stakeholders into account when formulating strategies and plans. For a procurement and supply chain manager, stakeholder management is likely to be helpful in several ways.

- It enables you to gain expert input from stakeholders at the planning stage of a project, to improve the quality of your decisions.
- Stakeholders are more likely to 'own' and support plans to which they have had input: this will make ongoing collaboration easier.
- Gaining the support of powerful stakeholders may, in turn, mobilise power and resources within the organisation in support of your plans.
- At the very least, sources of resistance to your plans (from stakeholders whose goals are different from or incompatible with yours) can be anticipated and planned for.

1.11 A simple but systematic approach to analysing and managing stakeholders is shown in Table 5.1.

Table 5.1 *Stakeholder analysis and management*

Identify	Use individual or team brainstorming and consultation to identify who your stakeholders are (in relation to the specific organisation, unit, plan or project in focus). Who is or will be affected by decisions? Who might have power or influence over them? Who might have an interest in success or failure?
Prioritise	Map and classify stakeholders (see later in this chapter). Which stakeholders will need to be the focus of leader attention? What engagement and management strategies are indicated by the priority and classification of each stakeholder group?
Understand	Analyse key stakeholder awareness, positions, interests and responses (where possible, by direct consultation). How are they likely to feel about your plans, decisions, initiatives? (Add designations such as 'blocker', 'critic', 'supporter', 'advocate' or 'neutral' to the stakeholder map) How are they likely to respond or react? How can they best be communicated with, engaged, influenced?

1.12 Stakeholder relationship management therefore involves processes such as the following.

- Gathering information about groups and their interests
- Prioritising groups which have most potential impact
- Establishing what each group may gain and lose from the procurement decision or plan – and using this information to (a) strengthen support and (b) mitigate losses and risks where possible
- Ensuring consistent and coherent communication with key stakeholder groups, in order to secure their 'buy-in' to plans and proposals
- Establishing opportunities for co-operation and synergy (where available)
- Continuously monitoring, evaluating and adjusting the relationship over time

1.13 The interests and expectations of stakeholder groups will often be different – and even conflicting. Shareholders, for example, will want to maximise profits (to increase the value of their shares), while suppliers will want to protect their own profit margins; interest groups may resist profit-taking at the expense of the environment; and employees may want to maximise their pay and conditions. Similarly, in the case of procurement stakeholders, the marketing function may want to maximise customisation and delivery-on-demand, while the operations function wants to be able to plan ahead and reduce variances, and the finance function wants to cut costs. You can't please all of the stakeholders all of the time.

1.14 Boddy (*Management: An Introduction*) concludes: 'The overall message is that it is important to the long-run success of organisations to embrace stakeholder expectations, but that the degree of priority they give to each is unequal and changing (over time).' The most common method of prioritising stakeholder relationships is stakeholder mapping.

2 Stakeholder mapping

2.1 A wide variety of tools has been developed to classify and analyse stakeholder groups, using different criteria. Where these utilise diagrammatic means (such as diagrams or matrices) to visualise and identify the 'positioning' of groups within classifications, they are known as 'stakeholder mapping' techniques. We will look at six influential perspectives, and related tools, in this section. You may come across others in your wider reading.

The power/interest matrix

2.2 Aubrey L Mendelow's power/interest matrix ('Stakeholder Analysis for Strategic Planning & Implementation' in *Strategic Planning & Management Handbook,* 1985) is perhaps the best known specialist tool of stakeholder mapping. It maps stakeholders according to their power to influence purchasing activity and the likelihood of their showing an interest in it: Figure 5.1.

Figure 5.1 *Mendelow's power/interest matrix*

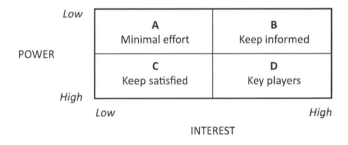

2.3 The technique is simple. Take a blank matrix and, for any given situation, write each stakeholder group into the quadrant which best describes their levels of power and interest.

2.4 Working through each of the segments in turn.

- Stakeholders with neither power nor interest (A) are a low-priority group: resources will not be wasted taking their goals or potential response into account. Small investors, or large suppliers with whom the organisation only does a small volume of business, may be in this category. So too may the local community or other organisational functions, in relation to particular decisions with low immediate impacts on them.
- Stakeholders in Segment B are important because of their high interest. They may have low direct influence, but unless they are kept 'in the loop' and understand the need for decisions, they may seek additional power by lobbying or banding together to protect their interest. Community, small supplier and employee groups may be in this category, in relation to decisions which impact significantly on their interests. The recommended strategy is to keep them informed of plans and outcomes, through stakeholder marketing, communication and education programmes (discussed later in the chapter).
- Stakeholders in Segment C are important because of their high influence. They currently have low interest, but if dissatisfied or concerned, their interest may be aroused. A large institutional shareholder, or large supplier, may be in this category, as may government agencies and regulatory bodies (if the organisation is broadly compliant). Senior managers in departments not directly affected by a procurement decision may also fall into this category. The recommended strategy is to keep these stakeholders satisfied, so that they do not need to exert their influence.
- Stakeholders in Segment D are known as 'key players'. They have influence and are motivated to use it in their own interests. Major customers, key suppliers and intermediaries, senior procurement managers and strategic allies or partners may be in this category. The recommended strategy is one of early involvement and participation, so that the stakeholder's goals can be integrated with organisational goals as far as possible – securing support, rather than resistance.

2.5 The purpose of the Mendelow matrix is basically to prioritise stakeholders according to their importance. This enables the procurement or supply chain function to:

- Identify stakeholders whose needs and expectations will define value and shape the function's priorities and policies (eg senior management or key suppliers)
- Identify stakeholders whose interests will be most affected by a decision or action, and towards whom the organisation may therefore recognise some moral or legal obligations (eg communities impacted by logistics operations)
- Identify stakeholders who will need to be informed, consulted or involved in the design or implementation of procurement exercises and policies (eg internal and external supply chain partners)
- Prioritise stakeholder interests, so that resources are utilised efficiently or leveraged for maximum advantage.

2.6 Further analysis may be carried out by determining, for each stakeholder group, whether they are likely to be for (+), against (−) or neutral (0) towards the strategy (or 'green' for supportive, 'amber' for neutral and 'red' for opponents). 'Key player' stakeholders who are against the strategy may be a barrier (or at least a challenge); high-interest, low-power groups who are supportive may be helpful in co-opting other support; low-interest, high-power groups who are supportive may be worth getting interested – and so on.

The power/dynamism matrix (Gardner *et al*)

2.7 A similar analysis is provided by Gardner, Rachlin and Sweeny (*Handbook of Strategic Planning,* 1986), but substituting 'dynamism' (the extent to which their stance is open to change) for 'interest': Figure 5.2.

Figure 5.2 *The power/dynamism matrix*

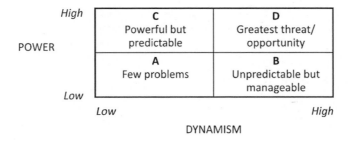

2.8 Working through the segments:

- Segment A stakeholders (low power, low dynamism) pose few problems, responding predictably and with little influence.
- Segment B stakeholders (low power, high dynamism) may react in unpredictable ways to an issue, but pose few problems because of their low influence.
- Segment C stakeholders (high power, low dynamism) are important because of their power, but their stance on an issue is predictable, so their expectations can often be met and managed relatively easily.
- Segment D stakeholders (high power, high dynamism) represent the greatest risk, being powerful and unpredictable or changeable in their stance on an issue: this will be the focus of managerial attention. These stakeholders may need to be consulted on new strategies, before final decisions are made.

Stakeholder salience

2.9 Mitchell, Agle and Wood ('Toward a theory of stakeholder identification and salience: defining the principles of who and what really counts', *Academy of Management Review,* 1997) developed a slightly more nuanced model based on identifying the 'salience' of stakeholder groups. 'Salience' in this context may be defined as 'the degree to which managers give priority to competing stakeholder claims' (ibid). In other words, salience is a measure of the 'importance' or priority of stakeholder groups to the organisation: the degree to which they require or deserve its attention and consideration when making plans.

2.10 In the model proposed by Mitchell *et al*, stakeholders are classified based on three variables, which together determine salience.

- **Power**: the extent to which the stakeholder is able to influence the organisation's actions (eg by virtue of positional power, bargaining power, or resources which can be offered or withheld)
- **Legitimacy**: the extent to which the stakeholder has a legitimate interest in the organisation's actions (eg by virtue of legal or contractual rights, or 'moral' rights which may arise from investment of finance or participation, or from being impacted or affected by organisational plans)
- **Urgency**: the extent to which the stakeholder's interest or concern is time-critical (for the stakeholder), and therefore the extent to which it is prepared to be 'demanding' in pursuing its claims or exercising its power

2.11 These three 'sets' of characteristics intersect and interact in various ways, creating seven classifications: Figure 5.3.

Figure 5.3 *Stakeholder salience*

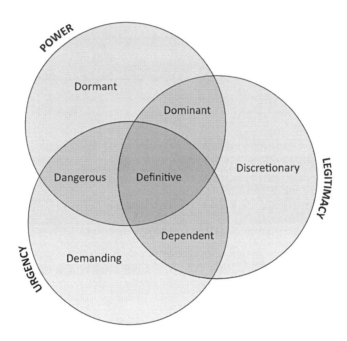

2.12 Working through the classifications:

- Stakeholders possessing just one of the characteristics are known as **latent** stakeholders. 'Latent' means existing, and having potential, but not yet developed or manifested.
  - Dormant stakeholders are powerful – but inactive, because their claims lack legitimacy and urgency.
  - Discretionary stakeholders have a legitimate claim – but the organisation can choose whether to respond, at its own discretion, because the claim lacks both urgency and power.
  - Demanding stakeholders have an urgent claim – and may make a lot of 'noise', but this at best has nuisance value, as they lack power and legitimacy.
- Stakeholders possessing two out of three of the characteristics are defined as **expectant** stakeholders, because they have a strong and more active claim.
  - Dominant stakeholders are in a strong position, because they have a legitimate claim – and the power to back it up (though the issue is not urgent).
  - Dependent stakeholders have a legitimate and urgent claim – but are dependent on the organisation's response, because they lack power.
  - Dangerous stakeholders have an urgent claim (even if it lacks legitimacy) and the power to back it up: they may be in a position to force concessions.

- **Definitive stakeholders** have the strongest claim and leverage to shape organisational decisions, because they have power, legitimacy and urgency on their side.

Awareness, support and influence

2.13 Turner, Kristoffer and Thurloway (*The Project Manager as Change Agent: Leadership, Influence and Negotiation,* 2002) propose strategies for project managers to communicate with project stakeholders, based on three variables.

- **Awareness:** whether the stakeholder is aware or ignorant of the plan or project
- **Support:** whether the stakeholder is supportive or opposing of the plan or project
- **Influence:** the extent to which the stakeholder has power to influence the plan or project

2.14 This is broadly similar to a power/interest model, in that 'interest' is a function of awareness and stake or viewpoint (for or against).

Stakeholder perceptions

2.15 Fletcher, Guthrie, Steane, Roos and Pike ('Mapping stakeholder perceptions for a third sector organisation', *Journal of Intellectual Capital,* 2003) propose a process for analysing stakeholder perceptions and expectations. This has specific relevance for third sector or not-for-profit (NFP) organisations, which typically have a much wider range of complex stakeholder constituencies than private sector firms (whose priorities are strongly focused on shareholders and customers), and therefore need a more consensus-based model of stakeholder management.

2.16 Stakeholder perceptions and expectations are analysed in regard to:

- **Value hierarchies**: the essential elements which represent value, from the stakeholder's point of view. The construction of a value hierarchy involves identifying stakeholder needs; identifying elements that satisfy those needs (value objects); and determining the relative priority of those elements. In a case study for the Australian Red Cross blood donation organisation, for example, Guthrie identified 'a primary concern for sufficient and safe supply of blood; a secondary concern for public confidence; and a third concern for internal operations'.
- **Key performance areas (KPAs)**: the essential elements likely to contribute to performance, from the stakeholder's point of view. Responses from stakeholders are plotted on a bar chart. The vertical axis (height of the bars) depicts scores for relative importance, and the horizontal axis identifies KPAs: for each KPA, there is a cluster of bars, with one bar for each key stakeholder.

Supplier segmentation

2.17 A particular form of stakeholder mapping may be used in buyer-supplier relationships, to indicate the extent to which collaborative or competitive influencing approaches will be appropriate to the buying organisation's aims from the relationship.

2.18 The Kraljic procurement positioning matrix, for example, may be used to identify strategic procurements, in relation to which adversarial or leverage-based supplier influencing may not be the most appropriate approach – and 'leverage' procurements, for which (as the term suggests) more 'push'-based influencing may be appropriate to secure price or cost advantage: Figure 5.4.

Figure 5.4 *The Kraljic matrix ('procurement positioning' tool)*

Complexity of the supply market

	Low		High	
High	**Procurement focus** Leverage items	**Time horizon** Varied, typically 12-24 months	**Procurement focus** Strategic items	**Time horizon** Up to 10 years; governed by long-term strategic impact (risk and contract mix)
	Key performance criteria Cost/price and materials flow management	**Items purchased** Mix of commodities and specified materials	**Key performance criteria** Long-term availability	**Items purchased** Scarce and/or high-value materials
Importance of the item	**Typical sources** Multiple suppliers, chiefly local	**Supply** Abundant	**Typical sources** Established global suppliers	**Supply** Natural scarcity
	Procurement focus Non-critical items	**Time horizon** Limited: normally 12 months or less	**Procurement focus** Bottleneck items	**Time horizon** Variable, depending on availability vs short-term flexibility trade-offs
	Key performance criteria Functional efficiency	**Items purchased** Commodities, some specified materials	**Key performance criteria** Cost management and reliable short-term sourcing	**Items purchased** Mainly specified materials
Low	**Typical sources** Established local suppliers	**Supply** Abundant	**Typical sources** Global, predominantly new suppliers with new technology	**Supply** Production-based scarcity

2.19 Working through the segments:

- For *non-critical or routine items* (such as common stationery supplies), the focus will be on functional efficiency, with low-maintenance routines to reduce procurement costs. Arm's length approaches such as vendor managed inventory, blanket ordering (empowering end users to make call-off orders against negotiated agreements) and e-procurement solutions (eg online ordering or the use of purchasing cards) will provide routine efficiency.
- For *bottleneck items* (such as proprietary spare parts or specialised consultancy services, which could cause operational delays if unavailable), the priority will be control over the short-term continuity and security of supply. This may suggest approaches such as negotiating medium-term or long-term contracts with suppliers; developing alternative or back-up sources of supply; including incentives and penalties in contracts to ensure the reliability of delivery; or keeping higher levels of buffer or 'safety' stock.
- For *leverage items* (such as local produce bought by a major supermarket), the priority will be to use the buyer's power in the market to secure best prices and terms, on a purely transactional basis. This may mean taking advantage of competitive pricing; standardising specifications to make supplier switching easier; and using competitive bidding and/or buying consortia to secure the best deals.
- For *strategic items* (such as core processors bought by a laptop manufacturer), a more complex set of business needs (for strategic alignment, lifetime cost and value, long-term security of supply and competitive supply) will be met by developing long-term, mutually beneficial, and potentially interdependent, strategic relationships with suppliers.

Further analysis

2.20 Once key or priority stakeholders have been identified and classified, it is possible to conduct further analysis, as appropriate to the situation. Some generic techniques are described below.

- **Force field** analysis (covered in Chapter 8): mapping stakeholders as forces for a change or initiative ('driving forces') or as forces resisting a change or initiative ('restraining forces') of different strengths
- **SWOT** (Strengths, Weaknesses, Opportunities and Threats) analysis, to determine the stakeholder's relative strength and potential impact in a given situation or environment
- **Network** diagrams (or **actor influence** diagrams): mapping the formal and informal connections and influencing relationships between members of a stakeholder network. (This will be important in identifying who the key influencers are; who has the ability to built supportive or resistant coalitions; and so on.)

2.21 More general analysis may be carried out in order to plan a management strategy for key stakeholders.

- **Goal analysis**. What motivates these stakeholders? What financial and/or emotional interests are at stake for them? What are their goals or desired outcomes from your plans? What fears or issues might your plans raise for them? Where might they support you – and where might they oppose you?
- **Desired outcomes.** What do you want or need from these stakeholders? What information or levels of support do you want from them? What role(s) would you want them to play in your project or plans?
- **Stakeholder marketing.** What messages or information will you need to convey to these stakeholders? What is the best way of communicating with them? How can you sell the benefits of what you are proposing or doing to them? How can you confront and overcome any resistance?
- **Relationship management.** How will you manage communication to, and input from, each of these stakeholders? How will you keep your key supporters motivated? How will you win over or neutralise resistance? How will you engage the interest of potential supporters?
- **Issues management.** How will you raise potential issues and problems, where stakeholders' goals may differ from yours? How will you gain stakeholders' early involvement, and collaborate with them in minimising or managing the impacts?
- **Danger signals.** What kinds of behaviour or responses might indicate resistance or lack of commitment and support from your key stakeholders?

3 Stakeholder influencing

3.1 In this section, we return briefly to our analysis of proactive influencing tactics (Yukl and Falbe), introduced in Chapter 3 and applied to upward, downward and lateral leadership in Chapter 4.

Influencing suppliers

3.2 In the case of suppliers and outsourced-service providers, non-personal forms of power and influence may be exercised in the form of:

- Purchase contracts and service level agreements
- Incentive and penalty clauses to ensure commitment to (or at least compliance with) delivery and quality requirements
- The offer of approved or preferred supplier status, accreditation or public acknowledgement for high levels of service
- The potential for ongoing business (and the corresponding threat of non-renewal or withdrawal)
- Competitive pressure to meet price and non-price criteria (eg in the case of public sector competitive tendering)
- Commercial or operational incentives to integrate or adapt systems and procedures (eg for quality assurance, training or e-procurement), which creates greater dependency (or interdependency).

3.3 In addition, however, interpersonal forms of leadership influence may be required in the negotiation and management of all these structural or contractual issues – and this is where interpersonal influencing styles and techniques come into play.

3.4 Given that suppliers and collaborators have their own goals and objectives, **exchange** may be the most effective influencing tactic. Hence the importance of **negotiation** in supplier relationships, as the nature of the exchange, bargain or *quid pro quo* is established. The nature of exchange-based influence should be strictly defined, however, in order to maintain professional ethical standards of integrity and objectivity. (Exchange involves a commercial relationship of mutual benefit to both organisations: *not* personal inducements to influence contract awards and other decisions.)

3.5 Consultation will also play a key role in supply chain management, especially in more developed collaborative or partnership relationships.

Influencing customers

3.6 In the case of customers, influence may be exercised through the **marketing mix**, in the form of factors such as the following.

- Advertising, public relations and corporate identity messages, appealing to the needs, wants, values and concerns of customers and users
- Sales or trade promotions and other purchase incentives
- Personal selling (using a mix of persuasive and negotiating techniques), particularly in business-to-business markets, where this promotional tool is most used
- Competitive or differential pricing strategies
- Competitive product and brand offerings (distinctive features, quality, identification with aspirations and values)
- Ease of availability and quality of service experience (eg e-commerce, speed of delivery, self-service or service-enhanced, customer care and so on).

3.7 Note that **customer communication** typically uses a wide range of influencing tactics: rational persuasion (product and price comparisons); inspirational appeal (value-laden branding); consultation (seeking customer feedback); ingratiation (congenial advertising, relationship marketing); exchange (sales promotions such as discount offers); personal appeal (personalised communications, loyalty programmes); and so on.

4 Stakeholder communication and engagement

Securing stakeholder buy-in to supply chain strategies

4.1 Taylor *(The Naked Leader)* argues that securing stakeholder commitment, ownership and 'buy-in' is necessary at all levels of leadership. 'Once a decision is made it must be bought into by everyone in the department [or project or supply chain]. Unity of purpose and direction is the most elusive yet one of the most powerful ways forward for all departments, teams and organisations.'

4.2 Supply chain strategies can be communicated in various ways, ideally using multiple communication media or vehicles.

- They can be formally incorporated in policy statements, sourcing plans, and other documents (eg intranet and extranet pages) – and articulated at briefings and forums of various kinds (including staff conferences, 'meet the buyer' events, and meetings with new and existing suppliers). Strategies should be consistently expressed across internal and external stakeholder communications.
- Ownership of the strategy must be modelled by management from the top down. Where possible, key influencers and leaders in the organisation (not necessarily in managerial positions) can be co-opted

to this process, as part of what Johnson and Scholes call the 'guiding coalition'. Strategic 'champions' may be used to articulate, sell and reinforce the message.

4.3   The key point in gaining 'buy-in' or ownership will be the **articulation of the strategy**, and **negotiation of collaboration or compliance**, in a way that:

- Is compelling, resonant and impactful for stakeholders
- Creates goal congruence, alignment or integration, by highlighting areas in which the goals and outcomes of the strategy dovetail with the goals and interests of stakeholders. In other words, emphasising 'win win', where possible.
- Creates incentives, by highlighting potential value gains, benefits or rewards – from the point of view of the target stakeholder audience. In other words: 'What's in it for them?'
- Creates momentum and urgency, by highlighting costs, threats or problems – from the point of view of the target stakeholder audience – which the strategy is designed to avert. In other words: 'What's the need?'
- Minimises potential for misunderstanding and insecurity, by transparent and targeted information and education, so that people have the information they need (and *feel* they need) to implement the strategy successfully
- Maximises ownership and identification with strategic values and goals, by utilising consultation and participation in strategy development, refinement, implementation and improvement or innovation, where possible. Stakeholders are considered more likely to support changes if they are encouraged to own them through having participated in the decision-making process.

4.4   We will discuss these issues in more detail in Chapter 9, as an aspect of change management.

4.5   It will also be important to support commitment and implementation, by removing perceived barriers, and facilitating the desired response. Ownership of plans and decisions may therefore be supported and reinforced by relevant systems (for internal and external stakeholders).

- Employee and supplier selection and appraisal criteria (so that stakeholders either 'buy in or get out')
- Human resource and supplier development activities (briefing, training, coaching, guidance, resourcing and so on)
- Governance and management structures (delegating authority, and allocating responsibility and accountability for implementation)
- Reward and incentive arrangements (with additional incentives for 'committed' levels of performance) and sanctions or penalties for non-compliance
- Ensuring that strategies are adequately resourced (in terms of deployment plans, policy guidance for implementation, managerial resources, finance and so on)

4.6   Individual leaders and managers can also reinforce the strategy by constant re-expression and refreshing (adding new examples, spreading new success stories); and recognising, acknowledging and celebrating individual and team expressions and achievements of the strategy. Many modern writers on leadership emphasise this myth-creating and celebratory role: 'catching people doing something right' (rather than wrong), praising, offering small but symbolic rewards, 'making heroes' and so on.

Stakeholder communication programmes

4.7   In addition to routine stakeholder communication (such as upward reporting to your manager on a regular basis, or communicating with supplier-side contract management teams or account managers), there may be a need for a planned series of information flows or communication initiatives on a particular subject, in order to inform stakeholders, engage their interest and support (or 'buy-in'), and shape their response to the information. Such a planned series of information flows is called a 'communication programme'.

4.8   Communication programmes are often planned in situations involving the management of change. Examples might include the introduction of new technology; a change of key supplier or distributor;

corporate restructuring, redundancies or changes in work methods; the adoption of new procurement policies (eg environmental or ethical standards); the launch of a new or modified product or service; or response to a potential public relations crisis (eg a product recall, environmental disaster or allegations of unethical behaviour).

4.9 It is necessary to establish a formal, systematic plan for communication with stakeholders in such situations, in order to ensure the following outcomes.

- The correct audience is identified and targeted (eg using stakeholder mapping to prioritise those most affected, or with most influence on the success of the plan being communicated).
- All affected stakeholders are reached with the information (ideally, at the same time, so that no-one has to find out 'by accident' from a less direct, reliable or positive source).
- Information is spread to the right people at the right time in the right way to achieve the most positive effect.
- Information is spread efficiently and cost-effectively.
- Information can be updated regularly where necessary.
- Messages are coherent and consistent (especially important when multiple channels are being used).
- Confidential information is spread on a 'need to know' basis, and sensitive information (eg company plans and financial data) and intellectual property (eg new product designs) are protected where relevant.
- Inaccurate rumours and misinformation are neutralised as far as possible.
- Opportunities are given, where appropriate, to gather feedback and deal with concerns or resistance on the part of stakeholders.
- The process is monitored and later reviewed, so that lessons can be learned for future communication programmes.

4.10 A **stakeholder communication plan** might include the following elements.

- A list of all stakeholders and their information requirements
- Communication mechanisms to be used (advertisements, written reports, newsletter, emails, briefing and consultation meetings, workshops, conferences, general meetings, media releases and communiqués, the website, intranets and extranets and so on) – taking into account the need for feedback and dialogue where appropriate
- Key elements of information to be distributed by the different mechanisms, and the level and frequency of communication required
- Roles and responsibilities of key individuals in ensuring that communication is adequate, appropriate and timely
- Identification of how unexpected information from other parties (eg media reports or internet discussion) will be handled within the scope of the activity

4.11 There may also be policies to protect the confidentiality and integrity of information, and to ensure that the organisation presents coherent and consistent messages – both to employees and to external stakeholders. Such policies may specify:

- Who has the authority to issue certain types of information, or to act as a contact point with particular audience groups
- What checking and authorisation is required before release of particular types of information
- Who will act as a point of contact for queries on information released
- What legal disclaimers may be required to protect the organisation from liability for any consequences arising from unauthorised communications. (You often see such disclaimers at the end of corporate email messages, for example.)

Why communication programmes fail

4.12   Communication programmes may fail for a number of reasons.

- Lack of planning (eg failure to identify the correct target audience; failure to ensure the consistency and coherence of messages over time; wrong timing)
- Lack of resources (eg finance, time) allocated to the programme, perhaps because of competing priorities
- Lack of opportunity for questions, concerns, arguments or suggestions to be raised by stakeholders (increasing insecurity, minimising 'ownership' and often driving resistance underground)
- Poor communication techniques: use of inappropriate media or channels; use of inaccessible language; information overload; and so on
- Lack of managerial and cultural support for the message being communicated (eg commitment not being modelled by senior management, values not being backed up by organisational policies and practices)
- Political or cultural resistance to the message, because of conflicting interests or values (eg staff not buying in to the need for restructuring or new work methods)

Stakeholder communication techniques

4.13   Stakeholder communication often involves reaching large numbers of people (or their representatives). It also often requires two-way communication: that is, opportunities for questions, concerns and views to be aired. (Being heard is important to stakeholders – just as their feedback and input is important to the organisation.) These two imperatives dictate the kinds of media and channels used in stakeholder communication programmes.

4.14   **Focus groups** are often used to gather qualitative data, views and feedback from stakeholders, particularly customers or potential customers. They consist of a group of 5–25 representatives of a target stakeholder population, together with a facilitator who encourages the group to discuss a list of relevant topics in an otherwise free and unstructured way.

4.15   This is a form of group **depth interview**, used for gathering complex qualitative information about attitudes, opinions and responses to organisational proposals and actions (such as advertising campaigns). Focus groups may be used to generate ideas for new product concepts and new products; to explore consumer responses to promotional or packaging ideas; or to conduct preliminary research into customer knowledge and opinions (which may be followed up with more extensive customer surveys, say).

4.16   Various **consultation forums** may be used to inform stakeholders about plans, and encourage the airing of questions, suggestions, concerns and feedback. In employee relations, for example, joint consultative committees or works councils may be used for discussion of issues of concern between employee representatives and management. Similarly, public consultation forums may be set up to allow discussion of community concerns about the environmental impacts of site developments or policy changes.

4.17   **Briefings, seminars or conferences** may be used to give information and presentations to stakeholders, and to solicit feedback. These can be used on a small scale (eg team briefings, cascading information down the organisation) or on a large scale (eg the annual general meeting of shareholders, or an industry conference).

4.18   In addition to these techniques, you may be able to think of a number of others, using written and electronic (rather than face-to-face) communication. Here are some examples.

- Briefings, updates, notifications and requests for feedback delivered by email or in personalised 'standard' letters to stakeholders
- Information and updates, and feedback mechanisms, delivered via the corporate website, intranet or extranet

- Shareholder reports, delivered via mail or posted on the website, to the key target audience of shareholders and investors
- Corporate advertising and public relations, in the form of advertisements, events, exhibitions, sponsorships, press releases and so on, to various target audiences including customers and the media.

Issues management

4.19 Issues management is a proactive process of identifying and analysing emerging controversies and issues which could potentially impact on corporate reputation or stakeholder interests, and initiating action to manage stakeholder perceptions about them. It endeavours not just to combat stakeholder perception problems as they arise, but to: proactively initiate dialogue with stakeholders to identify potential sensitivities and issues of concern; educate stakeholders in the organisation's position on issues; and establish networks of goodwill and support – in advance of conflict.

4.20 Issues management may be the responsibility of the corporate communication department or risk management function, but procurement may have direct responsibility for managing supply market issues. Issues management consists of seven main phases (Michael Regester & Judy Larkin).

- Monitoring: establishing an early warning system by scanning research findings, media coverage and 'what is being said' by stakeholders and influencers
- Issue identification: identifying trends and stakeholder cues signalling potentially reputation-damaging issues
- Issue prioritisation, on the basis of risk, impact and immediacy assessment (how likely, how costly, how urgent?)
- Issue analysis and preparation: determining how the issue is likely to develop; auditing the company's present position on the issue; appointing 'issue champions' (individuals who will develop authoritative, up-to-date knowledge of the issue); building influential relationships with supportive stakeholders; and setting up an issue task force to define and manage issue response strategies
- Response strategy formulation: deciding what the organisation's response to the issue should be
- Action programming and implementation: formulating policy and co-ordinating resources to support the response strategy
- Evaluation: assessing the success of response policies and programmes; capturing learning from failures and successes to inform future issues management.

Internal stakeholder communication

4.21 Internal stakeholder communication is particularly important.

- Organisations depend on their employees (the human resources of the business) to implement plans and deliver services. Employee awareness of, engagement in and commitment to organisational goals is essential to support external customer satisfaction and business success.
- People need to work together across functional boundaries in effective internal supply chains. There therefore needs to be both systematic communication between functions, and 'internal marketing' so that different functions understand each other's needs and contributions.
- Good employee communication enhances job satisfaction, and may help to create positive 'employer brand': that is, a reputation as a good employer, which may help to attract and retain quality staff.
- Employee communication, consultation and involvement is, in many countries, provided for by law (eg in the EU, in regard to consultation about redundancies, and the use of works councils to discuss matters of concern to employees).
- Communication is a cornerstone of positive employee relations, building stable and co-operative relationships between management and employees, and minimising conflict.

5

4.22 Some of the methods used for employee and cross-functional communication include: office manuals and in-house newsletters; a corporate intranet (staff-only web pages); team meetings, briefings, presentations and conferences; bulletins and announcements on noticeboards (and their website equivalents); personalised emails, letters and memoranda; day-to-day information passed on by managers to individuals and teams; and so on.

4.23 Tools which may more specifically encourage feedback or upward communication include: formal negotiating and consultative meetings (eg with employee representatives); suggestion schemes; performance appraisal interviews (where opportunities are given to discuss problems, issues and suggestions for improvement); quality circles and other consultation or discussion groups; employee attitude surveys; management participation in informal networks; and so on.

5   ICT tools for stakeholder communication

5.1 As suggested above, a number of information and communication technology (ICT) tools may be used to support both one-to-one and one-to-many stakeholder communication – and to facilitate the sharing and exchange of information within and between stakeholder groups. Here are some examples.

- Web conferencing and pod casting
- Virtual meeting and document or desktop sharing software
- Shared-access online database systems
- E-mail
- Social media communication tools
- Corporate websites and limited access networks such as intranets and extranets
- Internet-based e-sourcing and e-commerce systems

5.2 The syllabus highlights ICT tools through which an organisation can post or publish information for stakeholders, or make shared data accessible to shareholders: specifically, web-based information sharing via the internet and intranet.

The corporate website

5.3 The internet is a worldwide computer network allowing computers to communicate via telecommunications links. The network can also be accessed from laptop computers, personal digital assistants (such as Palm Pilots) and 3G mobile phones. The internet has exploded in recent years as a business tool, for:

- Marketing: supporting advertising, direct marketing, customer communication, public relations and market research (eg using online surveys and browsing or transaction histories).
- Direct distribution: of products (through online product ordering, or the downloading of electronic products such as music, video or educational content) and services (eg information, ticketing, consultancy and e-learning).
- Customer service and technical support: through email enquiries, FAQs (frequently asked questions), access to database information etc.
- Partnership development: through better information-sharing and communication with suppliers and business networks.

5.4 Some corporate websites are designed solely to provide information about products, services, sourcing policies, corporate social responsibility initiatives, career opportunities or other matters. They might provide contact details for would-be customers, suppliers, employees or other interested stakeholders to make direct enquiries, or to find a local office. A transaction-supporting website, however, can be a 'virtual' retail outlet, warehouse, supermarket, auction room or market exchange.

5.5 The term 'e-commerce' (short for electronic commerce) refers to business transactions carried out online via ICT – usually the internet. E-commerce has facilitated direct marketing, linking customers directly with suppliers across the whole value chain. It is a means of automating business transactions and workflows – and also streamlining and improving them. (However, it must be remembered that at some point, goods may have to be physically transported from the producer to the purchaser – and at this point, the speed of transaction-processing may not be matched by the speed of delivery.)

5.6 More sophisticated users of e-commerce can engage in 'electronic value chain trading': information on their entire value chain from customers via partners to suppliers is opened up for collaboration and co-operation on finding new and better ways of doing things.

5.7 Websites offer particular advantages for the publishing of stakeholder communications for the following reasons.

- They potentially reach a very wide global audience – but also have the facility to select target audiences, where required, through limited-access areas of the site (eg 'member only' pages) and clearly identified pages for target audiences (eg pages for investors, job seekers, suppliers etc).
- They make communication accessible 24 hours per day, 7 days per week and across international time zones and business hours.
- They support the use of a wide variety of rich, potentially engaging and compelling, communication media. Examples include: interactive surveys and tools; searchable information databases; a forum for user or stakeholder generated content; video presentations (eg personal messages for important issues-management or change leadership statements from a spokesperson or figurehead); visual and graphic aids; music (adding emotional appeal); community-building tools (such as discussion boards); and so on. Appropriate tools can thus be selected for target audiences and particular purposes.
- They support personalisation of the website/stakeholder interface, eg through various 'recognition' tools (utilising data-based information to recognise returning visitors or users and tailor messages and offers to their interests), interface customisation tools and loyalty programmes (eg services and rewards for registered members). This can be used to develop a sense of ongoing relationship and engagement in stakeholders using the site (Philip Kotler, *Marketing*).
- They support control and evaluation of communication, through embedded monitoring tools: measuring the number of 'hits' on the site, which pages were browsed, whether visitors made requested responses and actions and so on
- They support the gathering and analysis of stakeholder data and feedback (for stakeholder mapping and analysis), through a variety of tools including voluntarily supplied log-in data; online attitude and feedback surveys; and online message boards and discussion forums.
- They offer wide-ranging flexibility in the style and content of information that can be posted for stakeholder access (swiftly, in response to change or crisis, where necessary), allowing the web administrators control over stakeholder messages. (Where the website seeks genuinely to engage in dialogue with stakeholders, or to provide a transparent forum for them to contribute feedback or content, there is a risk of loss of control over the message. Even so, it is arguably preferable to have divergent or hostile messages hosted where they can be readily identified and countered – rather than 'out there' in the blogosphere or on Twitter...)

Intranets

5.8 The internet and the world wide web are an accepted framework for implementing and delivering information system applications. The internet is a global collection of telecommunications-linked computer networks, which has revolutionised global communication and commerce through tools such as email, and interactive, transaction-enabled websites. However, the same network protocols can be used more locally as a tool for internal and external supply chain communication.

5.9 An **intranet** is a set of networked and/or internet-linked computers. This private network is usually only accessible to registered users, within the same organisation or work group. Access is restricted by passwords and user group accounts, for example.

5.10 Intranets are used in internal supply chain and employee communication: only authorised internal users are able to access relevant web pages and dedicated email facilities (as well as having access to the wider internet).

5.11 Intranets may provide employees with access to a wide range of internal information: performance databases and reporting systems; induction and employment information (online policy and procedure manuals, job vacancies and training opportunities); noticeboards (for posting messages, announcements and bulletins); internal email facilities; mailings of employee newsletters and work updates; internal training software; and so on.

5.12 Intranets also offer significant advantages for integrating internal supply chain communications.

- Supporting multi-directional communication and data-sharing, and the formation of knowledge banks and communities of practice
- Linking remote sites and workers in 'virtual' teams
- Allowing authorised access to shared database and e-procurement platforms
- Giving employees wider access to corporate information (for personal identification, ideas-swapping and culture-creation)
- Encouraging more frequent – because more convenient – use of reference sources (such as procurement manuals, standing orders and policies) and updating of information
- Saving on the costs of producing and distributing the equivalent printed documents and messages

Extranets

5.13 An extranet is an intranet that has been extended to give selected external partners (such as suppliers) authorised access to particular areas or levels of the organisation's website or information network, for exchanging data and applications, and sharing information. Examples you might be familiar with include the registered-user-only pages of corporate websites, and the member-only pages of professional bodies' websites (like the CIPS website's student and member areas).

5.14 Supplier access to a buyer's extranet system is generally protected, requiring defined verification of identity (eg via a user ID), supplier codes and passwords.

5.15 Extranets are particularly useful tools for relationship management, inter-organisational partnerships and direct e-procurement transactions (which might have previously been carried out by EDI protocols).

5.16 An extranet may be used to publish news updates and technical briefings which may be of use to supply chain partners; publish requirements and/or conduct e-tenders or e-auctions (via a market exchange portal); exchange transaction data for electronic P2P processes (orders, payments, delivery tracking and so on); share training and development resources (eg as part of collaborative quality or sustainability management); and so on.

5.17 Procurement-focused extranets usually provide suppliers with the following facilities.

- Real-time access to inventory and demand information, enabling them to proactively manage the buyer's needs, rather than merely reacting to spot orders
- Authorised report information eg their vendor rating analysis – enabling them to be proactive in managing and improving their performance and competitiveness

5.18 Business Link lists the following potential benefits that can be gained from using extranet systems.

- Assists in achieving improved supply chain integration via the use of online ordering, order tracking and inventory management
- Reduces operational costs, for example by making manuals and technical documentation available online. This reduces cost and increases the speed of inter-business communication.

- Improved collaboration and relationship potential by enabling involved parties to work online using common documentation; again this accelerates the business process as well as saving cost by reducing the need to hold expensive meetings.
- Suppliers can directly access authorised business information which often enables them to resolve their own queries.
- Provides a single user interface between business partners.
- Improved security of communications since exchanges take place under a controlled and secure environment.

5.19 However, integrating supply chain processes via extranets still poses challenges and risks. In recent years, many extranet initiatives have failed to deliver tangible value. Research indicates that common reasons for failure can be identified as: inadequate planning and preparation; unrealistic expectations; and lack of a clear business case for how the extranet will support organisational objectives. It is easy for extranets to become nothing more than glorified chat groups. It is therefore important that the extranets provide tangible benefits. For best value, such benefits should be aligned to support and achieve overall business and supply chain objectives.

5.20 Extranet security is another critical design consideration. Hackers increasingly probe connected computers for weaknesses in their security, and data corruption, loss or theft – eg through the use of 'malware' – is a key issue for risk management.

Virtual teamworking and supply chain relationships

5.21 'Virtual' teams and organisations are interconnected groups of people who may not be present in the same office, site or organisation (and may even be in different areas of the world), but who:

- Share information and tasks (eg technical support provided by a supplier)
- Make joint decisions (eg on quality assurance, demand forecasts or production and delivery schedules)
- Fulfil collaborative functions: ie working together.

5.22 Information and communications technology has facilitated this kind of collaboration, simulating the dynamics of teamworking via tools such as teleconferencing, video-conferencing, web-conferencing, and internet linkages.

5.23 Partners in the supply chain, for example, can use such technology to access and share up-to-date product, customer, stock and delivery information (eg using web-based databases and data tracking systems).

5.24 Electronic meeting management systems allow virtual meeting participants to see and talk to each other using web-conferencing facilities, while sharing data and using electronic 'whiteboards': all on their PC, laptop, tablet or internet-enabled mobile phone. This supports enhanced supplier relationships and the management of outsourcing, particularly international outsourcing (or 'offshoring'): you don't need to be within reach of people to monitor their performance, stay in touch – or even have meetings.

6   The communication plan

Template for a communication plan

6.1 It is worth highlighting the practical component of the learning outcome for this section of the syllabus. You are required to be able to '*create a communication plan* to influence personnel involved in a supply chain'. That is, in a given case study scenario, you may be asked to identify an issue which requires stakeholder communication, and to develop and present a plan for leading and influencing stakeholders (especially employees and suppliers) appropriately.

6.2 The relevant assessment criterion (2.3) clearly sets out a template for this communication plan – which basically embraces everything we have discussed so far in this chapter. It would certainly be worth keeping this template in mind for use in an exam case study scenario – or in an essay question where you are asked to develop a communication plan for a stakeholder issue of your choice.

6.3 To wrap up this topic, therefore, we will simply highlight the elements of the template set out by the syllabus: Figure 5.5.

Figure 5.5 *Stakeholder communication plan*

	STAKEHOLDER COMMUNICATION PLAN
1. **Introduction**	*[Prepared by… for… Date… Purpose/terms of reference for plan eg identified stakeholder 'issue' if known]*
2. **Stakeholder analysis**	*[Major/relevant stakeholder groups identified and classified/mapped using an appropriate stakeholder mapping tool – eg Kraljic, Mitchell et al, Mendelow.*
	Brief text justifying the classification/positioning of each stakeholder: eg sources/ degree of power, nature of interest/stake]
3. **Engagement strategy**	*[Recommended engagement/management/communication approach for each stakeholder group, according to classification/mapping model: eg 'keep informed', 'keep satisfied', 'move from opponent to supporter']*
4. **Influencing approach**	*[Identification and justification of appropriate influencing styles and tactics, as relevant to relationship and direction of leadership*
	How stakeholder 'buy in' will be sought/secured]
5. **Communication plan**	*[Key messages to be conveyed to each stakeholder group*
	Key issues or pressure points for each group: possibly requiring proactive issues management
	Personnel to be responsible for stakeholder communication and contacts
	Communication media and tools to be used (including ICT tools to support stakeholder communication)]
6. **Evaluation**	*[Measures which will be used to evaluate success of the influencing/communication programme: desired outcomes and responses]*

Chapter summary

- Stakeholders are individuals and groups who have a legitimate interest or 'stake' in an organisation, process, project or decision. The stakeholders in a supply project include the owner or sponsor; customers and users; participating staff; suppliers and collaborators; and secondary stakeholders in the external environment.
- Stakeholder management recognises the need to take stakeholder needs and views into account when formulating plans, through activities such as: stakeholder mapping and analysis; stakeholder marketing and relationship management; and issues management. Mendelow's power/interest matrix may be used to map stakeholders according to the extent of their influence and interest in a given plan.
- Techniques of stakeholder influencing are relevant in the management of both suppliers and customers.
- Formal stakeholder communication programmes are particularly important in situations of change management. Relevant techniques include focus groups, depth interviews, consultation forums, briefings, seminars and conferences.
- Increasingly, stakeholder communications are managed by means of ICT tools (the corporate website, intranets and extranets etc.)

Self-test questions

Numbers in brackets refer to the paragraphs where you can check your answers.

1   Distinguish between (a) internal, connected and external stakeholders and (b) primary, secondary and key stakeholders. (1.5, 1.6)

2   In what ways is stakeholder management likely to be helpful for a procurement and supply manager? (1.10)

3   Sketch Mendelow's power/interest matrix. (Figure 5.1)

4   What are the three variables by which stakeholders are classified in the model developed by Mitchell *et al*? (2.10)

5   List mechanisms by which a buyer can exercise influence over a supplier. (3.2)

6   Give examples of situations in which formal stakeholder communication programmes would be desirable. (4.8)

7   List reasons why stakeholder communication programmes might fail. (4.12)

8   List examples of ICT tools that can assist in stakeholder communication. (5.1)

9   What are the advantages of intranets for internal communication? (5.12)

10 What are the potential benefits of using extranet systems? (5.18)

CHAPTER 6

Developing Leadership Effectiveness

Assessment criteria and indicative content

Section headings

Introduction

In this chapter we gather together various references in the syllabus to leadership skills and the management and development of leaders. The syllabus refers to this as 'leadership techniques... to influence personnel involved in the supply chain' – but the indicative content strongly suggests a focus on the management, measurement and development of leadership effectiveness. (Techniques for leading and influencing in the supply chain have already been discussed extensively in Chapters 3 and 4.)

We start with a general survey of some of the skills and values most commonly associated with effective leadership. We then follow up with a cluster of competencies which may be regarded as a 'meta-skill', enabling the leader to exercise all other skills effectively in the leadership context: emotional intelligence or EQ.

We then turn to the management of performance, recognising that this is something that is done *by* leaders (managing performance within their teams) and something that is done *to* leaders (as a way of enhancing leadership effectiveness). We start with the model of management by objectives, before looking at the broader concept of performance management which has largely replaced it in business contexts, and the challenges of defining and measuring leadership effectiveness.

Finally, we explore the dimensions and techniques of leadership learning, training and development: how leaders can be 'grown' in organisations and supply chains.

1   Leadership skills and competencies

1.1   There is no universally accepted definition of leadership skills. The demands made on leaders differ according to their position and role in the organisation; the nature of the task; the maturity of the team; the direction of leadership; the culture of the organisation – and so on.

1.2   Whetten and Cameron (*Developing Management Skills*) survey a number of research studies which cite different lists of skills recognised as key contributors to leadership effectiveness. They suggest that leadership skills can be differentiated from other kinds of 'leadership characteristics' (such as ambition, drive or integrity) because they are:

- Behavioural (observable and identifiable sets of actions that individuals perform)
- Controllable (able to be consciously practised, improved or avoided by individuals)
- Developable (amenable to learning, practice and feedback, in pursuit of higher levels of competency).

1.3   John Adair and Melanie Allen *(Time Management and Personal Development)* note that management development in recent decades has seen 'a drive towards lifetime learning, flexible self-development, continuous improvement and competence or core skills based training, linked directly to business goals'.

1.4   Competence-based qualifications for management and leadership were originally developed in the UK by the Management Charter Initiative, as the basis for vocational qualifications in management and team leading. In 2005, the Management Standards Centre took over the work of developing and championing a new set of National Occupational Standards (NOS) for management and leadership.

1.5   The Standards cover six functional areas of management and leadership, which broadly reflect the themes of this Course Book (with the exception of 'using resources', which is arguably a function of management rather than leadership).

A   Managing Self and Personal Skills
B   Providing Direction
C   Facilitating Change
D   Working with People
E   Using Resources
F   Achieving Results

1.6   However, Mullins argues that the education and training of management also needs to emphasise 'not only interpersonal skills, but also a flexibility of approach, diagnostic ability and the realisation that the most effective form of leadership behaviour is a product of the total leadership situation'. In other words, as we saw in Chapter 2, leaders need to develop the awareness and behavioural flexibility to adjust their leadership style to the demands of the task, the readiness of the team and the context of leadership.

1.7   In this section, we will look briefly at some of the interpersonal skills and values or attitudes most commonly identified with leadership. (We have already considered some of the 'micro' skills identified with influencing, in Chapter 3: refresh your memory of skills such as rapport building if you need to.) In Section 2, we will look further at the issue of awareness and flexibility, through the concept of 'emotional intelligence'.

Interpersonal and communication skills

1.8   As an interpersonal or relational process, leadership depends to a large extent on interpersonal skills. These can be seen at two levels.

- **First-order skills:** observing, listening, questioning, establishing rapport, expressing empathy, communicating assertively, giving and receiving feedback
- **Second-order skills**, in which the first-order skills are *applied* in specific contexts or for specific

purposes: negotiation, influencing and persuading, teamworking, managing conflict, managing people through change, coaching – and leading (which may involve any or all of these).

Think of the effective leaders you know – and you will probably recognise them as effective communicators: people who are 'good with people'.

1.9 Key communication skills for leadership include the following.

- **Promotion**
  Leaders 'sell' visions, goals, desired outcomes and values – in the same way that marketers promote products. They express them in a way that makes them look attractive, desirable and beneficial for the people who will have to adopt or implement them. To use a well-known marketing model (AIDA), they create Attention, Interest and Desire leading to Action.

  People-focused, anecdotal leadership literature strongly features leadership skills in value-laden goal articulation, positive thinking, good news swapping, 'catching people doing things right' (emphasising praise rather than blame) and so on.

  There is also an element of self-promotion, or image management, in effective leadership: creating a role model and impression of success that will inspire confidence and followership – and attract power and opportunity.

- **Influencing and persuasion**
  Influencing and persuasion (and their use in negotiation) are central skills in leadership (getting things done through other people).

  Various forms of power may be applied (as we saw in Chapter 3) to influence people: organisational authority, superior knowledge and expertise, personal charisma, the power to give or withhold rewards and so on. Persuasion is influencing *other* than by using authority or power: for example, by logical argument or emotional appeal. Authority and power 'push' people to change, despite their beliefs and goals: persuasion aims to 'pull' or lead people to change by bringing their beliefs and goals into alignment with those of the influencer.

- **Negotiation**
  Negotiation is widely recognised as a key skill for procurement and supply professionals – and is also identified as fundamental to leadership. Buy-in, followership and attitude change may be more readily secured by appealing to people's interests (offering something they value) than by appealing to logic or emotion.

- **Inspiration**
  Inspirational communication involves the expression of powerful values and compelling visions of the future, which appeal to the aspirations of followers.

- **Support and challenge**
  Individual and team motivation depends on a balance between supportive communication from the leader (coaching, facilitating, team-building, praise, encouragement, empathy) and challenging communication (goal articulation, constructive feedback, thought-provoking questions, continuous improvement targets, stretching opportunities for development). Without support, team members may lose confidence and experience stress; without challenge, they may lose motivation, cease to develop or lapse into dangerous complacency.

Leadership values

1.10 Values are things we attach importance to. They are a mixture of our beliefs, emotions and positive and negative judgements about things. They represent our personal and collective moral standards (in our families, organisations and cultures) – and are the foundation on which our attitudes, goals and personal preferences are formed and on which we take decisions.

1.11 Individuals and groups develop values – as do professions and organisations. Organisational values are often identified with organisation culture. Peters and Waterman suggested that a 'handful of guiding values' could be a powerful unifying force and a non-threatening form of leadership control in an organisation. Where individuals can be brought to buy into the values of the team, they are likely to be more satisfied and effective, with performance based on commitment, rather than compliance.

1.12 Taylor (*The Naked Leader,* 2002) uses the term **values-based leadership** to describe leadership based on 'perception, people and passion' – rather than 'process, product or projects'.

'People will only ever buy into an idea if they believe in it... Placing value, and values, at the heart of our organisation, is important for so many other reasons, beyond people, culture and leadership. Most companies are realising the importance of corporate and ethical responsibility to their customers, their stakeholders, society and to each other. Integrity and trust have taken on a new significance... Ethics and success just became powerful partners.'

1.13 Mullins identifies a number of key values (or 'underlying philosophies') that contribute to successful leadership, in terms of team satisfaction and task performance.

- Consideration, respect and trust
- Recognition and credit (where it is due)
- Involvement and availability: empathy for the responsibilities and challenges of team members, and taking an active and supportive interest
- Fair and equitable treatment
- Individual consideration: treating team members as individuals
- Emphasis on end-results: focusing on target outcomes, contributions and achievements, not process compliance
- Mutual satisfaction and co-operation: ensuring that team members' needs are met where possible, because this supports task performance and customer satisfaction

Integrity and ethics

1.14 Integrity is a cultural construct: people define it according to specific values about what constitutes 'good' behaviour in their culture. However, it is often used to refer to a cluster of behaviours to do with:

- **Consistency:** you can be relied on to do what you've said you will do
- **Openness:** your decision-making processes are transparent (within the bounds of professional and personal confidentiality); you are willing to share and face difficult truths, and to share information to support performance and learning
- **Honesty:** your conduct models high standards of personal and professional ethics
- **Respect for people:** you are committed to treating people fairly and with professional courtesy, upholding their right to dignity, choice and justice
- **Authenticity** (Goffee & Jones, 'Managing Authenticity – the Paradox of Great Leadership' in *Harvard Business Review,* 2005): the perception by followers that a leader's word and deeds consistently match. The paradox is that, as we see in relation to contingency theory (in Chapter 2), a leader may have to present a different face to different audiences in different circumstances. Goffee and Jones argue that authentic leaders do not 'fake' values or personality traits: they are merely intentional about which ones they should reveal and emphasise to particular audiences, in order to lead effectively.
- **Credibility:** the ability to inspire trust and confidence in followers. Kouzes and Posner ('The Janusian Leader', in *Management 21C)* argue that 'credibility is the foundation of leadership'. People would willingly follow leaders with 'integrity and trustworthiness, with vision and a sense of direction, with enthusiasm and passion, and with expertise and a track record for getting things done.'

1.15 Leaders also have a responsibility to communicate and promote ethical standards and practices in the internal and external supply chain, as part of:

- Their duty to comply with national and international law – including the need to avoid corporate liability (among other negative outcomes) for wrongdoing
- Their duty to comply with professional and corporate ethical guidelines and codes of practice
- Their responsibility for fulfilling corporate objectives (including ethical objectives) and maintaining constructive, sustainable and responsible ongoing trading (and employment) relationships
- Their responsibility for developing staff and managing discipline in the organisation.

2 Emotional intelligence

2.1 Mullins notes that 'until recently, workplaces were seen as rational, logical places where emotions were excluded or seen in a negative light.'

2.2 'Intelligence' has always been prized in the work context – often defined in terms of cognitive abilities (that is, mental processes such as perception, mathematical ability, verbal fluency and reasoning) and measured by IQ or **intelligence quotient**. However, the work of Howard Gardner (*Frames of Mind)* challenged the narrow definition of IQ, arguing that it oversimplifies the wide range of intelligent behaviours observable in individuals. Gardner developed a model of 'multiple intelligences' which included new categories such as spatial capacity (design awareness), kinaesthetic ability (physical ability) and musical ability. He also introduced the category of 'personal intelligences':

- *Intrapersonal intelligence*: knowing one's inner world; the ability to form an accurate self-concept and to be able to use that model to operate effectively in life
- *Interpersonal intelligence*: the ability to understand other people, what motivates them and how to work co-operatively with them.

2.3 The concept of personal intelligences was further developed (eg by P Salovey & JD Mayer, and Daniel Goleman) specifically to include feelings and emotions, which were said to express processes occurring in different parts of the brain than purely intellectual or cognitive processes. This gave rise to the concept of 'emotional intelligence'.

The work of Daniel Goleman

2.4 Daniel Goleman has popularised the argument that leadership success depends not only on technical ability and mental dexterity (IQ), but on emotional awareness and maturity: the ability to be aware of and regulate one's emotions – and to manage relationships with sensitivity to what others are feeling.

2.5 A basic definition of emotional intelligence is 'the capacity for recognising our own feelings and those of others, for motivating ourselves, and for managing emotions well in ourselves as well as others' (Goleman, *Emotional Intelligence,* 1996).

2.6 Goleman's five basic components (or 'domains') of emotional intelligence are shown in Table 6.1.

Table 6.1 *Goleman's domains of emotional intelligence*

Self awareness	'Knowing what we are feeling in the moment, and using those preferences to guide our decision making; having a realistic assessment of our own abilities and a well-grounded sense of self-confidence'
Self regulation	'Handling our emotions so that they facilitate rather than interfere with the task at hand; being conscientious and delaying gratification to pursue goals; recovering well from emotional distress'
Motivation	'Using our deepest preferences to move and guide us toward our goals, to help us take initiative and strive to improve, and to persevere in the face of setbacks and frustrations'
Empathy	'Sensing what people are feeling, being able to take their perspective, and cultivating rapport and attunement with a broad diversity of people'
Social skills	'Handling emotions in relationships well and accurately reading social situations and networks; interacting smoothly; using these skills to persuade and lead, negotiate and settle disputes, for co-operation and teamwork'

Goleman's leadership styles

2.7 Goleman's research *(Goleman, Boyatzis and McKee, Primal Leadership, 2002)* supported the contingency view that effective leaders are able to master and use distinct leadership styles at appropriate times, depending on the business situation.

2.8 The particular focus of Goleman's work is 'resonance': being attuned to, and able to 'tap into' the emotions of others, in such a way as to draw their attention, identification and emotional arousal.

2.9 Goleman identifies six leadership styles based on different components of emotional intelligence, which help to achieve resonance, build commitment and improve the emotional climate of the organisation: Table 6.2. The more styles that can be deployed, the more effective performance and morale will be.

Table 6.2 *Goleman's resonant leadership styles*

STYLE	RESONANCE BY	IMPACT	APPROPRIATE
Visionary Provides long-term vision and direction Empathises and inspires Explains people's contribution to vision	Moving people towards a shared vision	Very positive	When radical changes require new vision and direction
Coaching Develops human resources for the long term Listens, counsels, encourages, delegates Helps people identify their own strengths and weaknesses	Creating goal congruence: connecting people's goals with team goals	Very positive	To support competent, motivated personnel in improving performance via long-term team capability
Affiliative Builds relationships, harmony and co-operation within the team and work place Friendly, empathetic Resolves conflict, boosts morale	Creating harmony by connecting people to each other	Positive	To heal conflicts To motivate during challenging times To strengthen collaboration
Democratic Builds commitment through consultation and consensus decisions Listener, team worker, collaborator, influencer	Appreciating input and gaining commitment through participation	Positive	To build support or consensus To gain input for decision quality

Continued . . .

STYLE	RESONANCE BY	IMPACT	APPROPRIATE
Pace-setting Sets challenging goals and pushes to accomplish tasks and improve performance Strong personal standards, initiative and need to achieve Can be low on empathy and collaboration; impatient; micro-managing; numbers driven.	Realising challenging and exciting goals	Can be negative, if used exclusively or poorly	To get high-quality results from a motivated, competent, secure team (eg in sales)
Commanding Demands compliance Can be controlling, threatening, discomfort-creating	Giving clear direction in an emergency	Often negative, disempowering or driving away talent	In crisis, or with problem employees For urgent corporate turnaround In authoritarian cultures (eg military)

EQ and leadership effectiveness

2.10   Goleman defines **emotional competence** as a *learned capability* which translates emotional intelligence into skilled behaviours, resulting in effective work performance *(Emotional Intelligence at Work)*. Working with the Hay Group, Goleman developed the Emotional Competence Inventory (assessment instrument): a questionnaire measuring emotional competencies relevant to organisational management and leadership, as shown in Table 6.3. This may be used as a framework for leadership recruitment and selection, and management or leadership development.

Table 6.3 *The emotional competence inventory framework*

DIMENSION	COMPETENCIES
Self awareness	Emotional self-awareness Accurate self-assessment Self-confidence
Self management	Emotional self-control Transparency Adaptability Achievement orientation Initiative Optimism
Social awareness	Empathy Organisational awareness Service orientation
Relationship management	Developing others Inspirational leadership Change catalyst Influence Conflict management Teamwork and collaboration

2.11   The concept of EQ links strongly to leadership skills.

- Effective influence and persuasion is supported by qualities such as empathy: 'enabling us to get inside the minds of other people and be effective in our communication with them' (Borg, *Persuasion: The Art of Influencing People,* 2004). Communication skills, without the underlying values and attitudes to back them up, will not be effective in promoting positive relationships and successful, ethical influencing.
- Emotional intelligence underpins a range of leadership qualities such as confidence, perseverance, tolerance of stress, behavioural flexibility and so on.

- Social skills, as defined by Goleman, explicitly underpin leadership skills such as inspiring, persuading, motivating, leading, negotiation, conflict management and teamworking.
- Emotional intelligence is particularly influential in effective change management, because it supports a *transformational* leadership approach (inspiring and supporting change in the beliefs, attitudes and values underlying people's behaviour) rather than a merely transactional approach (getting people to change their behaviour, often temporarily, in exchange for offered rewards).
- Goleman suggests that emotional aptitude is a meta-ability, determining how well we can use *whatever* other skills we have.

2.12 Extensive research has shown that high emotional intelligence both distinguishes 'outstanding' leaders (and 'star' teams), and correlates strongly with effective business performance. Emotional competencies are now listed among the most important selection factors for senior managers worldwide.

EQ in procurement and supply

2.13 Malcolm Higgs and Andrea Reynolds (*Do Purchasing Professionals Need Emotional Intelligence?*, 2002) have adapted this model for a procurement setting as follows.

- **Self-awareness:** the awareness of your own feelings and the ability to recognise and manage these
- **Emotional resilience:** being able to perform well and consistently in a range of situations and when under pressure
- **Motivation:** the drive and energy which you have to achieve results, to balance short-term and long-term goals, and to pursue your goals in the face of challenge and rejection
- **Interpersonal sensitivity:** the ability to be aware of the needs and feelings of others, and to use this awareness effectively in interacting with them and arriving at decisions impacting on them
- **Influence:** the ability to persuade others to change their viewpoint on a problem or issue
- **Intuitiveness:** the ability to use insight and interaction to arrive at, and implement, decisions when faced with ambiguous or incomplete information
- **Conscientiousness and integrity:** the ability to display commitment to a course of action in the face of challenge, to act consistently and 'in the line'.

3 Managing performance

3.1 This topic area is placed in the syllabus among 'leadership techniques' for influencing personnel in supply chains: in other words, it includes processes and techniques that can be **used by leaders** in the management, improvement and development of performance in teams and supply chains.

3.2 However, it is also placed alongside 'measures of [leadership] effectiveness', and 'leadership development': in other words, it also includes processes and techniques that can be **applied *to* leaders** in an organisation, in order to manage, improve and develop *their* performance as leaders.

3.3 Try to bear this dual focus in mind as you read on – and as you apply these concepts in the exam...

Management by objectives

3.4 Developed by Peter Drucker *(The Practice of Management,* 1955), management by objectives (or MbO) was an influential early attempt systematically to integrate individual performance goals with corporate strategic objectives, as part of an ongoing programme of goal-setting and performance review involving all levels of management.

3.5 Drucker argued that managers often get so involved in operational activity that they forget the purpose or objective of that activity (the 'activity trap'). In order to improve the unity of purpose and direction of an enterprise, it is necessary both to:

- Align the objectives of individuals with team, functional and corporate objectives and
- Keep objectives, and the purpose of activities, at 'front of mind', by measuring and directing individual performance against agreed objectives.

3.6 The overall process of MbO involves the following steps.

- Developing a coherent strategic plan, with clear organisational goals and objectives
- The cascading of organisational goals and objectives down through the organisation: from enterprise level to business unit to function to team to individual
- The management of performance through a classic planning and control cycle: setting objectives; action planning; performance review and evaluation; and adjustment in the following planning period.
- Collaboration between managers and team members in setting objectives and standards, implementing plans (with managers providing support as required), reviewing results and planning adjustments

3.7 At the individual management level, steps in an MbO process are as follows.

- Collaboratively define each individual's major **areas of responsibility** and the purpose of their role within the corporate plan.
- Jointly define and agree the **key tasks** which are directly related to the achievement of the objectives, and in which any performance shortfall would negatively impact on success.
- Jointly define and agree, for each key task, **key results** (which must be achieved in order for the key tasks to be successfully performed and objectives met) and methods of monitoring and measuring performance in these areas (key performance indicators).
- Agree individual (or unit) **performance improvement plans** for a defined planning period: developing or selecting SMART improvement objectives for each key task and formulating action plans to achieve those objectives.
- Implement **monitoring, self-evaluation and periodic review** of performance at agreed intervals, and revise objectives, targets and action plans as required.

3.8 Advocates of MbO argue that such a process is helpful in clarifying organisational and unit goals; focusing attention on priority areas; systematically converting strategic plans into co-ordinated managerial action plans and budgets; securing the involvement and commitment of individuals to defined targets and areas of accountability; and supplying systematic information for managerial planning and control, individual performance appraisal and development planning.

3.9 Critics of MbO argue that there is a danger of rigidity because of the effort and investment put into integrated planning. Plans must be flexible – especially in complex and dynamic environments (where objectives may change) and in flexible work roles (where individual contributions may vary with requirements). There may be employee relations problems, if staff perceive that they are being made more accountable for performance without a corresponding increase in empowerment or involvement.

3.10 Although the process in its original form is no longer fashionable, for these reasons, MbO forms a foundation for broader performance management systems thinking.

Performance management

3.11 Performance management is the process by which shortfalls and weaknesses in individual and team performance are identified and addressed through various types of improvement or development intervention, on an ongoing basis. The same generic process can also be applied to supplier and supply chain performance.

3.12 Michael Armstrong *(How to be an even better manager)* provides a useful overview of the performance management process.

'Performance management is a continuous and flexible process which involves managers and those whom they manage acting as partners within a framework which sets out how they can best work together to achieve the required results. It focuses on future performance planning and improvement rather than retrospective performance appraisal. It provides the basis for regular and frequent dialogues between managers and individuals or teams about performance and development needs.'

3.13 There are four key activities in internal performance management (although you should be able to see how they might also be applied to managing the supply chain).

- **Preparation of performance agreements** (also known as performance contracts). These set out the individual's or team's objectives, how performance will be measured, the competencies needed to achieve the objectives and the organisation's core values.
- **Preparation of performance and development plans**. These set out identified performance and personal development needs in order for performance agreements to be met.
- **Management of performance throughout the year**. This involves the continuous process of providing feedback on performance; conducting informal progress reviews; and dealing with performance problems as necessary, using interventions such as motivation and reward, counselling, coaching, training and disciplinary action. Problem-solving and adjustment of the work situation, methods and technology may also be required.
- **Performance review and appraisal:** taking a view of an individual's progress to date and reaching an agreement about what should be done in the future. Performance appraisals should be collaborative, problem-solving, developmental discussions – not 'interviews'. They should ideally be separated from performance evaluations for the purposes of setting rewards, in order to remove the potentially judgemental and adversarial element from the discussion, and to keep it developmentally focused. Needs for learning, improvement, development and problem-solving can thus be identified – to start the planning cycle again, on an ongoing basis.

Establishing key performance indicators

3.14 Key performance indicators (KPIs) are clear qualitative or quantitative statements which define adequate or desired performance in key areas (critical success factors), and against which progress and performance can be measured. The important point about KPIs is that they state performance goals in a way that is capable of direct, detailed, consistent measurement at operational level, using available data collection systems. Eight to ten well-formulated objectives may be realistic for any given planning and control period.

3.15 Setting effective goals and objectives – at all levels – is important for organisational reasons.

- They promote unity of direction, aiding co-ordination and efficient organisation: reducing overlaps and gaps in activity.
- They enable limited resources to be intentionally allocated to optimise corporate performance (rather than potentially sub-optimal performance due to competition between units and individuals).
- They provide an objective measure against which performance can be evaluated and accountability maintained.
- They support flexibility, by focusing on key end results or critical success factors, rather than inputs (which may change) and processes (which may cause a bureaucratic, inward focus).

3.16 Goal-setting is also important, at an individual and team level, for behavioural reasons.

- Goals enable tasks to be broken down into manageable, time-bounded 'chunks', while at the same time giving people a sense of their role and contribution to the whole activity of the organisation.
- Goals are important in motivation: people are motivated by the decision that it is worth expending

effort to reach desired outcomes (goals), and by feedback information telling them to what extent they have achieved those goals. For the same reason, goals are also vital in learning and change.

3.17 A popular framework for ensuring that KPIs (and other objectives) are effectively formulated is the acronym 'SMART'.

- **Specific:** clear and well-defined statement of precisely what the desired outcomes or deliverables are, so that people know what they are committing to and accountable for.
- **Measurable:** susceptible to monitoring, review and measurement (ideally in quantitative or numerical terms) so that people can meaningfully assess progress and achievement.
- **Attainable:** achievable and realistic, given the time and resources available – even if the aim is to be 'stretching' or to stimulate improvement, attainment of the required level of performance must be possible!
- **Relevant:** performance measures should (as stressed by MbO) be relevant to, and aligned with, the strategic objectives of the organisation; the policies and objectives of the procurement function; the critical success factors of the organisation and supply chain; the business need and so on.
- **Time-bounded:** given defined timescales and deadlines for completion (or review) – ie not 'open ended'.

3.18 Some versions of the SMART model substitute, or add, the following.

- **Stretching:** performance measures may deliberately be made challenging enough to motivate personnel and stimulate committed performance, learning, development and improvement (eg as part of individual or supplier development and improvement agreements)
- **Sustainable** (or responsible): KPIs should take into account potential impacts on key stakeholders, in the light of the unit's (and organisation's) ethical responsibilities towards them
- **Agreed:** incorporated in a contract, agreement or charter (formal or informal), in order to secure joint commitment and accountability.
- **Rewarded:** attainment of KPIs may be linked to positive incentives or rewards of some kind, as part of the performance management or supplier motivation process.
- **Reviewed:** KPIs should be periodically reviewed, so that they can be adjusted if circumstances or requirements have changed – or if they are designed to be 'movable' to stimulate continuous improvement.

3.19 A simple process for developing KPIs is summarised in Figure 6.1.

Figure 6.1 *Developing key performance indicators*

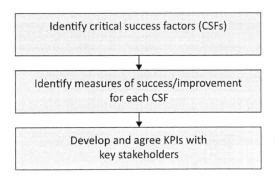

Benefits and limitations of KPIs in improving performance

3.20   Some of the benefits of using KPIs (for leaders, for team members *and* for suppliers) are as follows.

- Increased and improved (results-focused) communication on performance issues. (Essentially, 'what gets measured, gets managed'.)
- Motivation to achieve or surpass the specified performance level (particularly with KPI-linked incentives, rewards or penalties). Motivation is in any case stronger where there are clear targets to aim for.
- Support for integrated, collaborative performance measurement and improvement (with KPIs on both sides of the leadership or supply relationship, to encourage two-way feedback and problem-solving)
- The ability directly to compare year on year performance, to identify improvement or deterioration trends
- Focus on key results areas (critical success factors) for the team, unit or supply chain
- Reduced conflict arising from causes such as goal confusion and unclear expectations.

3.21   It is worth noting that KPIs can have some disadvantages as well. The pursuit of individual KPIs can lead to some dysfunctional or sub-optimal behaviour: cutting corners on quality or service to achieve productivity or time targets, say, or units focusing on their own targets at the expense of cross-functional collaboration and co-ordination. Targets will have to be carefully set with these potential problems in mind.

3.22   Common problems with objectives and objective-setting, which must be addressed by managers, include: constantly changing focus and targets (or, conversely, failure to review and adjust targets); poorly-constructed (un-SMART) objectives; a limited range of objectives (neglecting qualitative criteria such as ethics and relationships); not enough flexibility within the boundaries set by objectives; inadequate information for, or attention to, measuring performance against objectives; and setting too few or insufficiently challenging objectives.

Performance appraisal and feedback

3.23   In all organisations, the performance of each employee is assessed by someone. Often this is a subjective, *ad hoc* activity carried out by the individual's immediate superior in the course of day-to-day operations.

3.24   Managers and supervisors should be constantly monitoring the performance of the individuals and teams within their authority – if only by requiring regular reports on key results and deviations from plan, according to a system of reporting by exception. In practice, many managers prefer to stay closer to what is going on in their section, observing and listening to the flow of work and work relationships to get a sense of individual and teamwork patterns, styles, capabilities and results.

3.25   Leaders have a key role in giving ongoing feedback to team members in a way that enhances performance, morale and motivation: this is an important leadership skill. Feedback may be of two broad types.

- **Motivational** feedback (praise, encouragement) is given to acknowledge, reward and encourage positive behaviour or performance by the team member (or leader). Its aim is to boost *confidence*.
- **Developmental** feedback (constructive criticism, coaching or counselling) is given when an area of the team member's (or leader's) performance requires improvement, helping the individual to identify the problem and plan for change. Its aim is to increase *competence*.

3.26   Informal performance monitoring, reviews and discussions should therefore take place on a continual basis, as part of the relationship between the leader and the team. There may be little formal documentation of this process – although feedback, agreed improvement goals and learning undertaken may be written down in an individual's learning or development 'log' or journal, say.

3.27   Increasingly, however, organisations are choosing to formalise the assessment process and use it in a proactive attempt to improve business performance and manage the potential of employees for ongoing skill and career development.

3.28 Such a process requires managers to understand individual contributions to departmental and organisational goals; to form a coherent, complete and objective view of each individual's performance in comparison with agreed standards; to offer specific, development-focused feedback; and to engage in collaborative problem-solving and improvement planning. These processes in turn are likely to:

- Support performance management and improvement: dovetailing individual objectives with organisational goals; setting realistic performance targets; comparing actual performance against standards to identify and motivate improvements; providing a context for collaborative problem-solving, to resolve barriers to improved performance; and so on
- Enhance manager-employee relations and communication
- Form a basis for continuous learning, quality or service improvement, innovation and employee empowerment: providing a context for open discussion of performance issues and encouraging upward communication to harness employee 'front line' knowledge and commitment
- Help to identify (and increase the visibility of) the contribution of the purchasing function to organisational competitive advantage, providing a business case for purchasing disciplines.

3.29 Systematic performance measurement and evaluation also provides benefits to individual team members.

- Clear goals, targets and standards, so they know what they are expected to achieve, and how their role and performance contributes to departmental and organisational objectives
- Regular, objective, relevant performance feedback, which is essential to learning and motivation (providing positive reinforcement of progress and achievement, and identifying areas for improvement)
- Opportunity to discuss work problems, frustrations, expectations and training and development needs – potentially leading to performance improvements (and resulting rewards and satisfactions) and training or development opportunities.

Formal appraisal systems

3.30 The most common approach to formal performance appraisal is evaluation by the appraisee's immediate superior, who usually has the most detailed knowledge of the tasks carried out by the individual, and their work context, and is therefore in a good position to assess how well the appraisee performed and to appreciate any problems that may have affected performance. The appraisal can then be seen as part of the ongoing process of performance management. However, appraisal by a superior alone, if not well managed, may be liable to unchecked subjective judgements, and may affect (and be affected by) the working relationship between the parties concerned.

3.31 In order to get a more rounded picture of individual performance, feedback assessments may be sought from a range of key stakeholders in the leader's performance.

- **Peer appraisal** is useful as an element of a more comprehensive appraisal process, particularly in regard to inter-personal criteria such as ability to work with others, communication, conflict resolution, lateral influencing and so on, which can best be assessed by those 'on the receiving end'. This method may be awkward to implement, however, because of peers' reluctance to judge or 'betray' a colleague by conveying negative feedback to management.
- **Upward appraisal** (by the leader's line subordinates) is not widely used, but on the increase. It is a particularly useful tool for appraising the effect of a manager's leadership style on team members. Again, however, it may be difficult to elicit feedback, because of fears of retribution.
- **Internal customer appraisal** may be relevant in procurement and supply, to assess the quality of service and relationship management provided to other departments. Internal customer satisfaction should be a key performance measure for procurement leaders.
- **Appraisal by suppliers** may be particularly useful feedback, since it may be important for the organisation to maintain 'good customer' status (and the benefits it brings) with key suppliers. Suppliers will be in a good position to provide feedback on the effectiveness and impact of a

manager's influencing, relationship-building and leadership style. However, again, it may be difficult to gather meaningful feedback if suppliers are reluctant to alienate a supply chain manager on whom they rely for business.

3.32 **360-degree feedback** (or **multi-source appraisal**) is designed to enable a range of stakeholders in a leader's style and performance (including the leader himself) to comment and give developmental feedback. The information is usually collected (anonymously, where appropriate) through questionnaires. The advantage of multi-source feedback is that it offers a rounded picture of a leader's performance. It gives a more complete and relevant assessment and reduces the risk of bias. It also increases the amount and openness of task and performance-related communication in the organisation.

Performance improvement and development

3.33 A range of performance improvement and development processes can then be applied, as required.

- Performance gap analysis and learning or development needs identification
- Management interventions to address performance or learning gaps, including: discipline handling; grievance handling; motivation and reward; learning, training and development; supervision, coaching and leadership; and/or employee counselling and support for change

4 Measures of leadership effectiveness

4.1 Because leadership is not always a defined role, or associated with a defined position in the organisation, there may not be formal measures of leadership performance or effectiveness.

4.2 Mullins emphasises that since management (and leadership) involves getting work done through the efforts of other people, managers (and leaders) are likely to be evaluated not just on their own performance but on the results achieved by their subordinates or followers.

4.3 An 'effective leader' might therefore be identified with generic measures such as the following.

- The performance of the team or suppliers and supply chain for which the leader is responsible, or in which the leader is involved and has influence – which will partly reflect the effectiveness of leadership. Measures of this may include: customer or supplier satisfaction ratings, complaints and other feedback; meeting project milestones and deadlines; meeting or exceeding quality or cost management targets; levels of output and productivity; innovation performance; and so on.
- The motivation, commitment, loyalty and satisfaction of team members, suppliers and other stakeholders – which will partly reflect the effectiveness and acceptability of the leader's style. Indirect measures of morale and motivation may include: staff turnover, absenteeism, poor timekeeping, disciplinary and grievance actions – or, with suppliers, poor service, supplier turnover, contractual disputes and so on.
- The development and improvement of individual, team and/or supply chain capability and performance over time – which will partly reflect the leader's effectiveness in directing, motivating and developing
- Internal and external stakeholders' awareness and understanding of the vision, goals and objectives of the team, organisation or supply chain – which will partly affect the leader's effectiveness in vision and goal articulation and stakeholder communication
- The effectiveness and ease with which change is introduced and maintained in the team, organisation or supply chain – which will partly reflect the effectiveness of change leadership
- The quality of relationships, trust and communication in the team, organisation or supply chain – which will partly reflect the effectiveness of leadership in creating a positive communication 'climate'
- The extent to which individuals, teams and suppliers are willing and able to respond flexibly to changing demands; to exercise initiative and responsibility; and to develop and implement innovative solutions – which will partly reflect the effectiveness of leadership in developing, delegating and directing through vision, values and guidance (rather than stifling controls).

The balanced scorecard

4.4   The balanced scorecard model was developed by Robert Kaplan & David Norton *(The Balanced Scorecard: Translating Strategy into Action)* who essentially argued that purely financial objectives and performance measures are not enough to control organisations effectively. Indeed, they tend to encourage short-term, limited thinking, because leaders are judged by criteria which do not measure the long-term, complex effects of their decisions. Other parameters and perspectives are needed for more balanced performance management.

4.5   The balanced scorecard is an approach to performance measurement that combines traditional financial measures with non-financial measures; it uses both quantitative and qualitative metrics. The balanced scorecard approach to performance measurement provides management with a more integrated and balanced framework of metrics that can be cascaded to all levels of the business and used in pursuit of overall corporate objectives.

4.6   The balanced scorecard can offer a powerful catalyst and motivator in the pursuit of continuous organisational and supply chain improvement.

4.7   Kaplan & Norton proposed four key perspectives for a balanced scorecard, focusing on long-term 'enablers' of corporate (and supply chain) success.

- *Financial:* financial performance and the creation of value for shareholders
- *Customers:* how effectively the organisation delivers value to the customer, and develops mutually beneficial relationships with customers and other stakeholders
- *Internal business processes:* how effectively and efficiently value-adding processes are carried out throughout the supply chain
- *Innovation and learning:* the skills and knowledge required to develop distinctive competencies for future competitive advantage and growth.

4.8   This is depicted in Figure 6.2.

Figure 6.2 *The balanced scorecard*

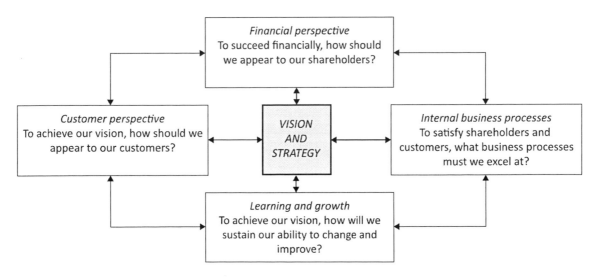

4.9   The 'balance' of the scorecard is thus between: financial and non-financial performance measures; short-term and long-term perspectives; and internal and external focus. This offers strong motivational potential, as a spur to continuous improvement – both for internal units and within the supply chain. (Linked buyer/supplier scorecards could be used to integrate strategy, performance measurement and feedback across key supply chain partnerships.)

4.10 Working with a balanced scorecard requires identification and description of several factors for each perspective selected.

- The organisation's long-term goals
- The critical success factors (CSFs) in achieving those goals
- The key activities which must be carried out to achieve those success factors
- The key performance indicators (KPIs) which can be used to monitor progress

4.11 The problem within many businesses is that the approach to the 'customer' is very generic in nature: they attempt to serve all customers in the same manner. There is little or no differentiation that will provide possible competitive advantage in the market. To develop KPIs from the **customer perspective,** the organisation (and its leaders) must define its target customers and define value from their point of view. Typical indicators may include measures such as customer satisfaction, customer retention and market share.

4.12 From the **internal process** perspective, the task is to identify the key processes the organisation must excel at in order to continue adding value in the eyes of customers and other stakeholders. Having identified these key processes the next step is to develop the most appropriate performance measures with which to track progress. It may be necessary to consider more innovative solutions, rather than concentrating efforts and resources on incremental improvements to existing activities. All internal and external supply chain activities should be considered within this perspective.

4.13 From the **innovation and learning** perspective, the key focus initially should be on the 'enablers' that underpin business success, since people skills, knowledge and learning provide the foundations for all future development. A 'gap analysis' should be carried out to identify shortfalls between the current business infrastructure and that required to achieve future objectives. Performance measures for innovation and learning are then targeted to closing any identified 'gaps'.

4.14 From the **financial perspective**, measures should be designed to indicate the extent to which corporate and supply chain strategies, and the way they are being executed, are achieving improved profitability and shareholder value. It is no good focusing on improved customer satisfaction, say, if this does not have a measurable effect on sales revenue, profits or market share.

Limitations of the balanced scorecard

4.15 Having defined performance criteria related to the four business perspectives, it is important not to view this purely as a static list of metrics, but rather as a framework for implementing and aligning complex programmes of change, that will constantly evolve over time. The strategic-level scorecard must be cascaded through the organisation, and expressed in, or aligned with, functional and operational plans.

4.16 The scorecards developed for individual functions should contain only performance measures that they can actually influence. As the scorecard system is cascaded deeper into the organisational structure this will often mean fewer performance measures are posted.

4.17 There are drawbacks and limitations to the balanced scorecard approach in practice. Developing and implementing the scorecard is a complex and time-consuming exercise. It will often imply radical change of management style and organisation culture – for which resources and support may not be available. Commitment from senior management must be genuine and consistent to avoid 'mixed messages' (eg if lip service is paid to the balanced scorecard, but procurement leaders are still judged mainly on their ability to reduce costs...)

The Triple Bottom Line

4.18 John Elkington is one of the earliest and most respected advocates of corporate sustainability. In 1987, he co-founded SustainAbility, a strategic consultancy, research and advocacy organisation, 'offering a range of services and undertaking advocacy in order to create financial value at the same time as addressing environmental, social and governance issues in an integrated manner'.

4.19 Elkington coined the term 'Triple Bottom Line' (TBL) in 1994. Based on the accounting concept of 'the bottom line' (profit), the term was designed to engage business leaders, raising awareness that corporate activity not only adds economic value, but can potentially also add environmental and social value – and, more importantly, create environmental and social costs (previously regarded as 'externalities', not accounted for in the performance measurement of organisations). Traditionally, these have been borne financially by governments and experientially by communities: in TBL thinking, businesses which cause costly social and environmental impacts should share (or at least recognise) these costs.

4.20 The triple bottom line (also called TBL, 3BL, and later 'People, Profit, Planet') recognises the need for businesses and leaders to measure their performance not just by how well they further the interests of their primary stakeholders (shareholders) through profitability (the 'economic bottom line'), but also by how well they further or protect the interests of their secondary stakeholders (including wider society), in relation to social and environmental sustainability. TBL accounting means expanding the traditional reporting framework of a company to take into account ecological and social performance, in addition to financial performance.

Limitations of TBL

4.21 The triple bottom line concept has been hugely influential in bringing sustainability to the fore. However, it has been criticised, and the main arguments against it are as follows.

- Specialisation promotes efficiency, knowledge management, development and (in international trade) comparative advantage. Companies need to focus on their distinctive, value-adding competencies: to 'stick to the knitting' (as Peters and Waterman put it, in *In Search of Excellence*).
- Concern for environmental issues is a luxury for corporations in less affluent economies: the need to survive inevitably takes precedence over global, long-term concerns.
- Nationalism – the view that you look after your own citizens first – may get in the way of consensus on sustainability (which is seen as a global issue).
- Sustained economic downturn or recession inevitably refocuses businesses on economic indicators, in the interests of survival.
- Application, in monetary-based economic systems, is a major weakness of TBL, according to *The Challenge of TBL: A Responsibility to Whom?* (Fred Robin). It is difficult to make a genuine business case for TBL, when the costs of sustainability improvements are tangible – and their value is difficult to measure.

5   Leadership development

5.1   As we discussed in Chapter 2, theories of leadership no longer suggest that 'leaders are born, not made': attention has shifted to how management and leadership skills can be developed. Management development is 'an attempt to improve managerial effectiveness through a planned and deliberate learning process' (Alan Mumford).

Management development

5.2   Increasing attention has been focused on systematic management development in recent decades, for a number of reasons (as we suggested in Chapter 1).

- Management development can promote improved performance capability – both for the managers *and* for the teams and processes they manage and lead. Managers (and perhaps even more so, leaders) are responsible for aspects of processes and performance which can – arguably – not be optimised in any other way. Quality of leadership is a critical success factor – and a competitive differentiating factor – for many organisations.
- Leaders have a unique responsibility for vision and culture creation in organisations and supply chains. Managers must be developed and equipped to articulate and secure 'buy-in' to compelling a vision, and to develop the culture and capabilities of the enterprise for future needs.
- Leaders are uniquely placed to optimise customer and shareholder value, by driving both incremental and transformational improvement in the organisation and supply chain.
- As we have seen, there is a particular need for effective leadership in complex, dynamic environments. In order to drive and support change in the organisation and supply chain, managers need to develop skill sets for change leadership (creating vision for change, supporting people through change, mobilising resources for change, and so on) and transformational leadership (energising and empowering people to own and drive change).
- Management development supports management succession and business continuity: proactively and systematically creating a pool of promotable individuals who can fill leadership gaps when people are promoted or transferred, retire or leave.
- Organisational support for, and investment in, leadership development may help the organisation to attract and retain quality managerial talent.

5.3   Management development programmes have traditionally involved some form of formal management education and training – from short skill-based training courses (eg in time management or team leadership) to ongoing competence development (eg using in-house or nationally-accredited competence frameworks) to the pursuit of formal qualifications such as an MBA.

5.4   In addition, there is likely to be the use of developmental tools such as the following.

- Management by objectives and performance management (to develop managerial competencies through ongoing goal-setting, coaching and mentoring) – as discussed earlier
- Experiential learning
- Mentoring
- Group learning.

'Deep' leadership development

5.5   Keith Grint (*Leaders are trained and not born)* argues that organisations should focus not just on the development of individual leaders, but on collective or 'deep' leadership programmes, which nurture the potential for all employees to be leaders. 'Subordinates need to be given as much exposure as possible to leadership and the opportunity to make mistakes and learn from them. Empowerment programmes which simply push leadership responsibility out to subordinates who are unprepared and untrained for it, are bound to fail.'

5.6 Other authors also emphasise the importance of developing leadership skills throughout the organisation, not just in identified 'talent' or senior people: creating a 'leadership culture' (Tim Melville-Ross) that supports ideas-generation, personal initiative, self-motivation and positive influencing.

5.7 Meanwhile, research surveys by the CIPD (*Global Comparisons Leadership Forecast*) suggest that less than 50% of existing leaders have a development plan – although organisations with high-quality leader development programmes and formal succession management programmes can be shown to achieve superior business performance. 'Leaders in the UK, though resilient, often lack dedicated attention from their superiors to help them develop in a planned fashion through continuous learning, both from job experiences and more formal training activities.'

5.8 Pedler, Burgoyne and Boydell *(The Learning Company: a Strategy for Sustainable Development)* popularised the term **learning organisation** to describe an organisation 'that facilitates the acquisition and sharing of knowledge, and the learning of all its members, in order continuously and strategically to transform itself in response to a rapidly changing and uncertain environment'.

5.9 Yukl *(Leadership in Organisations)* proposes a number of features of learning organisations through the lens of effective management and leadership practices.

- Leaders developing methods for understanding and interpreting business processes
- People at all levels being empowered to deal with problems and suggest better working methods
- Knowledge being made available throughout the organisation and people being encouraged to apply it in their work
- Top management championing changes, and suggestions for change, initiated by lower levels of the organisation
- Resources being invested in the promotion of learning and entrepreneurship

5.10 Adair *(How to Grow Leaders,* 2005) identifies seven principles of leadership develpoment that can be applied across a wide range of organisations, based on his Action-Centred Leadership model (discussed in Chapter 2).

- Develop a strategy for leadership development at operational, strategic and team level
- Identify and select people with high leadership potential
- Train people for leadership, based on identified business learning needs
- Manage career development, giving people progressive practice in leadership roles
- Utilise line managers as coaches and mentors to develop leaders within their teams
- Create a corporate culture that supports self-development in leadership
- Ensure that senior management champion leadership development.

Career development

5.11 A career may be defined as the pattern of work-related experiences that span the course of a person's working life. Career development processes enable individuals to be intentional about the purpose and direction of their personal development, and their contribution to the work organisation.

5.12 Management development includes career development and succession planning by the organisation, which in turn requires attention to a number of issues.

- The types of experience a potential leader will have to acquire: experience in different business functions, for example, or in general (as opposed to functional) management, or in different international divisions.
- The individual's guides and role models in the organisation. Individuals with potential should be encouraged to measure themselves against peers (assessing their own weaknesses and strengths) and to emulate desirable role models.
- The scope and variety of opportunities and challenges offered to the developing employee. Too much

responsibility too early can be damagingly stressful, but if there is insufficient challenge, the employee may never be stretched towards his full potential.

- The provision of career management programmes, such as: management succession planning; identification of career paths within the organisation; career planning guidance, information and advice; development programmes; formal mentoring; and help with adjustment to mid-career issues (such as career plateau) and late-career issues (such as approaching retirement).

5.13 The current trend for delayered, decentralised structures has increased the difficulty of creating career opportunities for *upward* progression in the formal organisation structure. Alternative career moves may have to be considered, including sideways transfers, secondments to project groups, short external attachments and so on. However, the concept of leadership development also suggests that individuals can be offered increasing responsibility and career challenges through leadership opportunities in *any* job role, by developing and exercising leadership in their own context.

Personal development

5.14 Personal development, taking account of employees' wider needs and aspirations, may seem like an unnecessary luxury, but businesses are increasingly offering employees wider-ranging development opportunities, rather than focusing simply on skills required to do their current job better. Personal development creates more rounded, competent employees, who may contribute more innovatively and flexibly to the organisation's future needs, and develop their leadership potential. It may also help to foster job satisfaction, commitment and loyalty, and to create a culture in which learning and flexibility are valued: a learning culture.

5.15 Here are some tools of personal development.

- **Personal development plans** (PDPs) are action plans for people's career development which make employees responsible for seeking and organising learning and development opportunities.
- The use of a **personal development journal (PDJ)** or learning log: a structured approach to using the experiential learning cycle, by reflecting on identified problems and critical incidents (as potential learning needs) in writing. This enables the individual to capture experience; bring unknown behaviours into conscious awareness; analyse the effects of behaviours; and plan to modify unsuccessful behaviours in future.
- **Self-development and support groups,** which meet to discuss personal development and work issues, give each other feedback and so on
- Seeking and using **feedback information**: self-analysis questionnaires, self-appraisal processes, personal SWOT analysis – and so on – to increase self-awareness and identify learning and development needs
- The use of **experiential learning** to turn everyday work experiences into opportunities for reflection, learning and change
- The use of **knowledge sharing** systems, such as the internet and corporate intranet; other people (especially coaches and mentors); and communities of practice (formal or informal groups of people sharing knowledge, best practice and 'tips' with others in similar roles, or facing similar problems).

5.16 Continuous development programmes are often based on the use of negotiated **personal development plans** (PDPs) or **learning contracts**. A PDP is generally prepared by the individual and his or her line manager or mentor.

5.17 The process of personal development planning may be summarised as follows.

- **Analyse your current capability profile**; eg using personal SWOT (strengths and weaknesses) analysis; competence review; or self-assessment of learning needs
- **Formulate learning and development goals**
- **Develop an action plan**: including SMART objectives; methods to be used; and timescales and methods for progress review and final evaluation.

- **Agree the action plan as a 'learning contract'** with a coach, mentor or line manager, to promote accountability, and gain assistance with resourcing, monitoring, feedback and evaluation.

Professional development

5.18 Professional and managerial techniques are continually developing, becoming more sophisticated and complex. Professional institutions such as CIPS have formally recognised this situation by providing for their members to keep up to date with developments.

5.19 **Continuing professional development** (CPD) is a self-managed process, with the individual continually reassessing his learning needs in the light of changes, and seeking to meet those needs via available avenues. Membership of a profession requires an undertaking to develop and maintain standards of competence and ethics on an ongoing basis. Team leaders may act as mentors or supervisors for team members' CPD – as well as seeking similar support, guidance and feedback for themselves.

Experiential learning

5.20 Experiential learning is learning by experience – or 'learning by doing'. David Kolb *(Experiential Learning)* is an influential proponent of the idea that effective learning could start, not just from abstract concepts or theories, but from concrete experience. He formulated the 'experiential learning cycle' to demonstrate how everyday work experiences can be used for learning, personal development and performance improvement, through the process of 'learning by doing': Figure 6.3.

Figure 6.3 *The experiential learning cycle*

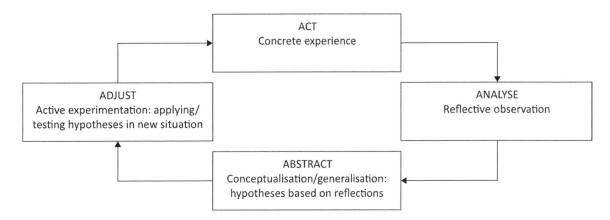

5.21 Working through the cycle:

- The learner has a concrete experience of the technique or concept to be learned. (For example, a procurement team leader chairs a meeting of supply partners.)
- He thinks back over the experience later, perhaps using a personal development journal. (The leader notes that the meeting split into side-issue arguments on several occasions, and ponders what sorts of behaviour may have allowed this to happen.)
- Using theory and experience, he develops some abstract concepts of what might have been going on, and sets up a hypothesis for future action. (The leader realises that the facilitator is responsible for controlling a meeting, and that this can be achieved only by being the focus of all communications.)
- He applies and tests the hypothesis in a new situation. (The leader plans to facilitate the next buying group meeting in a more directive style, in which he requests that all communications be routed via the chair.)
- The learner is thus supplied with a new or adjusted concrete experience, from which to begin the cycle again.

5.22 Experiential learning allows any experience or situation to become an opportunity for learning and development, enabling a potential leader to manage his own learning. It also provides a systematic and effective approach to 'learning to learn', and emphasises the nature of learning as a continuous process or cycle. It engages different learning approaches, preferences and 'styles': experimentation, practice, theorising, watching and reflecting – and so on. And it builds in transfer or application of learning from the original learning context to other contexts: reinforcing and embedding learning on the job.

5.23 Experiential learning can be supported by a number of methods.

- Temporary promotions or 'assistant to' positions: individuals experience or observe more challenging roles
- Project or committee work: individuals might be co-opted to project teams or committees to gain experience of relevant areas of the organisation's activities, as well as multi-functional team processes and problem-solving.

Mentoring

5.24 Mentoring is a relatively long-term one-to-one developmental relationship, focused on broader issues of personal, career and leadership development. It is typically carried out by a more senior member of the organisation (often not the mentee's immediate manager, so that there is greater freedom to discuss concerns and issues.)

5.25 A mentor may occupy a role as the individual's 'wise (or critical) friend', teacher or coach, counsellor, role model, spur to action and improvement, encourager and supporter in the organisation, as the leader (and the relationship) develops over time. A mentor should help a trainee leader achieve greater self-awareness; encourage him to formulate and clarify career and personal development goals; and support him in taking responsibility for self-development.

Group training (T-group) methods

5.26 The purposes of group learning are generally as follows.

- To give each individual a greater insight into his own behaviour and how he appears to other people, via feedback from other group members
- To give an understanding of intra-group processes and dynamics, including communication, influence, leadership and so on
- To develop each individual's skills in controlling and participating in intra-group processes and dynamics
- To develop appreciation and management of diversity, through raising awareness and building relationships between people whose interactions might otherwise be based on prejudices and stereotypes
- To encourage people to learn from each other, sharing knowledge and skills, to build the team and foster a continuous learning orientation.

5.27 Group training (using T-groups) is based on 'encounter groups', which allow people to practise their interpersonal skills in a controlled group and receive feedback from group members, guided by a facilitator. The T-group is usually small (8–12 participants), leaderless and unstructured, with no agenda or planned activities. The facilitator draws the group's attention to its behaviour as it struggles to cope with this situation. Participants are encouraged to be more receptive to the feelings, behaviours and needs of others. The main mechanism for learning is feedback received from other members of the group on how an individual is communicating, relating and responding.

5.28 This is a popular tool of **sensitivity training**, which focuses on helping individuals to:

- Understand their own behaviour; gain insight into how others perceive them; and understand the consequences and effects of their behavioural choices
- Develop behavioural flexibility, so that they can adapt their behaviours to the requirements of a particular situation or relationship, in order to gain more effective outcomes (agreement, co-operation and so on).

5.29 It is also the foundation of **action learning:** a method of leadership training in which 'working in small groups, people tackle important organisational issues or problems and learn from their attempts to change things' (Pedler, Burgoyne and Boydell, *A Manager's Guide to Leadership)*.

5.30 In action learning, a small group of 4–5 people meets together regularly, with each participant bringing a leadership or managerial problem they want to deal with. Group members generate, explore and evaluate solutions – *and* learn about the interpersonal and managerial processes involved in problem-solving and consulting. Project teams and quality circles may offer action-learning type processes.

Identifying leadership development and learning needs

5.31 Many leadership development requirements may emerge relatively informally in the course of work.

- Critical incidents (problems or events which affect a key area of a team's effectiveness) may be observed or reported and then analysed. These may suggest that there is a need for leadership development: for example, loss of a key supplier, or disciplinary, grievance or conflict problems in a team.
- Developmental discussions (such as performance appraisals, coaching or mentoring) may be used to focus on the individual's leadership aptitudes and opportunities, strengths and weaknesses, goals and aspirations and to identify learning (or other interventions) needed to attain them.
- Self-assessment and personal development activities may lead individuals to identify areas in which they are not satisfied with their leadership performance, or in which there is potential for growth. This may involve informal self-nomination for advertised leadership skills courses, say, or it may be more systematic (eg using learning needs questionnaires, leadership competence definitions or 360-degree feedback appraisal reports).

5.32 Training needs may also, however, need to be more systematically assessed. A wider, more objective viewpoint will allow the leader (and the organisation as a whole) to take into account the organisation's future leadership requirements, given its strategic and human resource plans. It will also enable greater integration of training and development, to support overall performance (rather than merely individual improvement).

Chapter summary

- Leadership depends to a large extent on interpersonal skills, particularly communication skills. Authorities on the subject also emphasise leadership values, based on 'perception, people and passion' rather than 'process, product or projects'.
- Daniel Goleman has popularised the idea that leadership success depends not only on technical ability and mental dexterity, but on emotional awareness and maturity (emotional intelligence or EQ).
- Management by objectives attempts to integrate individual performance goals with corporate strategic objectives. This is argued to be helpful in clarifying organisational, departmental and individual goals. However, many authorities have identified problems with setting key performance indicators.
- Measuring performance has often been limited to monetary aspects. Kaplan and Norton highlighted the shortcomings of this perspective and developed a 'balanced scorecard' approach to address them.
- Increasingly, organisations have recognised social environmental responsibilities. John Elkington attempted to capture this insight in his 'Triple Bottom Line' model.
- There is an increasing emphasis on systematic development for managers and leaders. This arises from a modern rejection of the view that 'leaders are born, not made': researchers are increasingly convinced that leadership abilities can be acquired.

 ## Self-test questions

Numbers in brackets refer to the paragraphs where you can check your answers.

1   Distinguish between first-order and second-order interpersonal skills. (1.8)

2   List values that contribute to successful leadership. (1.13)

3   Define 'emotional intelligence'. (2.5)

4   Explain the link between emotional intelligence and leadership skills. (2.11)

5   List steps in the process of management by objectives. (3.6)

6   Explain why it is important to set effective organisational goals and objectives. (3.15)

7   Describe groups of stakeholders who may be able to contribute to a leader's performance appraisal. (3.31)

8   What are the four key perspectives in Kaplan and Norton's balanced scorecard? (4.7)

9   Suggest limitations of the TBL concept. (4.21)

10 Give reasons why organisations increasingly focus on systematic management development. (5.2)

11 List tools of personal development for leaders. (5.15)

12 Describe the stages in Kolb's experiential learning cycle. (5.21)

CHAPTER 7

Equality, Inclusion and Diversity

Assessment criteria and indicative content

 3.3 Analyse how equality and diversity issues relating to the supply chain can be managed to improve the effectiveness of the supply chain

- Defining diversity, equality and inclusion
- The benefits of diversity in organisations
- The impact of discrimination, harassment and victimisation
- Developing and implementing policies to enhance diversity

Section headings

1 Definitions
2 Benefits of diversity
3 The legislative framework on diversity
4 Enhancing diversity
5 Leading diverse teams

Introduction

Equality and diversity are hot topics in organisations, partly because they remain high on the agenda of legislative and regulatory bodies. The impact of EU social policy is still being felt in the UK, in the form of new and revised legislation on discrimination in the workplace.

Diversity is partly a 'productivity through people' issue for leadership. The avoidance of discrimination, harassment and victimisation in the workplace helps to maintain employee morale, motivation, commitment and loyalty. And heterogeneous (diverse, multicultural) teams have been shown to out-perform homogeneous (non-diverse) teams in the long term.

However, equality, diversity and inclusion can also be seen as an issue of personal and corporate ethics, and corporate social responsibility. Leaders treat people fairly, and respect their differences, because this is an ethical and humane way to behave – and to preserve working relationships.

In this chapter we look at the performance, ethical and legal rationale for equality and diversity, and suggest how diverse workforces and supply chains can be supported by procurement leaders.

1 Definitions

Equality

1.1 Equality is the principle that people should be treated fairly and without bias or discrimination in their access to rights and benefits, compared to other groups. It is particularly applied to the equal rights of minority, or under-represented, groups in society and the workplace.

1.2 Two key areas of equality are addressed by the European and UK legal framework.

- Equal opportunity: non-discrimination on the basis of sex, race, religion and belief, disability and age (among other criteria) in the provision of access to employment rights and opportunities
- Equal pay: the right of women (specifically) to receive equal pay for performing work of equal value to that of men

Inclusion

1.3 Inclusion involves positive action to include the interests of all stakeholders in planning and decision making, and specifically to reduce the inequalities suffered by the least advantaged groups: closing 'opportunity gaps' and ensuring that support is given to those that need it most.

1.4 This may include intentional support for the following groups.

- Potentially disadvantaged categories of workers, including disabled people, under-represented minority groups, those with language barriers, and adults struggling to access education and learning opportunities in order to enter or re-enter the work place
- Potentially disadvantaged suppliers, including small and medium enterprises (SMEs), which face a range of barriers to participation in contracts: lack of information about contracts, lack of production capacity for large contracts, lack of resources to comply with onerous pre-qualification and standards certification criteria etc
- The most vulnerable workers at the lowest tiers of the supply chain: for example, ensuring that lower-tier suppliers have, maintain and enforce adequate labour standards (working conditions, health and safety, contracts, working hours); fair wages for employees and prices for suppliers; and so on.

Diversity

1.5 Diversity is the 'visible and non-visible differences [between people] which will include sex, age, background, race, disability, personality and work style. It is founded on the premise that harnessing these differences will create a productive environment in which everybody feels valued, where their talents are being fully utilised, and in which organisational goals are met.' (Rajvinder Kandola & Johanna Fullerton, *Managing the Mosaic: Diversity in Action*).

1.6 As an HRM policy, diversity reflects the belief that the make-up of an organisation's workforce should broadly reflect that of the external labour market or society as a whole – and ideally, therefore (from a strategic point of view), that of the target customer base – in order to be able to meet the challenges posed by those environments.

1.7 The UK workforce is becoming increasingly diverse, not just in terms of national and ethnic backgrounds, but in: the wider representation of women in the workforce; the wider variety of educational experiences and pathways leading to employment; and legislative support for the recognition of workers' rights to equality of opportunity, regardless of sexual orientation, religious affiliation, family structure, age and disability.

1.8   A 'managing diversity' orientation argues that an organisation should proactively seek to understand, appreciate and manage the needs of a diverse workforce. This may mean: supporting tolerance of individual differences (and outlawing discrimination and harassment); taking diversity into account when designing reward systems (eg offering flexible menus of benefits) and development programmes (taking into account potential education and qualification issues); adjusting work arrangements and environments in order to accommodate diverse family responsibilities and disabilities; and enhancing employee communications.

1.9   'Diversity management goes beyond what is required by legislation designed to promote equal opportunities and prevent discrimination. It comprises an approach which recognises and values differences and aims to make positive use of the unique talents and perspectives within the workforce. The focus is on individuals, rather than minority groups' (Chartered Management Institute).

Characteristics of diversity

1.10   Hellriegel, Slocum & Woodman (*Organisational Behaviour*) include 'Diversity competency' as a core competency for leaders, alongside self-competency, across-cultures competency, communication competency, teams competency and change competency. They define 'diversity competency' as 'the knowledge, skills and abilities to value unique individual, group and organisational characteristics, embrace such characteristics as potential sources of strength, and appreciate the uniqueness of each'. Diversity competency enables individuals, teams and organisations to be effective in the following activities.

- Fostering an environment of inclusion of people who have different characteristics
- Learning from individuals, teams or organisations with different characteristics and perspectives, to stimulate creativity and innovation
- Developing awareness, attitudes and behaviours that support diversity in the workplace
- Demonstrating commitment to work with team members and value their contributions, regardless of personal attributes or differences

1.11   Hellriegel *et al* suggest that individuals may vary on a wide range of characteristics, which may affect individual, team and organisational behaviours. They propose a categorisation of diversity characteristics (based on the work of S Bradford's Fourteen Dimensions of Diversity) commonly faced in organisations: Figure 7.1.

Figure 7.1 *Hellriegel, Slocum & Woodman's characteristics of diversity*

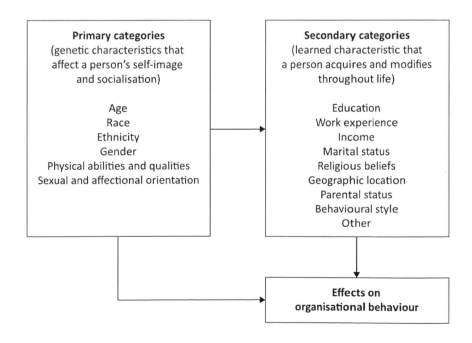

2 Benefits of diversity

2.1 The benefits claimed for developing a diverse workforce include the following.

- Widening the recruitment pool: giving the organisation access to more skills (particularly in the face of regional or specific skills shortages) eg from women returning to work, older workers and so on. There may be specific benefits from some of these previously underutilised skill sectors: older workers, for example, may offer experience and loyalty which more than compensate for age-related loss of performance.
- Performance benefits of being able to draw on (and support full contribution from) people with diverse skills, experiences and viewpoints. A diverse team or workforce can support better communication, decision-making, learning, change and innovation, through the following means.
  - Widening the range of ideas and information which is taken into account in decision-making and problem-solving. This may enhance the quality and creativity of solutions, and their acceptability (where required) to a wider constituency.
  - Controlling the risk of blinkered and complacent thinking (a phenomenon called 'groupthink'), by challenging and testing dominant or unquestioned viewpoints.
  - Opening processes and methods to fresh scrutiny, questioning and criticism – as the basis for learning and continuous improvement
  - Creating a group climate in which ideas and feelings can be safely expressed, and differences are welcomed and respected. (This may be essential to support the contribution of all members.)
- Reflecting the diversity of external stakeholders. Employing representatives of different groups, cultures and viewpoints allows the organisation to anticipate the needs and concerns of similarly diverse stakeholders. This is most obviously beneficial in being able to anticipate the needs of the market and customer base (to target market and customer segments more effectively). However, it may also be beneficial in building rapport and relationships within the supply chain – particularly in areas such as cross-cultural negotiation and contract management.
- Benefits for staff morale and performance, as previously under-represented groups feel supported and valued, and are able to contribute fully
- Enhanced customer satisfaction and loyalty, both among minority groups (better represented in customer service teams, and more likely to have their needs taken into account in marketing strategies) and among consumers generally (who increasingly demand corporate ethics and responsibility over and above mere compliance with legislation)
- Enhanced employer brand (as an ethical and diverse employer): the ability to attract and retain quality talent
- Compliance with equal opportunities legislation and codes of practice (which are used by Employment Tribunals in arbitrating employee grievances and industrial disputes)
- Enhanced flexibility and learning. 'The more open we are to difference, the greater is the learning potential and the greater the ability to embrace change and development. Difference and diversity therefore hold the key to many of the aspirations of leadership. (Pedler *et al: A Manager's Guide to Leadership)*

2.2 The benefits of diversity can be summarised as: legal, moral and social benefits; business benefits (better understanding of market segments; positive employer brand; attraction and retention of talent); and employee benefits (more representative workforce; value and respect for people; opportunity to contribute fully; enhanced creativity).

The impact of discrimination, harassment and victimisation

2.3 Conversely, an organisation which does *not* take proactive measures to develop and support diversity will suffer corresponding potential consequences.

- Inability to target key market segments; reputational damage (affecting the employer brand, corporate image and business relationships)
- Reduced staff morale, loyalty and contribution, with potential for low productivity, unnecessary absenteeism and loss of talent through high employee turnover
- Inability to attract and retain talent in competition with other employers
- An impoverished organisation culture: lacking key ethical and social responsibility values, and based on a mono-cultural identity
- Distortion of decisions and resource allocations due to 'crony-ism': favouritism among groups and cliques
- Workplace conflict, arising from discrimination, harassment and victimisation
- Potential for lawsuits, arbitrations and appeals as a result of claims of discrimination, harassment and victimisation under relevant legislation

Drawbacks of diversity

2.4 Potential drawbacks of diversity are based on the idea that difference presents a challenge to organisation and management. However, these should be seen clearly as management challenges – *not* arguments against diversity.

- Burdens and costs of formulating and administering diversity policies and practices (including policy task forces, diversity monitoring, training, more extensive recruitment and more rigorous selection processes, implementation of job evaluation for equal pay and so on)
- Difficulties of managing and communicating effectively in ethnically diverse teams: differences in cultural values and norms, language, and interpersonal styles (for example, in negotiation or management style) – compounded by the difficulties and costs of training team leaders to cope.
- Difficulties and costs of managing a workforce with increasingly diverse family structures and responsibilities (introducing flexible working; equal rights for part-time workers; childcare support and so on)
- Confronting issues of literacy, numeracy and differences in different nations' qualification and training schemes (with implications for recruitment, training and development)
- Adapting the work environment, processes and task organisation to support contribution from disabled employees. (Adjustments may also have to be made to support an increasingly aged workforce.)
- Potential for misunderstanding, miscommunication and conflict arising from differences which have not been effectively managed

2.5 Some of these drawbacks are simply costs that must be absorbed as an investment in the potential benefits. Others, however, can be minimised by effective management, as we will see in the final section of this chapter.

The impact of equal opportunities legislation

2.6 The positive influence of diversity and equal opportunities legislation on the leadership of procurement and supply can be seen from a number of points of view: that of managers (how has legislation made the task easier?); the organisation (how has it improved performance?); and the employee (how has it improved the quality of working life?).

2.7 Several arguments may be cited for the positive influence of such legislation, from each of these viewpoints.

7

- It enhances the ability of the organisation to attract and retain quality, skilled staff, by broadening the labour pool and creating a positive employer brand and climate for a diverse workforce.
- It enhances the appeal of the organisation and its brands to an increasingly diverse consumer base, by making the organisation more representative of its market.
- It supports fairness and justice in the workplace. This is not a purely ethical issue, since enhanced rights for employees are also intended to be beneficial for management and organisations. For example, consultation with employee representatives on issues of concern can facilitate change management and foster innovation and problem-solving.
- It provides minimum standards of protection for all parties in the workplace eg in regard to health and safety at work, and reduced compliance risk.
- It enables individuals (including managers) to develop work/life balance eg through family-friendly policies and the right to request flexible working.
- It creates transparency within organisations, in the interest of stakeholders and the general public.
- It supports managerial decision-making, policy development and compliance. Stakeholder consultation, legislative provisions and related Codes of Practice give purchasing managers clear guidelines for good practice within the employment relationship.

3   The legislative framework on diversity

3.1   'Equal opportunity' in an employment context means that everyone has a fair chance of getting a job, accessing training and benefits and competing for promotion, regardless of individual differences or minority status. It is, effectively, non- or anti-discrimination. Below we look at the framework of UK legislation in this area. If you are not based in the UK, it would be worthwhile to research similar legislation in your own country.

3.2   In the UK, after years of review and planning, the complex and varying protections given by separate pieces of sex, race, disability, religion and age discrimination legislation have been harmonised and consolidated within a major new piece of legislation: the **Equality Act 2010**. This Act provides a cross-cutting legislative framework: 'to protect the rights of individuals and advance equality of opportunity for all; to update, simplify and strengthen the previous legislation; and to deliver a simple, modern and accessible framework of discrimination law which protects individuals from unfair treatment and promotes a fair and more equal society.'

3.3   One of the key aims of the Act is to make discrimination law easier to understand and comply with, removing unnecessary burdens on organisations in order to support economic recovery in the wake of the 2009 recession. It applies to discrimination in relation to the full range of protected characteristics: age, disability, gender reassignment, marriage and civil partnership, pregnancy and maternity, race, religion and belief, sex and sexual orientation.

Forms of discrimination and harassment

3.4   There are five basic types of unlawful discrimination under the legislation.

- **Direct discrimination**: where a job applicant, employee or former employee is treated less favourably than another because of a protected characteristic. (In the case of pregnancy and maternity, direct discrimination can occur simply if the person *has* the protected characteristic – without needing to compare treatment to anyone else. A difference is also made in the case of *age:* an employer can make decisions based on age, if it can show that it is objectively justified.)
- **Indirect discrimination**: where an employer does something which has (or would have) a worse impact on people with a protected characteristic than on people who do not have that characteristic – *unless* they can show that what they have done, or intend to do, is *objectively justified.* (For example, an employer may offer applicants for a job a single time for interview, and an observant Muslim might not be able to attend at the allocated time, for reasons of religious observance. Unless the employer

can objectively justify the lack of flexibility, this may be indirect discrimination because of religion or belief. Similar examples might concern changing shift patterns to include early morning starts, which would disadvantage women responsible for childcare.)

- **Victimisation**: where a person is treated badly because they have complained about discrimination, or have done anything to uphold their own or someone else's equality law rights. (For example, if an employer refuses to shortlist a qualified person for a job interview, because he had accused the employer of discriminating against him in the past.)
- **Harassment**: an employer must not harass a job applicant, employee or former employee. Harassment is defined as unwanted conduct which violates a person's dignity, or creates an intimidating, hostile, degrading, humiliating or offensive environment for a person. Protection has been extended to third parties: ie those who are not directly subject to the conduct, but are impacted by the intimidating or degrading environment.
- **Discrimination arising from disability**: a new definition, where an employer treats a disabled person unfavourably because of something connected to their disability, if (a) they cannot show that the treatment is objectively justified and (b) they knew or could reasonably have been expected to know that the applicant is a disabled person. (For example, an employer might tell a visually impaired person who uses an assistance dog that they are unsuitable for a job because the employer is nervous of dogs.)

The employer also has a duty to make **reasonable adjustments** to ensure that a disabled person has the same access, as far as is reasonable, to everything that is involved in getting and doing a job as a non-disabled person. (For example, a disabled person may have to eat at set times to manage their diabetes: different break times need not impact negatively on their ability to do the job, so this would be a reasonable adjustment.)

3.5 There are several legitimate **exceptions** to these provisions.

- If an employer can show that a particular protected characteristic is central to a particular job (a **genuine occupational requirement**), they can insist that only someone who has that particular protected characteristic is suitable for the job. Examples might be authenticity in dramatic performance; reasons of decency or privacy (eg same-sex counsellors or changing-room attendants); or reasons of legal or customary restrictions (eg in work outside the UK).
- An employer can take into account a protected characteristic where *not* doing so would break another law. (For example, a driving school would have to reject a 19-year-old job applicant on the basis of age, because driving instructors must by law be over 21.)
- An employer can take protected characteristics into account if there is a need to safeguard national security.
- If an employer is a religion or belief organisation, it may require a job applicant to hold a particular religion or belief, or (in the case of posts such as a minister of religion) to have or not have a particular protected characteristic, where this is necessary to avoid conflict with the strongly held religious convictions of a significant number of followers.
- Other organisations, such as educational establishments, and the civil and armed services, may be able to require particular characteristics (eg woman teachers, or people of a specific nationality).

3.6 The legislation does *not* permit **positive discrimination**: actions which give preference to people with protected characteristics, regardless of genuine suitability or qualification for the job. However:

- *Disabled people* may be treated more favourably than non-disabled people, in acknowledgement of the additional barriers to work that they face
- The Act encourages **voluntary positive action**: steps taken by an employer to encourage people from groups experiencing disadvantage or low participation to take up employment opportunities, including jobs, training, promotion, transfer or other development opportunities.

Specific provisions

3.7 In regard to **recruitment and selection**, employers:

- Must avoid all forms of discrimination in all aspects of recruitment, and make reasonable adjustments for disabled people
- May take 'positive action' to encourage people from groups with a track record of disadvantage or low participation to apply for jobs
- May not ask job applicants about their health or any disability, until they have been offered the job (outright or conditionally). Questions are only permissible if they are asked to support reasonable adjustments for the recruitment process; if they relate directly to a person's ability to carry out a core function of the job; or if a specific impairment is an occupational *requirement* (eg if the employer wants to recruit a Deafblind project worker with personal experience of Deafblindness)
- May not refuse to employ a woman because she is pregnant, suffering pregnancy-related illness, or on maternity leave; and may not ask a woman whether she intends to have children, whatever her age or marital status. (This should not be taken into account in deciding suitability for the job.)

3.8 In regard to **working hours, flexible working and time off**, *employment law* sets out people's rights to rest breaks; annual leave; paternity, maternity, adoption and parental leave; family emergency leave; time off for public duties and trade union responsibilities; and the right to request flexible working arrangements (part-time, term-time, working from home some of the time, working flexi-hours and so on) and have those requests seriously considered. From the point of view of *equality* law, employers:

- Must avoid all forms of discrimination when making decisions about what hours an employee should work, whether to allow them to work flexibly and when to allow them time off
- Must make reasonable adjustments for disabled people
- Must objectively justify any inflexibility in regard to working hours, where requests for changes relate to religion and belief (eg breaks for prayer times)
- Must not treat people less favourably if sickness absence is related to disability or pregnancy
- Must not discriminate (eg on the grounds of sexual orientation or age) in responding to requests for maternity, paternity, adoption or parental leave.

3.9 In regard to **pay and benefits,** employers:

- Must avoid all forms of discrimination in decisions on pay and benefits
- Must apply objective criteria (such as market rate for the job, skills and qualification or performance in the job) fairly. The Equality and Human Rights commission recommends that employers: make sure why they are paying people differently; use an equal pay audit to check the impact of decisions on pay and benefits; and implement a transparent, structured pay system based on job evaluation (rather than just managerial discretion).

3.10 In regard to **career development** (training, promotions, and transfers), employers:

- Must avoid all forms of discrimination in all aspects of career development, and make reasonable adjustments for disabled people
- Must not stop someone doing training because they are pregnant or on maternity leave, unless a specific risk to health and safety has been identified
- Must not deny someone access to promotion opportunities because they are pregnant or on maternity leave.

3.11 Further detailed provisions are made in relation to additional management issues such as:

- Access to facilities (eg prayer rooms or breast-feeding facilities)
- The non-discriminatory application of dress codes
- The non-discriminatory use of appraisal, performance management and disciplinary procedures
- The application of procedures and decisions regarding dismissal, redundancy (eg selection for redundancy) and retirement.

4 Enhancing diversity

Diversity programmes

Diversity Training

4.1 At the organisational level, there should be a plan to evaluate the dimensions of diversity and to implement programmes to encourage: managerial and employee awareness of areas of difference and sensitivity; behavioural flexibility (being able to use multiple-solution models rather than 'one best way' approaches); and constructive communication, team-building, conflict resolution and problem-solving.

4.2 Diversity training may be required to ensure that managers and staff appreciate the value of diversity, respect individual differences and treat all team members with respect. As with any culture change initiative, there will have to be sponsorship and support from top management, in order to secure buy-in and embed diversity as a core value of the organisation.

4.3 It may be necessary or desirable to reinforce communication and awareness training with guidelines or Codes of Conduct for cultural sensitivity and respect for diversity. Other mechanisms of organisation culture may also be used: using diversity awareness criteria in recruitment, selection, appraisal and reward; planning diversity learning experiences as part of training and development programmes; and so on.

Formulating a positive diversity policy

4.4 In addition to responding to legislative provisions, many employers have begun proactively to address the underlying problems of equal opportunities. The formulation and promotion of an effective equal opportunities and diversity policy requires buy-in from key stakeholders.

4.5 Implementing an effective policy may require measures such as the following.

- Analysing the business environment, to determine whether and how far the organisation reflects the population and the customer base
- Carefully defining diversity and its business benefits
- Appointing equal opportunities champions at a senior level to put issues higher on the corporate agenda, and ensuring that diversity values are included in corporate strategy
- Establishing a representative working party to formulate policies and codes of practice
- Communicating and promoting the policy, involving staff at all levels (diversity handbook, awareness training, discussion groups, mentoring schemes, training, intranet pages and so on)
- Supporting implementation of the policy through HR processes: including diversity in selection criteria, training and coaching (especially for leaders), career management and reward
- Monitoring and benchmarking progress at regular intervals (diversity score cards, employee surveys, statutory monitoring and reporting where required).

Proactive measures to promote equal opportunity and diversity

4.6 **Flexible policies** on working hours and career shapes facilitate employment for women with family responsibilities. Flexible hours, part-time working, term-time or annual-hours contracts (to allow for school holidays) may be used. Career-break and return-to-work schemes may be developed, including training for women-returners. The provision of workplace childcare facilities is another possibility for larger organisations.

4.7 The **accelerated development** of women and minority groups can be achieved by fast-tracking school leavers (as well as graduates) and posting managerial vacancies internally, giving more opportunities for movement up the ladder for groups currently at lower levels of the organisation. Positive action may be taken to encourage protected groups to undertake training in which they have previously been under-represented. The Metropolitan Police, for example, piloted a scheme of pre-training training (in literacy, numeracy, current affairs, physical fitness and interpersonal skills) to prepare applicants from minority groups to compete on an equal basis for training places.

4.8 In the area of **disability**, similar positive action policies may include the provision of wheelchair access, braille or large-print versions of documentation, text-based telecommunications systems, interpreters and so on.

- In the area of **religion and belief,** organisations are still working out the full implications of equality provisions in practice, but they may raise issues such as:
- Handling requests for time off for religious observances and holidays
- Rights to wear religious head-gear and symbols (which may conflict with corporate dress codes)
- Protecting employees from religious harassment and vilification (including offensive jokes) and counselling offenders
- Some proactive organisations have gone further: for example, setting aside space for prayer and providing kosher and halal meals in corporate canteens.

4.9 More generally, many organisations attempt to address underlying discriminatory attitudes and behaviours: offering awareness and/or sensitivity training to educate managers and staff on the nature and effects of discriminatory or harassing behaviour; establishing counselling and disciplinary frameworks to manage offensive behaviours; and perhaps offering assertiveness training for women and minority groups. Leaders will also have a crucial role in values articulation, role-modelling and championing equality, diversity and inclusion in the work place.

Diversity and inclusion in the supply chain

4.10 The issue of **supplier diversity** is seen as increasingly important for the sustainable procurement agenda. This is driven by the recognition that in the interests of sustainability *and* commercial advantage, buyers should consider increasing the accessibility of contracts to a wider supplier base.

4.11 Supply base diversity can:

- Support strategic alignment, by ensuring that the supply base reflects (and can respond with knowledge and insight to) the increasing diversity of the customer base
- Help build stakeholder relations and generate goodwill (eg among diversity-aware consumer groups)
- Support corporate image and reputation by demonstrating commitment to equality and inclusion
- Contribute to improved supply chain performance: a wider pool of suppliers can generate competition and innovation.

4.12 A sustainable procurement orientation argues that procurement professionals should seek to remove unnecessary barriers to participation for smaller or less established suppliers who might nevertheless:

- Have the technical capability to fulfil requirements, especially if supported through supplier development
- Be able to add value through qualities such as responsiveness, innovation and entrepreneurship, understanding of consumer segments, and quality of service (due to eagerness to win and retain business).

4.13 In the first instance, it may be necessary for procurement leaders to:

- Appreciate the value of **widening and developing the supply market** through increasing diversity and participation
- Consider whether **sourcing policies and practices** (such as international sourcing, the use of technical specifications, the aggregation of orders into large contracts to secure economies of scale, or the requirement for high-level quality accreditations) may act as a barrier to participation
- Appreciate the **frustration** of suppliers unable to compete for business, and facilitate access where

possible (eg through advance notice of upcoming contracts, information about sourcing processes, or the giving of post-tender feedback)

- Appreciate the **ethical issues** in fair access to contracts. Appraisals, quotations and tenders cost prospective suppliers time, effort and money – and it is unethical to subject them to this cost frivolously or manipulatively: that is, if there is not a genuine, fair and open opportunity for them to win the business.

4.14 Here are some proactive approaches to improving supplier diversity.

- Removing barriers to participation in competing for contracts: publicising contracts widely; refreshing approved supplier lists; educating diverse suppliers on how to compete for business (eg via 'selling to...' or 'doing business with...' web pages and 'meet the buyer' events); ensuring that sourcing procedures and pre-qualification requirements are appropriate to the size and complexity of the requirement; dis-aggregating contracts; and encouraging first-tier contractors to use SMEs as subcontractors (particularly where they can provide specialist or innovative products)
- Positive action **supplier diversity programmes**, whereby suppliers in certain under-represented groups are targeted to offer opportunities to compete for contracts. Johnson & Johnson, for example, have a programme to identify and provide opportunities for qualified minority-owned, woman-owned, and 'disadvantaged' suppliers.
- Encouraging or requiring suppliers to have diversity policies in place for their own supply chains: another form of supply chain leadership.

Diversity and inclusion in global supply chains

4.15 Sensitivity to **cross-cultural diversity issues** is also important in international and global supply chains, for developing relationships of trust. Respect for cultural and linguistic differences may be seen as an issue of responsibility, ethics and inclusion.

- Assumptions of cultural superiority reflect a potential power imbalance or 'asymmetry' in negotiation and buyer-supplier relationships, which may weaken the less powerful party's ability to be heard, and to protect its interests (an ethical issue). It may also cause resentment and resistance, and weaken the potential to seek genuine win-win solutions (a sustainability issue for organisations seeking collaborative and committed supply chains).
- In addition to creating risks of communication failure, insensitive use of the buyer's language (without adequate translation or interpretation for the supplier's language and cultural context) may exacerbate power imbalance in buyer-supplier dealings: making it difficult for the most vulnerable voices to be genuinely heard.

4.16 **Grievance mechanisms** (or dispute mechanisms) are structured processes to address grievances, problems or disputes that arise between two or more parties engaged in contractual or commercial relationships. A range of grievance mechanisms is commonly provided for in contracts, in order to ensure that performance and relationship issues can be dealt with – ideally *without* recourse to costly and relationship-damaging litigation.

4.17 However, grievance mechanisms may also be used as a tool for establishing open, transparent and equitable communication channels between *businesses and communities,* as part of a responsible organisation's approach to sustainable development and community relations, based on inclusion.

4.18 They can offer a channel for local communities to voice and resolve concerns related to development projects (such as human, labour rights or environmental concerns), and a way for companies to address those concerns. At the same time, such mechanisms and forums support the company in systematically identifying emerging issues and trends which may create risks in international development projects, as the basis for proactive issues management and reputational defence.

4.19 The World Bank argues that: 'Locally-based grievance resolution mechanism(s) provide a promising avenue by offering a reliable structure and set of approaches where local people and the company can find effective solutions together'. Such grievance mechanisms would typically recognise a range of internationally recognised human rights, labour and environmental standards, as the basis for desired outcomes and remedies.

5 Leading diverse teams

5.1 There has been increasing demand for managerial competence in working with (or within) different cultures in recent decades. Domestic skill shortages have encouraged international recruitment, supported by freedom of labour movement in blocs such as the European Economic Area. Meanwhile, communications technology and e-commerce have facilitated the globalisation of markets, and there has been an increase in internal mergers, acquisitions and joint ventures as organisations have sought to operate effectively across national boundaries.

5.2 Detailed guidance on cross-cultural management is beyond the scope of this syllabus, but you should be aware of the impact of cultural values and differences from your earlier studies.

5.3 Susan C Schneider and Jean-Louis Barsoux *(Communicating Across Cultures)* argue that 'rather than knowing what to do in Country X, or whether national or functional cultures are more important in multi-cultural teams, what is necessary is to know how to assess the potential impact of culture, national or otherwise, on performance'.

5.4 An effective culturally diverse team (or supply chain) requires leadership in the following areas.

- Acknowledging cultural conflicts when they arise (without attributing all conflicts to cultural differences) and encouraging mutual learning about assumptions, values and culture-based behaviours
- Identifying and focusing on shared values and common ground
- Clarifying expectations and gaining commitment to the group's shared goals and objectives
- Identifying individual interests, strengths and preferences, and showing appreciation and respect for different cultural contributions
- Flexibly exploring culturally appropriate ways of team building and rewarding excellence (in the process developing a shared group culture)
- Being sensitive to power imbalances (such as a dominant language which may not be the first language of all members, or culture-based reluctance to contribute to a meeting or contradict a leader) and supporting all-member contribution
- Facilitating communication and feedback processes, so that people are encouraged to learn, develop sensitivity and behavioural flexibility, and confront potential conflicts and power imbalances before they become dysfunctional.

5.5 In fact, the challenges of leading a diverse team are not *that* different from those of leading *any* team.

5.6 In particular, attention will have to be given to matters such as the following.

- **Managerial and leadership styles.** Managers' cross-cultural competence can be enhanced through: encouraging diversified work experience in international or multi-cultural settings (eg through management development); undertaking training exercises (reading, language learning, cultural briefings); networking with managers from other cultures and using them as consultants; and seeking to learn through all cross-cultural interactions.
- **Awareness training**. Relevant staff may be trained to understand the potential for problems arising from culturally-acquired assumptions: the need to recognise cultural stereotypes and move beyond them through new information and encounters with other people; the need to appreciate that 'different' does not necessarily imply 'wrong'.

- **Communication mechanisms**. Inter-cultural communication is the only way to bring cultural values and assumptions into the open, in order to limit potential misunderstanding. This cannot be done by single cultural profiles or briefings: it requires ongoing monitoring of messages, interpretations and areas of difference. Mechanisms for this kind of communication may include: cross-cultural teams; cross-cultural discussion, consultation and conflict resolution groups; cultural education and briefings; cross-cultural networking and forums (eg on the corporate intranet); and so on.

5.7 Mullins offers 'ten practical ideas' for managing diversity: Table 7.1.

Table 7.1 *Mullins's 'ten practical ideas for managing diversity'*

1	Test assumptions about people before acting on them
2	Ensure that organisational policies related to discipline and grievance are clearly understood
3	For all employees, but particularly new recruits, make sure that written and unwritten diversity policies are understood and acted upon
4	Maintain open channels of communication to try to locate possible issues before they become problems
5	Learn how to understand the views of all staff members and encourage open approaches
6	Be prepared to listen to varying methods of solving work-based problems
7	Learn about and have regard to any strongly-held beliefs (such as religious observances, food, relationships) that are held by individuals
8	Acknowledge all contributions to improving working environments and processes, whatever the source
9	Know your own cultural diversity biases – and work at not letting them affect the workplace
10	Take care that any workplace based social events can be enjoyed by all workers – especially relevant (but not restricted) to those with physical disability

Balancing diversity and cohesion

5.8 One of the benefits of maintaining team diversity, as we suggested earlier, is that it is possible for groups to become *too* cohesive. Charles Handy *(Understanding Organisations)* notes that 'ultra-cohesive groups can be dangerous because in the organisational context the group must serve the organisation, not itself'. If a group is completely absorbed with its own maintenance, members and priorities, it can divert energy and attention away from the task.

5.9 It can also become dangerously blinkered to outside information and feedback and may confidently forge ahead in a completely wrong direction. I L Janis *(Victims of Groupthink,* 1972) described this as 'groupthink': 'the psychological drive for consensus at any cost, that suppresses dissent and appraisal of alternatives in cohesive decision-making groups'. The cosy consensus of the team prevents consideration of alternatives, constructive criticism or conflict.

5.10 Here are some of the symptoms of groupthink.

- A sense of invulnerability – blindness to the risk involved in pet strategies
- Rationalisations for inconsistent information
- Moral blindness ('might is right')
- A tendency to stereotype all outsiders as enemies
- Strong group pressure to quell dissent and stop people rocking the boat
- A perception of unanimity – filtering out or ignoring divergent views
- Mutual support and solidarity to guard the decision

5.11 Since by definition a group suffering from groupthink is highly resistant to criticism, recognition of failure and unpalatable information, it is not easy to break such a group out of its vicious circle. It must, however, be encouraged to exercise self-criticism, to welcome outside ideas and evaluations and to respond positively to conflicting evidence. A member may be appointed to the role of 'devil's advocate',

7

to deliberately inject alternative viewpoints and energise conflict. It may help to rotate team roles (where possible), to encourage people to see the team's purpose and objectives from alternative viewpoints, and to reduce power imbalances that would stifle opposition or questioning. The *status quo* should continually be 'refreshed' in order to avoid complacency.

Leadership and gender issues

5.12 Gender is one of the most obvious 'dimensions' of difference between people, and as such is the basis on which individuals are easily categorised – and stereotyped. As Mullins asks: 'How does this perception affect our behaviour? What difference does it make if our work group is predominantly male or female? Do women and men have different experiences at work?'

5.13 Although the number of women in the workforce has increased in recent decades, they still do not have equal access to all occupations. The existence of predominantly 'male' or 'female' occupations is known as **gender segregation**.

- Horizontal gender segregation occurs where men and women are associated with different types of jobs.
- Vertical gender segregation occurs when women are disproportionately distanced from positions of power and the exercise of formal authority: in other words, women are less represented in managerial positions than men.

5.14 Many cultural assumptions about women's attitudes to work, and capabilities for various types of work, are being re-examined. Maureen Guirdham (*Interactive Behaviour at Work*) argues that 'Sex and gender are not strong predictors of work behaviour. Even when gender differences are found, they typically account for only 1–5% of the variance for any given outcome. Recent research suggests that femininity and masculinity are independent dimensions and that each dimension has multiple domains within it, including appearance, behaviour, personality and interests. There is evidence that gender stereotypes are not very accurate, because they are more extensive than actual sex differences, and they contain information based on exaggerations of minor differences between the sexes.'

5.15 In other words, it is not helpful to view 'men' or 'women' as homogeneous groups: there are wide differences in individual characteristics of diversity within each gender. It is therefore difficult to make meaningful generalisations about men's and women's experience of work and working life. However, research attempts have been made to identify distinctive communication and negotiation styles; relationship styles; and leadership styles. David Boddy cites the research of:

- Judy B Rosener (*America's Competitive Secret: Women Managers*), suggesting that male managers tend to adopt a transactional style of leadership (based on exchange and positional authority), while women tended to use a more relational style (based on persuasion, encouragement, support and personal qualities). She argues that the female 'facilitate and empower' model of leadership is more suited to modern, turbulent conditions than the male 'command and control' style.
- Sally Helgesen *(The Female Advantage: Women's Ways of Leadership)*, suggesting that women are better at developing co-operation, creativity and intuition than men; that women prefer to manage through relationships rather than positional authority; and that they listen and empathise more than men.
- David Knights and Fergus Murray *(Managers Divided)*, suggesting that a predominantly male management undervalues the strengths of women's style of leadership, and prevents women reaching senior positions. 'Managers who emphasise the value of hard analytical skills above soft interpersonal skills support, perhaps unwittingly, the progression of men and discourage that of women. Stressing competitiveness, tension and long unsocial working hours has a similar effect.' (Boddy)

5.16 The position of women in the workplace is thus a culturally and historically conditioned issue. It is also an issue of gender politics. Mullins emphasises the extent to which 'emotions and politics surround the issue of gender', pointing out that:

- Some people may be over-sensitive to gender issues and interpret any and all negative comments as if they are intentional (or symbolic) acts of discrimination
- Some people may be under-sensitive to gender issues, and may unwittingly perpetuate stereotyping, bias and discrimination
- Finding a balance between these extremes is an important skill in managing people at work. 'Perhaps the most positive approach to take is for an organisation to acknowledge the changing working pattern of *all* employees and to consider the best working practices for managing a diverse workforce as a whole.'

Chapter summary

- Equality is the principle that people should be treated fairly and without bias or discrimination in their access to rights and benefits, compared to other groups. Diversity acknowledges the visible and non-visible differences between people: it underpins the belief that an organisation's workforce should broadly reflect the diversity of its labour market and customer base.

- A diverse workforce offers advantages in: widening the skill pool; drawing on diverse viewpoints and experiences; reflecting the diversity of stakeholders; enhancing staff and customer satisfaction; complying with equal opportunity law; and enhancing organisational learning. There are costs and difficulties involved, but these should be seen as management challenges, rather than arguments against diversity.

- Equal opportunity in an employment context means that everyone has a fair chance of accessing employment, training and promotion opportunities, and rewards and benefits, regardless of job-irrelevant differences or minority status. EU and UK law prohibits direct and indirect discrimination, harassment and victimisation on grounds of: sex, marital status and sexual orientation; colour, race, ethnic origin and religious belief; disability; and age. The Equality Act 2010 integrates previous legislation across all these areas.

- The formulation of a diversity policy requires: presentation of a business case for diversity; champions at a senior level; representative working parties to draft the policy; and communication and support for the policy.

- Proactive measures to promote diversity and equal opportunity in practice include: flexible working arrangements, accelerated development, adjustment of work environments and systems for the disabled, and awareness or sensitivity training to adjust underlying attitudes and values.

Self-test questions

Numbers in brackets refer to the paragraphs where you can check your answers.

1   Explain what is meant by a diversity strategy. (1.5, 1.6)

2   List the activities where a diversity policy enables individuals, teams and organisations to be effective. (1.10)

3   List benefits of diversity in the workplace. (2.1)

4   List potential drawbacks of a diversity policy. (2.4)

5   Under UK legislation, what are the five basic types of unlawful discrimination? (If you are not UK based, can you identify similar types in your local legislation?) 3.4)

6   Suggest typical measures for implementing a diversity policy. (4.5)

7   List potential benefits of supply base diversity. (4.11)

8   List potential areas for management attention when leading diverse teams. (5.6)

9   List symptoms of groupthink. (5.10)

10   Describe the results of research into gender differences in organisational management and leadership. (5.15)

CHAPTER 8

Managing Change

Assessment criteria and indicative content

 Evaluate the main methods of change management that can be used to develop the supply chain

- The nature of organisational change
- Planned organisational change
- Dealing with resistance to change
- Effective change management

Section headings

1 The nature of organisational change
2 Analysing the change situation
3 Vision and objectives
4 Dealing with resistance to change
5 Planned change models
6 Managing cultural change
7 Skills and attributes of an effective change agent

Introduction

Technology, economies and markets, cultural values, government policy and other factors in the supply chain environment are subject to continuous and – it often seems – accelerating change. This chapter introduces various models of change and leadership of change.

We start by examining the nature of organisational change. We then work our way through the key elements of a systematic approach to leading change: analysing the change situation; articulating vision and securing stakeholder buy-in; and managing responses to change (in particular, resistance).

We evaluate a number of models of planned change. And, finally, we look at the role of the leader as an agent of cultural change, and at the skills and attributes of an effective change agent.

1   The nature of organisational change

1.1   For some people in some organisations, change is a positive and energising thing, as the title of Tom Peters's well-known book *Thriving on Chaos* suggests. For others, it means loss of security, loss of competence – perhaps loss of livelihood. As someone once said: 'We're all for progress – we just don't like change.'

1.2   The fact is that in today's fast-moving business and social environment – with its technological innovation, globalisation, ever-increasing competition and market sensitivity, demographic shifts and so on – change within organisations and supply networks is inevitable.

Triggers for change in the organisation or supply chain

1.3   Internal triggers for change are those factors that cause organisational disequilibrium: in order for equilibrium to be re-established, some element of the system will have to change. Such factors may include any of the following.

- Poor performance: the pressure to become competitive or cut costs may stimulate a move away from old processes and procedures. For example, the vision (or need) for improvement in procurement, supply chain management or supply chain performance and competitiveness may trigger a change programme or initiative.
- The presence of entrepreneurs, new senior management or other innovators who act as evangelists (leaders) for more modern approaches in the supply chain: for example, a new procurement manager with awareness of e-procurement, or a new supplier with innovation capability
- Changes in, or re-ordering of, organisational goals, processes and structures: for example, supply base optimisation, or the introduction of e-procurement.
- Favourable changes experienced in the past: for example, positive improvements in quality or cost gained through supply chain collaboration, resulting in continuous improvement or supplier development agreements
- Changes in knowledge or resources, enabling the adoption of different processes and technologies. (This includes the process of learning to learn, which supports continuous change and improvement.)

1.4   These internal triggers may, or may not, be related to external forces operating within the organisation's competitive ('micro') and wider ('macro') environments: often categorised using PESTLE (political, economic, socio-cultural, technological, legal and environmental) factor analysis. These may include: economic opportunities and threats; changes in the characteristics of the market and labour pool; increasing scarcity of natural resources and ecological concerns; technological developments; the opening of international or global markets; and amendments to the law and regulation of business activities.

1.5   Franco *(Leading and Influencing in Purchasing)* cites a systematic model (attributed to Anderson and Anderson) of seven drivers of change which can be used to analyse a change situation: Figure 8.1 (Each driver affects the next in the sequence, so this can also be seen as a model of 'stages of change', for change management purposes.)

1.6   You might practise applying this sequence to analysing a particular change objective in your own organisation, or organisations in different sectors and situations: an organisation offshoring its production facilities to a low-cost country, say, or introducing e-commerce or e-procurement.

Figure 8.1 *Seven drivers of change*

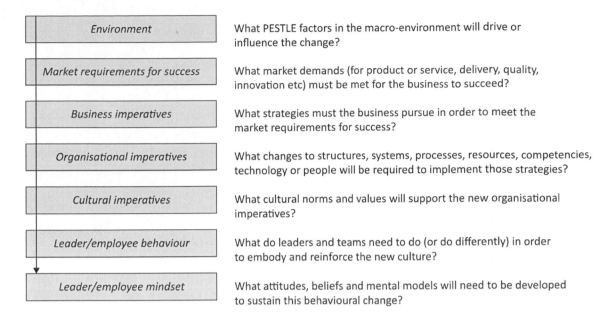

Environment	What PESTLE factors in the macro-environment will drive or influence the change?
Market requirements for success	What market demands (for product or service, delivery, quality, innovation etc) must be met for the business to succeed?
Business imperatives	What strategies must the business pursue in order to meet the market requirements for success?
Organisational imperatives	What changes to structures, systems, processes, resources, competencies, technology or people will be required to implement those strategies?
Cultural imperatives	What cultural norms and values will support the new organisational imperatives?
Leader/employee behaviour	What do leaders and teams need to do (or do differently) in order to embody and reinforce the new culture?
Leader/employee mindset	What attitudes, beliefs and mental models will need to be developed to sustain this behavioural change?

Incremental and transformational change

1.7 **Incremental (or evolutionary) change** is often used as a proactive approach, building on the existing situation (the *status quo*) in small steps over a long period of time. This is the basis of business improvement strategies such as *kaizen* (continuous improvement) and total quality management. Because it requires only realistic, small operational improvements and elimination of wastes, it can be implemented from the 'bottom up', involving employees through suggestion schemes, quality circles and self-improvement plans.

1.8 This makes it a particularly effective approach for building up organisational learning and core competencies: building the organisation's general responsiveness to change (such as shifting patterns of customer demand, sector dynamics and cultural change).

1.9 Incremental change has the following benefits.

- It builds on existing skills, routines and beliefs in the organisation: change is likely to be more efficient, less traumatic and more likely to win acceptance and commitment. There is likely to be less resistance, requiring less management.
- It allows flexibility and responsiveness to environmental changes and feedback, allowing constant re-alignment of strategy. Resources are not wasted on long-range plans which are undermined by uncertainty.
- It allows a continuous sense of progress, even through uncertainty and difficulty. Small changes may be easy to achieve – and may trigger (or help to emerge) bigger changes: 'Big strategies can grow from little ideas' (Mintzberg, *Strategy Safari*). This is the cornerstone of *kaizen* philosophies of learning and quality management.
- It empowers employees. 'Because big strategies can grow from little ideas... almost anyone in an organisation can prove to be a strategist' (ibid). Continuous improvement, and the power to make a small difference that makes a big difference, can be a powerful source of job satisfaction and employee commitment.

1.10 *Kaizen* itself is beyond the scope of this syllabus, but you should have encountered it elsewhere in your CIPS studies. Mullins defines it as 'a Japanese concept of a total quality approach based on continual evolutionary change with considerable responsibility given to employees within certain fixed boundaries'.

It relies on small-step incremental improvements: elimination of wastes (non-value-adding activities) and immediately accessible improvements to equipment, materials or team behaviour. It is essentially a cyclical approach to change, because it also incorporates reflection and evaluation (*hansei kaizen*) for future learning and improvement.

1.11 **Transformational (or revolutionary) change** is often a reactive approach, responding to 'disruptive' change, crisis or the need for a completely new paradigm. It seeks to overthrow (or throw out) the *status quo* and introduce radical transformation in a relatively short period of time. This is the basis of business improvement strategies such as business process re-engineering (BPR). Because it requires discontinuous and sweeping change across organisational structures and systems, it can only be implemented from the 'top down', with top management vision and leadership. Although it requires heavy investment, and some risk, it can achieve transformative improvements.

1.12 This makes it a particularly effective approach where the *status quo* has become dysfunctional for organisational survival or growth, and where sudden challenges require a radical response (such as the introduction of new technology, re-alignment of processes in response to competitive pressure, or re-structuring in response to take-overs or mergers). An extreme example would be an organisational turnaround situation, where there is a need for major structural change or cost-cutting to secure the organisation's survival through performance decline or competitive threat.

1.13 Again, BPR in detail is outside the scope of the syllabus, but you should have encountered it in your studies for other modules. Its developers, Hammer and Champy *(Re-engineering the Corporation)* defined it as: 'the fundamental rethinking and radical redesign of business processes to achieve dramatic improvement in critical, contemporary measures of performance, such as cost, quality, service and speed.' Its key features are as follows.

- 'Discontinuous thinking': breaking away from old rules and assumptions, and seeking a clean slate for radical change. (What, how, where, when, by whom is a task done? Why? What if it were done differently?)
- A horizontal approach, focused on processes which cross structural boundaries
- A strategic approach, which must be supported and driven by the strategic plan and the support of top management. A typical BPR model embraces managerial, organisational, social and technological ('MOST') aspects of the business.

Emergent and planned change

1.14 Johnson, Scholes and Whittington *(Exploring Corporate Strategy)* also distinguish between emergent change and planned change.

- **Emergent change** is allowed to develop naturally, often from the bottom up, in response to environmental influences. This is a 'fluid', ongoing approach, which by definition stays continually up to date with current developments. It focuses on continuous learning and responsiveness, and is suitable for organisations in fast-changing, dynamic environments.
- **Planned change** involves deliberately-formulated strategies and programmes for implementing change. This is said to be a 'frozen' approach, as it locks goals and plans into place for defined planning periods: while it is proactive (dealing with a forward period), it runs the risk of plans being overtaken by fast-changing events. It is primarily top-down, driven by change sponsors and agents in the organisation. This approach is necessary for operational changes such as new product development, in order to co-ordinate all the resources and activities required.

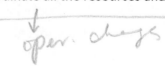

2 Analysing the change situation

The change context

2.1 Throughout this Course Book, we have emphasised a contingency or situational approach to leadership. There is no single success formula: it all depends on the context. This certainly applies to the complex business of managing change. A small, newly-formed research & development company, for example, under the leadership of an entrepreneurial team, would face quite different issues in managing change to a large, long-established corporation (or public sector body), with a formalised structure, traditional culture and miles of red tape...

2.2 We most often hear about 'resistance to change' (and we will consider, later in this chapter, how it can be overcome), but organisations can also create conditions that are favourable to the acceptance – or even welcoming – of change.

- Financial viability and stability: insecurity is a prime source of resistance. (However, it may also be argued that change is more readily complied with when it is perceived to be a necessity for survival.)
- Adaptable (or 'organic') organisation structures: task-focused or output-focused (rather than process or job-description focused); flexible (eg temporary, multi-skilled); and horizontal (eg networked and team-based, facilitating co-operation and communication across vertical barriers of departments and specialisms)
- Good multi-directional communication systems, and systems for formal and informal negotiation and consultation
- Vision, leadership and support from senior management: setting clear goals for, and benefits of, change – and modelling the flexibility of attitude and practice required to achieve it
- Supporting HR systems and procedures: selection, training, appraisal and reward systems which reinforce flexibility and willingness to change as a cultural value
- Supportive culture and attitudes: trust between management and staff; receptivity to new ideas, learning and information-sharing; tolerance of mistakes and shortfalls in the process of learning; and flexibility. These attributes are all (as we have seen) broadly characteristic of a **learning organisation**.

Factors in the change situation

2.3 Johnson, Scholes and Whittington (based on their work with Balogun and Hope-Hailey) helpfully summarise the kinds of contextual features that might require different approaches to change: Figure 8.2 (from *Exploring Corporate Strategy*).

Figure 8.2 *Contextual features which may influence strategic change programmes*

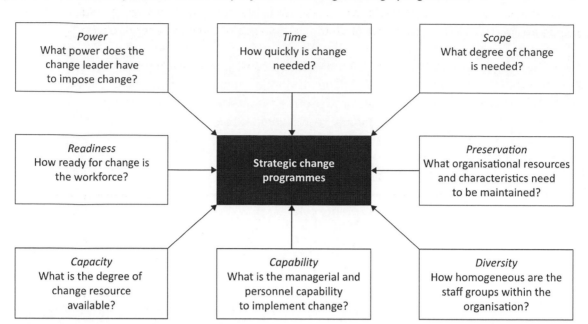

2.4 These kinds of contextual factors will help inform decisions about:

- Whether the organisation has the ability (capacity, capability, readiness and power structures) to achieve the desired change, of the scale, and in the time, required. (Change may need to be managed in incremental stages rather than a major one-off change initiative, for example. Or contextual factors may need to be adjusted – say, by enhancing capability and readiness – before change can be initiated at all.)

- *How* the change should be managed (styles and approaches), given the specific contextual constraints and opportunities.

2.5 Change leaders may need to analyse the change context in detail, in order to ascertain which factors can be used to support change – and which will act as barriers. We will discuss the most influential model for doing this (force field analysis) next.

Force field analysis

2.6 Force field analysis (Kurt Lewin) is a technique for identifying forces for and against change, in order to diagnose some of the change management problems that will need to be addressed, and some of the resources and dynamics available to support it.

2.7 Lewin recognised that at any time in an organisation there exist both forces for change (pushing towards a preferred state) and forces for maintaining the *status quo* (pushing back towards the way things are). The interplay of these forces determines the current state of the organisation (where the forces balance each other out, creating a temporary equilibrium) and the pace and direction of change (if one set of forces is stronger than the other) at any given moment.

- Driving forces (for change) encourage people to give up old ways of doing things and to try new behaviours. Examples include: the frustration or unpleasantness caused by customer complaints or inefficient processes; new technology becoming available; or influence and support from a powerful individual or group.

- Restraining forces (against change) support the *status quo*. Examples include: shortage of resources; opposition from powerful influencers or cultural values; already-installed technology and established systems; managerial preoccupation with day-to-day matters and so on.

2.8   Force field analysis suggests a method of visualising or mapping the forces for and against change using directional arrows, the thicknesses of which represent the strength of each force. (Numerical values can also be assigned to each force, to calculate the net balance of force in either direction.)

2.9   For a specific example, consider an organisation seeking to introduce a system of performance review: Figure 8.3.

Figure 8.3 *Force field analysis*

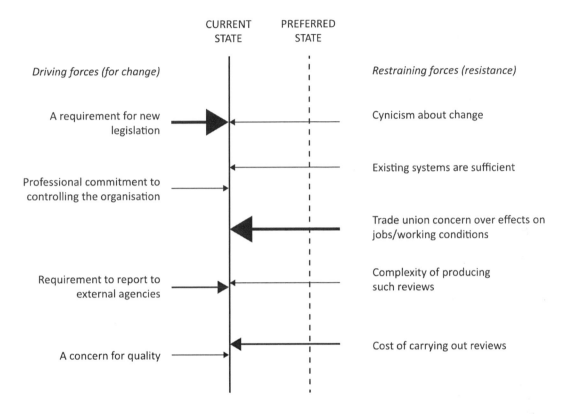

2.10   The force field model suggests that to implement change, managers should first understand the forces for and against change, and the strength of each (including the influence of individuals and groups who are opponents or allies of the change). One simple technique is to give a numerical value to each force, on a scale of 0 (neutral) to 4 (strong). If the totals on each side are the same, the *status quo* will be maintained.

(You might like to add some scores to the forces in our example – and see whether you think the change programme is currently viable or not.)

2.11   Managers can then select change management strategies and styles which concentrate either on strengthening driving forces ('adding forces in the desired direction'), or weakening restraining forces ('diminishing the opposing forces'), or both. Here are some examples.

- Driving forces can be strengthened by emphasising the needs and benefits of change (eg threat from competitors); developing people to cope with change; co-opting the support of influencers (including customers, by gathering feedback, say); raising confidence through a positive managerial style; and so on.
- Restraining forces can be weakened by participation (involving resistors in diagnosing and solving the problem), education and communication (persuading resistors of the need for change), coercion (applying power to silence resistors) or negotiation (offering concessions to buy resistors off).

2.12   Using the example above, we might decide on a programme of negotiation with the trade unions (to weaken one of the stronger restraining forces). This might add to the score for 'cost' – but reduce trade union concern. We could reinforce values about quality (perhaps using customer feedback), to strengthen concern for quality. Staff could be shown that performance review gives them more feedback and opportunities for development, creating a new driving force. And so on. This would add to the total 'driving' score and lower the 'restraining' score – giving preference to change.

2.13 Johnson, Scholes and Whittington suggest that: 'What typically emerges from such an exercise in diagnosing a change situation is that the routines, control systems, structures, symbols and power or dependency relationships can be both important blockages and facilitators to change. Deciding which are blockages and which are facilitators is a helpful diagnostic basis for managing change.'

The change equation

2.14 Another tool for analysing the change situation – aimed specifically at giving a quick initial impression of the possibilities for change – was popularised by Richard Beckhard and Reuben Harris (*Managing Complex Change,* 1987), based on the work of David Gleicher. The change equation or change formula argues that three basic components are required to gain the momentum to overcome resistance to change in an organisation.

- Dissatisfaction with the *status quo*
- Vision of what is possible in future
- First steps: achievable first-step action plans towards reaching the vision.

2.15 This can be expressed as a formula. Change will be possible if:

$$D \times V \times F > R$$

In other words, if Dissatisfaction × Vision × First Steps is *greater* than Resistance.

If any of the three values D, V and F is zero, or close to zero, the product of these 'drivers for change' will also be zero or near zero – and resistance to change is likely to dominate the dynamics of the situation.

Stakeholders in change

2.16 Gerard Egan (*Working the Shadow Side: A Guide to Positive Behind-the-Scenes Management,* 1994) divides stakeholders in a change into nine distinct groups, in relation to the leader or agent of change.

- Partners: those who support the change agent
- Allies: those who will support him, given encouragement
- Fellow travellers: passive supporters, who are committed to the agenda, but not to the change agent personally
- Bedfellows: people who support the agenda, but do not know or trust the change agent
- Fence sitters: those whose allegiances are not yet clear
- Loose cannons: people who may vote either way on agendas in which they have no direct stake
- Opponents: people who oppose the agenda, but not the change agent personally
- Adversaries: people who oppose the change agent and the agenda
- The voiceless: 'silent' stakeholders who are affected by the agenda, but lack advocates or power to influence decisions

2.17 Like Mendelow, Egan argues that different groups should be managed differently.

- Supporters (in various groups) must be encouraged and kept 'on side'. Partners may not require much interaction, but the organisation cannot afford to lose their interest or support. Allies require some encouragement, but infrequent contact (a 'light touch') is usually sufficient. Passive supporters (fellow travellers and bedfellows) require more intensive relationship-building contacts to mobilise their commitment.
- Fence sitters may or may not have the potential to become valuable supporters or harmful opponents. The potential value of their allegiance, or potential cost of their resistance, will determine how much is invested in communication.

- Opponents need to be 'converted' by persuading them of the merits of the change and addressing their reasons for resistance. This is often done via formal, structured communication (eg meetings for negotiation and conflict resolution). Adversaries, on the other hand, may be too difficult and costly to 'win over', and may have to be marginalised or otherwise neutralised, so they cannot mobilise further opposition.
- The view of corporate ethics and social responsibility is that the needs of the voiceless should also receive attention, despite their relative powerlessness. Again, low-frequency contact should be all that is necessary to monitor the response of these stakeholders or their advocates and allow them to feel heard.

2.18 An alternative model for stakeholder management is **Mendelow's power/interest matrix** (covered in Chapter 5). This model would support the need to consult with 'key players' (high interest, high power) when introducing strategic change which will affect them. In a procurement and supply context, these may include any of the following groups.

- Internal customers, such as the line managers directly affected by change in purchasing or supply policy: departmental users of purchased materials and resources; marketing managers (for promotion and pricing of altered product features); and so on
- Major external customers of the organisation, where relevant to the change being proposed, eg if it affects the quality or price of the product
- Major or first-tier suppliers, and suppliers of critical components and materials
- Buyers or buying teams which will be called upon to implement the change

3 Vision and objectives

Vision and values for change

3.1 Vision is a cornerstone of transformational change: change which affects the basic strategic direction of a business. It is also – as we saw in Chapter 2 of this Course Book – the basis of transformational leadership, which aims to influence 'from the inside out', by motivating and inspiring changed attitudes and directions. Transactional approaches to the leadership of change, by contrast, merely assume that stakeholders will comply with change plans and directives out of self interest: in exchange for offered rewards or the promised benefits of change.

3.2 Johnson, Scholes and Whittington *(Exploring Corporate Strategy)* argue that vision, as an overarching sense of what the organisation is about or is seeking to achieve, is particularly valuable in supporting change and innovation. It allows clarity in the communication of strategic intent to business units and external stakeholders. It offers a measure of control and organisational coherence (or focus), by creating a sense of direction and simple rules for action. At the same time, it is highly flexible, leaving room for diversity and the exploration of different options and pathways.

3.3 A clear sense of vision, or strategic intent, also helps to express the purpose of change: the aspirations or needs of the organisation (and its stakeholders) that the change is designed to achieve. This is essential in justifying the change and securing the buy-in of stakeholders to the change programme.

Building a compelling vision

3.4 As we suggested in Chapter 2, in connection with visionary leadership, a compelling vision is one that is shared, widespread, motivating and meaningful. Gino Franco has suggested ten steps to building a compelling vision: Table 8.1.

Table 8.1 *Ten steps to building a compelling vision*

Step 1	Assess the context: stakeholder needs and expectations; competitor strengths and responses and so on
Step 2	Look for trends: consider future needs and influences
Step 3	Think big: focus on key purposes and opportunities; create a challenge
Step 4	Think long term
Step 5	Envision: picture your desired future state vividly and in detail: 'dream' it.
Step 6	Check for passion: adjust the vision until it is meaningful, exciting, motivating
Step 7	Assess resource requirements: what competencies and resources will have to be sourced and mobilised to implement the vision
Step 8	Invite others in: involve people in the ideas, planning and implementation process
Step 9	Balance conviction and openness: believe in the rightness of the vision (for strength to lead and persevere) – but be open to ideas from others (for support and commitment)
Step 10	Stay objective: don't take criticism or rejection of your ideas personally: learn...

Communicating and reinforcing the vision

3.5 Vision can be communicated in various ways, ideally using multiple communication media or vehicles.

- It can be expressed overtly and specifically in **mission and value statements**; annual reports and shareholder meetings; and other stakeholder communications (customer charters, website 'About Us' statements, conference speeches, employee handbooks and so on). It can also be expressed through (or implied by) the organisation's mottos, slogans and stories about itself; and its corporate image, identity and branding.
- Commitment to the vision, and the behaviours it implies, must be **modelled by management** from the top down. Where possible, key influencers in the organisation (not necessarily in managerial positions) can be co-opted to this process, as part of what Johnson, Scholes and Whittington call the 'guiding coalition'.
- **Communication media** should be chosen for their capacity to facilitate understanding and maximise impact. For complex messages, for example, Robert H Lengel and Richard L Daft ('The selection of communication media as an executive skill', *Academy of Management Executives*, 1988) recommend 'rich' media, which allow instant feedback; are able to transmit complex, multiple verbal and non-verbal cues; use natural, accessible language; and have a personal focus. (The richest communication medium is face-to-face communication.)

3.6 Vision can be enhanced by powerful expression of the desired outcomes, or consequences of failure, at all levels. John P Kotter and Dan S Cohen *(The Heart of Change,* 2002) cite examples of the use of dramatic visual images to overcome apathy or inertia about the need for change. 'In one case, showing a video of an angry customer to employees sparked a sense of urgency that helped to overcome long-standing resistance to improving the product.... The main reason why change efforts of any size fail is that there is not a great enough sense of urgency about the need to change – and visual shocks can help break that barrier.'

3.7 The vision can also be reinforced using the human resource management and other systems of the organisation: embedding core values in recruitment and selection criteria; using training and development activities to foster core values and behaviours (including value expression by leaders); promoting and rewarding performance in line with the vision; and so on. Essentially, this is part of empowering people to act on the vision: removing obstacles to change (whether structure, systems or skills based) and encouraging the required ideas, activities and actions.

3.8 Individual leaders and managers can also reinforce the vision by constant re-expression and refreshing (adding new examples, spreading new success stories); and recognising, acknowledging and celebrating individual and team expressions or achievements of the vision. Many modern writers on leadership emphasise this myth-creating and celebratory role: 'catching people doing something right' (rather than wrong), praising, offering small but symbolic rewards, 'making heroes' and so on.

Change objectives and targets

3.9 Some change management models emphasise the need to set objectives and targets, in order to minimise risk and uncertainty and to move the organisation forward in a rational, planned and co-ordinated way. Other models emphasise the difficulties and dysfunctions of the rational-linear approach in a turbulent environment, arguing that the organisation needs to stay alert, flexible and adaptive to opportunities and threats which emerge in the environment in which it operates.

3.10 In so far as objectives are set in advance for a change programme, there are four key requirements for making them effective.

- They must be aligned or integrated: both vertically (with the strategic objectives of the business as a whole) and horizontally (so that they contribute to co-ordinated, consistent, coherent – and potentially synergistic – effort between the different units and functions in the organisation). A procurement department's objective to move to overseas sourcing, for example, must support strategic objectives for profitability and corporate social responsibility – and meet the production and marketing department's requirements for quality, price and delivery lead times.
- They must be effectively formulated (eg as SMART objectives).
- They should – where possible – be formulated with the participation or at least the agreement of key stakeholders, including team members who will have to implement changes, in order to secure buy-in and commitment.
- They should be flexible. Monitoring and feedback throughout the project may indicate the need not just to correct or adjust performance in line with objectives, but to adjust the objectives themselves: circumstances or needs may have changed. The longer-ranging the objectives are, in turbulent business environments, the less fixed objectives may have to be, in order to avoid dysfunctional rigidity.

The change plan

3.11 An integrated change plan will address, in one coherent statement, the following issues.

- The need for change: its contribution to the overall mission and objectives of the organisation
- The vision for change: its envisaged impact on structures, systems and culture
- SMART change objectives
- Resource requirements (financial, human and material) and how they will be sourced and allocated: in other words, a change budget
- The process and structure for implementation: accountabilities, monitoring and reporting, progress milestones and so on.

Securing stakeholder buy-in

3.12 One of the key implications of **strategic alignment** is that the vision and objectives for strategic change must be sold downward to contributing units and individuals, in order to secure co-operation or buy-in. Conversely, the vision and proposed plans of a particular leader or unit may need to be sold upward to strategic managers and other stakeholders. (This has been identified as a key issue for the procurement profession, particularly in organisations where its strategic potential is not yet recognised, or where it does not yet have influence at a strategic level.)

3.13 Taylor (The Naked Leader) argues that this is necessary at all levels of leadership. 'Once a decision is made it must be bought into by everyone in the department. Unity of purpose and direction is the most elusive yet one of the most powerful ways forward for all departments, teams and organisations.'

3.14 **Consultation** is the process of exchanging information with stakeholders as part of the change process. **Engagement** is the process of securing their interest, collaboration and support for the change programme. Consultation and communication (if done well) is a key tool for securing engagement.

3.15 The aims of effective consultation and engagement processes are as follows. *Stud*

- To allow the views and needs of stakeholders to be taken into account (in the interests of fairness and transparency, and for the development of trust and long-term working relationships with stakeholders)
- To develop change objectives and processes that are likely to be accepted or supported (or at least not strongly resisted) by stakeholders
- To ensure accountability for change decisions which affect stakeholders (particularly in the public sector)
- To enhance the quality of change plans through information inputs from expert and involved stakeholders (eg users)
- To provide for issues management: pre-empting conflict or negative public relations effects of foreseeable problems and adverse impacts (eg concern about potential redundancies arising from restructuring or supply base rationalisation)
- To provide for crisis management: dealing with unforeseen negative contingencies which affect stakeholders (eg disrupted production due to fire, systems failure or strike action; health and safety problems of new systems; or quality problems in new components leading to product recall). Established communication channels will allow the organisation to contact potentially-affected stakeholders early; to reassure them (on the basis of established trust); and to collaborate to solve problems and minimise damage.

3.16 As we have seen in Chapter 5 on stakeholder management, there is a wide range of mechanisms and media available for consultation and stakeholder marketing. The change agent may consider any of the following possibilities.

- Using steering groups, task forces, committees and cross-functional teams already set up for stakeholder communication, consultation and advice
- Setting up temporary advisory or task-force teams for the purpose
- Implementing consultation programmes targeted to key stakeholder groups or stakeholders in particular affected areas
- Issuing proposals and inviting the views and responses of interested parties. This may be done via public advertisement (via print media or the company's website) or direct contact with known stakeholders (via mail or email), or via workshops, meetings or public forums
- Unveiling proposals at meetings or seminars (eg annual general meetings or staff conferences) at which stakeholders will be present for discussion.

3.17 The choice of method will depend on the publics the organisation needs to reach (general community or specifically targeted); the mechanisms and channels already in place; the nature of consultation required (expert input or broad acceptance); and the time and resources available.

4 Dealing with resistance to change

4.1 Changes may affect individuals in many different ways: physically (eg different shift patterns or work methods), circumstantially (eg relocations), socially (eg re-establishing work relationships with a new team) and psychologically (eg the requirement to learn new skills). Change may create feelings of disorientation, insecurity, fear of loss of competence and so on.

4.2 Four factors affect the individual's **response to change**.

- Facts: what is known about the reasons for change, the change process and likely outcomes of the change. (So it helps if a rational case for change can be made.)
- Beliefs: whether individuals believe that change is necessary and potentially beneficial, that they have (or will be given) the resources to cope and so on. (So the case for change must be convincingly made, and trust earned by leaders and other change agents.)
- Feelings: emotional responses to the process or proposed outcomes of change. These may be negative – fear, insecurity, anger – or positive – excitement, pride or relief, say. (So change leaders need to anticipate, diagnose and manage such responses.)
- Values: the individual's positive and negative moral judgements around change, or specific change objectives. A move towards greater social responsibility may have positive values attached, say, while downsizing may be negatively regarded. (So change needs to be associated with positive values, in order to secure support and buy-in, while negative values are acknowledged and confronted.)

4.3 Reactions to proposed changes cover a wide range.

- Acceptance: enthusiastic espousal, willing cooperation, grudging cooperation or resigned compliance
- Indifference: apathy, lack of interest, inaction (usually where the change does not directly affect the individual)
- Passive resistance: refusal to learn, working to rule, absenteeism, delaying tactics, defensive responses
- Active resistance: deliberate spoiling, go-slows, sabotage or strikes

Resistance to change

4.4 Organisations often talk about 'resistance to change', but resistance strategy (the method of introducing and implementing the change charged with introducing the change) rather than the change itself may be welcomed as a form of feedback from those affected by ch used constructively to modify the change strategy.

4.5 John Hunt (*Managing People in Organisations*, 1982) highlights a like resistance on the face of things, but are nevertheless behaviou

- Pleas of ignorance ('I need more information before...')
- Delayed judgement ('Let's wait and see before...')
- Defensive stances ('This isn't going to work', 'It would be too e 'The unions will never accept...')
- The display of various personal insecurities, fears, anxieties, fr control over planning', 'I won't see my team any more', 'What'll happen to my job?', 'Nobody ever asks us what *we* think')
- Withdrawal, or disowning of the change ('Oh well, on their heads be it').

4.6 John P Kotter and Leonard A Schlesinger ('Choosing Strategies for Change' in *Harvard Business Review*, 1979) cite four common sources of resistance to change.

- Parochial self-interest: individuals or groups have a vested interest in maintaining the *status quo*, which is (or is perceived to be) threatened by the change. Change may pose a threat to established ways of working (and therefore to people's sense of competence); to existing social arrangements and relationships (eg breaking up a work team); or to economic advantage (eg changes to the way in which contracts are awarded, or policies on Fair Trade pricing).

- Misunderstanding and lack of trust: people do not understand the reasons for change, or its likely consequences, or lack trust in the change advocates. This resistance may be exacerbated where change is imposed, because people resent coercion and control.
- Contradictory assessments of the situation: people's perceptions of the nature and likely consequences of change differ from the information being given by change agents, or the culture as a whole denies the need for change.
- Low tolerance of change: individuals feel insecure in the face of uncertainty. This may take the form of self-doubt ('Will I be able to cope with the changes?') or exhaustion (if change is constant, without time to consolidate and regroup) even where the benefits of change in general are recognised. Low tolerance of change (and resulting inflexibility) also exists in organisation cultures: eg bureaucracies are highly resistant to change, as they depend on roles and rules and attract security-seeking kinds of people.

4.7 Mullins suggests a more detailed set of reasons for both individual and organisational resistance to change: Table 8.2.

Table 8.2 *Reasons for individual and organisational resistance to change*

INDIVIDUAL RESISTANCE	ORGANISATIONAL RESISTANCE
Selective perception, leading to biased views of the situation	Organisational culture: strong norms and values establishing the *status quo*
Habit, providing ease, comfort and security	A desire to maintain stability and predictability (especially in bureaucratic organisations)
Inconvenience, loss of control or reduced freedom of action	Resource requirements and priorities (economic feasibility, asset specificity)
Economic implications of change for pay, rewards or job security	Past and existing contracts and agreements, constraining changes in behaviour (eg long-term supplier contracts)
Nostalgia: value and security in the past, tradition, 'tried and tested' ways	Threats to the power or influence of interest groups (protecting functional territory or managerial power, say)
Fear of the unknown and insecurity	Blaming culture (discouraging experimentation) or deference culture (discouraging intiative).

Dealing with resistance to change

4.8 To overcome resistance, Kotter and Schlesinger propose six possible approaches.

- Education and communication
- Facilitation and support
- Participation and involvement
- Negotiation and agreement
- Manipulation and co-optation
- Explicit and implicit coercion

We will look briefly at each of these in turn.

Education and communication

4.9 This strategy relies on the belief that communication about the need for change, and its benefits, can be used to persuade employees to accept the change programme. Education and communication approaches are likely to be based on a strategy of promoting and justifying the compelling reasons for the change and the benefits (to the stakeholders themselves, where possible) expected to accrue from the change. This is one reason why it is easier to gain support for change in crisis situations, or in the face of serious threats to organisational survival: stakeholders in the organisation can more readily perceive the advantage to them of co-operating with the change programme – or the negative consequences of failing to do so.

4.10 It is important for the effectiveness of an educative approach, however, that the reasons and benefits being communicated are both compelling (creating sufficient motivation to buy in) and genuine – or at least plausible. Change leaders must promote, but cannot afford to overstate, the benefits likely to accrue from change: disappointed expectations will erode trust for future change initiatives. If there is already a lack of trust, the change leaders may need to back their arguments for change with solid evidence of the threat or opportunity; the likely effectiveness of the specific change plans to meet the threat or capitalise on the opportunity; and the resources that will be used to support their success.

4.11 Management's viewpoint may need support from a source perceived as neutral (eg external consultants or change agents) in order to be persuasive, and this may be time-consuming. However, the benefits of clear communication in advance of change are that it dispels unnecessary fears; gives key stakeholders some sense of control (reducing the insecurity that is a major source of resistance to change); and reduces the potential for demotivating and resistance-promoting rumours.

4.12 Johnson, Scholes and Whittington *(Exploring Corporate Strategy)* also emphasise that communication is a two-way process: 'feedback on communication is important, particularly if the changes to be introduced are difficult to understand or threatening, or if it is critically important to get the changes right.'

Facilitation and support

4.13 Through facilitation and support, change managers reassure those affected by the change that they will be helped to develop the necessary skills and will be given the necessary resources to achieve the change – and follow through on this reassurance with the coaching, training and other activities required.

- **Facilitation** involves assisting stakeholders to change (with training, coaching, resources or extra staffing, say).
- **Support** involves helping stakeholders to come to terms with the change psychologically – eg through counselling about change issues and help with coping (often used in the case of staff redundancies).

4.14 Although this process can be time-consuming and costly, it reduces fears of loss of competence and security, and demonstrates management's commitment to supporting stakeholders through the change. It may also be necessary or helpful to enable the change itself (eg through retraining employees). It is important that reassurances are actually followed through; otherwise it will be perceived as attempted manipulation.

Participation and involvement

4.15 As we have discussed elsewhere in this Course Book, stakeholders are considered more likely to support changes if they are encouraged to own them through having participated in the decision-making process. Quite apart from the advantages of enhanced commitment to change, participation may allow better quality decision-making by taking advantage of people's expertise and knowledge in relevant areas.

4.16 Class studies undertaken by Lester Coch and John RP French ('Overcoming resistance to change' in *Human Relations*, 1948) demonstrated the effectiveness of a participative approach in overcoming resistance to change. Changes were introduced in three production groups in a pyjama factory which had been experiencing resistance due to perceived loss of status and earnings.

- The non-participative group was informed about the change but not involved in the decision making. Resistance was immediate: conflict flared, efficiency remained low, and some members left.
- The representative group was given a hand in the change to the extent that after a preliminary

meeting of explanation, representatives were given appropriate training and subsequently trained fellow members. The group was cooperative and submissive, and efficiency rose rapidly.

- The total participation group also had a preliminary meeting, but all members then took part in the design and standard-setting for the new job. This group recovered its efficiency rating very rapidly, and then increased it to a level much higher than before the change, without conflict or resignations.

4.17 There are, however, some recognised drawbacks to a participative approach. It can be a lengthy process, particularly if consensus is sought, and a strong relationship of trust must exist between management and workforce if employee participation is to be genuine and effective. Where participation is genuine, management may be unacceptably constrained by resistance due to the contradictory assessment of change by workers or other stakeholders.

Negotiation and agreement

4.18 A negotiation strategy may be required where potential resistance groups have considerable power. It is often practised where the workforce is represented by recognised trade unions, and in interdependent buyer-supplier relationships. Opposing interest groups bargain towards an agreement based on compromise. Negotiation may be based on adversarial (win-lose) or partnership (win-win) bargaining strategies, and this will obviously affect the approach to change management.

4.19 The main advantage of a negotiation strategy is that (ideally) it allows conflicts of interest to be acknowledged and taken into account in a systematic fashion. Compliance can be insisted on, on the basis of a negotiated agreement – and if a genuine win-win outcome is reached through the process, it may encourage positive commitment and enhanced morale.

4.20 The main disadvantage of a negotiatory approach is that the process can polarise opposing positions, in order to allow for eventual compromise. This may be unnecessarily time-consuming and adversarial in style.

Manipulation and co-optation

4.21 Resistors are neutralised by co-opting them into the change process (eg by giving them a symbolic position in the change leadership team, or asking them to explain and 'sell' the change to others). The psychological dissonance caused by the incongruence of their personal attitude to the change and their public 'position' on the change will cause discomfort. In order to reduce this discomfort, they are more likely to bring their attitudes into line with their public position.

4.22 This may be regarded as a less than ethical approach to influencing, although the process of co-optation is based on positive techniques of attitude change: if a person's resistance is unreasonable, it may be for their ultimate good to manipulate them into changing their attitude through being asked to 'fake it' until they come into line.

Explicit or implicit coercion

4.23 It is important to remember that change leaders may have the option of simply applying various forms of power, according to the managerial prerogative, to implement whatever they perceive is required and to enforce compliance.

4.24 Despite the prevalence of more 'enlightened' HR approaches, more or less explicit coercion may be effective in certain contexts, as we saw in our discussion of autocratic leadership styles and push styles of influencing. The advantage of such an approach is that change decisions can be made and implemented with speed, as may be required by a crisis situation.

4.25 Its disadvantages are that coercive changes may (at best) secure mere compliance, where commitment has greater power to harness the positive energies and efforts of the human resource. A coercive approach basically fails to address resistance, and makes stakeholders feel powerless in the face of potentially threatening changes. Even if they are unable directly to prevent the implementation of changes, resistance and negative power may emerge in low morale, employee absenteeism or turnover, industrial or commercial disputes, sabotage and so on.

Change strategies and styles

4.26   Johnson, Scholes and Whittington identify five broad management styles for overcoming resistance to change.

- **Education and communication**: based on promoting and justifying the compelling reasons for the change and the benefits (to the stakeholders themselves, where possible) expected to accrue from the change. It is also based on management's sharing its perceptions, knowledge and objectives, in order to 'get the facts straight' about the change, and identify and confront opposing views. This may be done through a programme of coaching or training, counselling, group briefings and discussions, written communication and so on.
- **Collaboration**. Stakeholders are considered more likely to support changes if they are encouraged to 'own' them through having participated in the decision-making and implementation process. Quite apart from the advantages of enhanced commitment to change, participation may allow better quality decision-making and enhanced organisational learning and flexibility, making it suited to incremental (bottom-up) change.
- **Intervention**. A change agent drives, co-ordinates and controls the overall change process, while delegating elements of the process to project or task force teams (eg ideas generation, research or identification of critical success factors). The main advantage of this approach is that it allows participation, but at the same time maintains momentum, co-ordination and control: it suits both incremental and (non-crisis) transformational change situations. The main problem is that this may be perceived as manipulative.
- **Direction**. The change agent or senior leader uses personal managerial authority to establish a clear strategy and map of how change will occur: in other words, top-down change management. This has the advantage of setting a clear direction – particularly in complex, transformational change situations where speed is required. However, like all unilateral approaches, it may at best gain compliance – not commitment – from stakeholders, and may reflect the limited knowledge or perspective of a single individual.
- **Coercion**. The change agent or senior leader imposes the change, more or less as a *fait accompli*, and threatens some form of penalty or sanction for failure to comply. This is an extreme form of direction, and an overt use of power. While it may cause resistance and resentment, it may be effective in situations of organisational crisis, where rapid transformational change is required – and in established autocratic cultures.

4.27   Dexter Dunphy and Doug Stace ('The strategic management of corporate change' in *Human Relations,* 1993) identify four categories of change leadership style. (You may notice that these reflect our earlier discussion on leadership style in general.)

- Coercion: senior management forces or imposes changes, from the top down
- Direction: managers use their authority to make decisions about the future direction of the organisation or function, the changes required, and how change will be managed
- Consultation: employees are given limited involvement in setting change goals relevant to their own areas of responsibility and expertise
- Collaboration involves widespread employee participation and involvement in key decisions affecting their future (and that of the organisation as a whole)

4.28   Using a contingency approach, Dunphy and Stace suggested that different styles are appropriate, according to the scale and pace of the desired change. Huczynski and Buchanan *(Introduction to*

Organisational Behaviour) summarise their conclusions on a grid, as shown in Table 8.3. (Note that, again, while participative approaches may be 'ideal', they are not necessarily the most appropriate in all circumstances.)

Table 8.3 *Change strategies and styles*

	INCREMENTAL CHANGE	TRANSFORMATIVE CHANGE
Collaborative/ Consultative style	Participative evolution strategy Use when: • The organisation needs minor adjustment to environmental conditions • Time is available for participation • Key interest groups favour change	Charismatic transformation strategy Use when: • The organisation needs major adjustments to environmental conditions • There is little time for participation • There is support for radical change
Directive/Coercive style	Forced evolution strategy Use when: • The organisation needs minor adjustments • Time is available for participation BUT • Key interest groups oppose change	Dictatorial transformation strategy Use when: • The organisation needs major adjustments • There is no time for participation • There is no internal support for strategic change BUT • Change is necessary for survival

5 Planned change models

5.1   Mullins notes that: 'planned change represents an intentional attempt to improve, in some important way, the operational effectiveness of the organisation. The basic underlying objectives can be seen in general terms as: modifying the behavioural patterns of members of the organisation; and improving the ability of the organisation to cope with changes in its environment'.

The unfreeze-change-refreeze (behaviour modification) model

5.2   Kurt Lewin developed his force field model, working in collaboration with Edgar Schein, to draw up a three-step model for changing human behaviour: Figure 8.4.

Figure 8.4 *The planned change (unfreeze-change-refreeze) model*

5.3   Stage 1 is to unfreeze the existing restraining and driving forces which preserve equilibrium. This is the most difficult (and in many cases neglected) stage of the process, concerned mainly with motivating the change and confronting resistance. Hunt notes that: 'learning also involves re-learning – not merely learning something new but trying to unlearn what is already known.' If the need for change is immediate, clear and perceived to be associated with the survival of the individual or group (for example, change in reaction to an organisational crisis) the unfreeze stage will be greatly accelerated.

5.4   Here are some possible approaches to the unfreezing stage.

- Consulting team members about proposed changes, so that they take ownership of the evaluation and problem-solving process
- Confronting team members' perceptions, assumptions and feelings about the change, so that sources of resistance are confronted early and openly

- Positively reinforcing signs of willingness to 'unlearn': validating efforts, suggestions and new behaviours or insights with recognition and praise
- Removing individuals from their usual routines, sources of information and social networks, so that old behaviours and attitudes are less likely to be reinforced: for example, the change programme may be introduced at an off-site team conference or training course

5.5 Stage 2 is essentially to introduce imbalances, which allow the driving forces in the situation to outweigh the restraining forces (as discussed earlier). This phase is mainly concerned with:

- Communicating new, desirable behaviours and values clearly and positively
- Supporting and facilitating adoption of new behaviours and values (eg with information, opportunities for practice, pilot schemes and trial roll-outs, required resources and so on)
- Removing real and perceived barriers to the adoption of new behaviours and values (eg structural barriers to communication, unsupportive leadership, denial or resistance and so on).

5.6 Stage 3 is to refreeze the driving or restraining forces to hold the new equilibrium in place, through consolidation or reinforcement of the new behaviour. Positive and/or negative reinforcement may be used, together with coaching and training, repetition and practice, co-optation to teach the change to others, and the alteration of policies and procedures.

5.7 It is worth noting that Lewin's model is less applicable in fast-changing or turbulent business environments, where 'freezing' may be seen as counter-productive, hampering flexibility and responsiveness. Some organisations may need to exist in a constant state of unfreezing and changing, without re-hardening policies, procedures and practices.

5.8 Pedler *et al (Manager's Guide to Leadership)* argue that the model 'assumes that we can bring about the desired future as a new steady state, and that other things can be held steady whilst this is done. This model is still highly influential, but neither of these assumptions holds up in a rapidly transforming world, where the ground shifts under our feet even as we stand thinking about the changes we want to make. In the complex collaborations of alliances, value chains, multi-agency partnerships and networks that characterise the contemporary organisational world, such control is illusory.'

5.9 They argue that in the face of this lack of control, relational leadership is essential: building trust, working together and developing and empowering people, so that the team is equipped to respond effectively to challenges and changes as they present themselves. Vision, direction and simple rules or values can be specified in advance – but leave maximum room for manoeuvre.

Eight components of planned change

5.10 French, Kast and Rosenzweig *(Understanding Human Behaviour in Organisations,* 1985) suggest eight specific components of a planned change initiative, as a basic problem-solving model, related to the unfreeze-change-refreeze model: Figure 8.5.

Figure 8.5 *Eight components of a planned change programme*

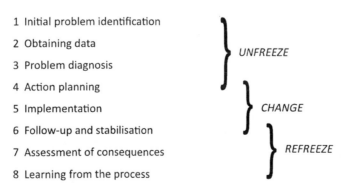

1 Initial problem identification
2 Obtaining data
3 Problem diagnosis
} UNFREEZE

4 Action planning
5 Implementation
} CHANGE

6 Follow-up and stabilisation
7 Assessment of consequences
8 Learning from the process
} REFREEZE

Eight steps to successful transformational change

5.11　There are a number of other change management approaches based on the concept of a phased project management structure: sequential steps or phases to implement change.

5.12　For example, change guru John Kotter ('Leading Change: Why Transformation Efforts Fail' in *Harvard Business Review*, 1995) identified eight reasons for the failure of change programmes.

- Allowing too much complacency (it's important to establish a sense of urgency)
- Failing to build a coalition of stakeholder support .
- Lack of a clear vision for the purpose and direction of change
- Failing to communicate the vision clearly
- Allowing resistance and barriers to gather
- Lack of short-term wins in the change plan (to create momentum and confidence)
- Stopping short (failing to consolidate changes or push for ongoing improvement)
- Failing to embed changes in the corporate culture

5.13　Kotter proposes a corresponding eight-step model for successful major or transformational change.

Step 1　Establish a sense of urgency and prioritise change objectives based on market and organisational imperatives

Step 2　Form a guiding coalition of influential stakeholders

Step 3　Create a compelling vision for change

Step 4　Communicate the vision as widely and clearly as possible

Step 5　Empower people to act on the vision by removing cultural, technological and structural obstacles

Step 6　Plan to create short-term wins (visible performance improvements, recognition and reward for participants) which foster momentum and buy-in

Step 7　Consolidate improvements to produce further change, keeping momentum going (eg next-step changes, developing staff, setting improvement goals)

Step 8　Institutionalise new approaches: embed them in culture, procedures and HR systems.

6　Managing cultural change

6.1　Lewin and Schein acknowledge that cultural change is the hardest to achieve, because it is difficult to target and motivate the 'unfreezing' of deeply-held, socially supported values and behaviours.

Mayo's three elements of cultural change

6.2　Elton Mayo advocated a simple model of cultural change, involving three interdependent elements.

- **Top management vision and determination**. Senior management must share and own the end goal, so that they visibly drive and articulate the changes needed.
- **Education and communication.** In order to change the way people think, first management and then personnel must be educated: encouraged to think through the implication of the desired cultural change for themselves, and to work out what they must do to help to achieve it.
- **Supporting systems and processes**. Recruitment, selection, training, promotion, reward, appraisal and all other HR systems and processes (and their equivalents in the supply chain) must support cultural change by positively reinforcing new cultural values and performance criteria – and negatively reinforcing 'old' values and behaviours.

Trice and Beyer's eight considerations in cultural change

6.3　HM Trice and JM Beyer *(The Cultures of Work Organisations,* 1993*)* argue that 'cultural innovation is... more difficult than cultural maintenance. When innovation occurs, some things replace or displace others... People often resist such changes.'

6.4 Trice and Beyer propose the following guidelines for changing organisational culture: Table 8.4.

Table 8.4 *Eight considerations in cultural change*

Capitalise on propitious moments	Eg competitive challenge or poor financial performance. Such moments provide momentum for change – provided that people actually perceive the need.
Combine caution with optimism	Create a positive vision of what the change will bring – while managing expectations
Understand resistance	Resistance is likely to occur: • At the individual level (eg as a result of fear of the unknown, self-interest, selective perception, habit, dependence etc) • At the group, organisational or supply chain level (eg as a result of threats to power and influence, lack of trust, different goals and perceptions, resource competition, inter-organisational agreements and so on)
Change many elements, while maintaining some continuity	Identify key principles that will remain constant, as a source of security and continuity
Recognise the importance of implementation	Attention will have to be given to: adoption (buy-in), implementation (roll out) and institutionalisation (reinforcement) of new values and behaviours. Initial acceptance and enthusiasm are not sufficient to carry through lasting change.
Select, modify and create appropriate cultural forms	Utilise all elements of Johnson & Scholes' 'cultural web': symbols, rituals and rites, stories, myths, metaphors, ceremonies, control mechanisms, power structures and so on.
Modify socialisation tactics	Socialisation is the process by which people are inducted into 'the way we do things around here', generally at the beginning of their employment or entry into a work team. This is the main way in which people learn, absorb and adopt culture. If these processes are changed (eg by induction training, supplier induction and so on), the organisation's culture will begin to change.
Identify and cultivate innovative leadership	If members are to be wiling to follow leaders in new directions (away from the *status quo* and their comfort zones), the leaders must project vision, conviction and confidence.

7 Skills and attributes of an effective change agent

7.1 In addition to organisational and cultural conditions supporting change, the success of a change programme depends to a large extent on the attributes and skills of the change agent or champion. The key attributes of a successful change agent may, in part, be identified with the key attributes of 'transformational leaders'.

- **Vision and leadership.** Change agents must be able to visualise where the organisation needs to be, and what it needs to look like, in order to be able to articulate and model the vision and goals to other stakeholders.
- **Team building skills.** Change programmes cannot be driven or completed single-handed. If only in order to co-opt key stakeholders and influencers into the process, the change agent will need to be ___ age teams for planning and implementing change.
  ___ l change management requires extensive interpersonal communication ___ culating goals and values, in order to motivate change; influencing, ___ n order to change attitudes; conflict management and resolution, in ___ nd opposition; supportive communication and counselling, in order to ___ .
  ___ anagers must themselves be open to challenge, uncertainty, risk and ___ to set an example and convince others of the benefits of change. ___ be required as part of the change programme. Setbacks and mistakes, ___ of change, should be regarded as learning opportunities and useful ___ ther by the change agent or by the affected employees.
  ___ nd stamina. A change programme is typically a long-term project, and ___ hroughout. Setbacks must be overcome and not allowed to derail the

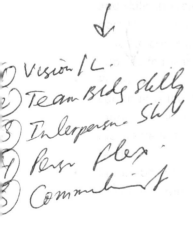

8

process. A positive outlook, and deep commitment to the organisation's future, are required to maintain focus and momentum.

7.2 Stuart Crainer (*Key Management Ideas: Thinkers that Changed the Management World,* 1998) emphasises seven skill areas for managing change.

- Managing conflict (stimulating diversity and disagreement, but resolving dysfunctional conflict). Conflict need not always be destructive (as we will see in Chapter 9). Change managers must be able to draw on the positive effects of conflict while minimising any damaging effects.
- Interpersonal skills – as discussed in the previous paragraph.
- Project management skills (complex planning and control and team or stakeholder management). This implies a mix of talents, partly to do with the technical aspects of project management, and partly with the team building and motivation skills to get the most from the project team.
- Leadership and flexibility (setting clear objectives, motivating people to achieve them – while appreciating the need to respond to contingencies). The latter aspect is particularly important in environments of rapid change.
- Managing processes (not just the content of change). It is not sufficient to understand the desired change outcomes; it is also important to achieve them by effective processes.
- Managing strategy (aligning changes to corporate objectives). During the change management process, the change agent must continually refer to overall corporate objectives to ensure that the changes implemented make a positive contribution towards them.
- Managing personal development (taking responsibility for one's own learning and growth). Crainer sees such development as a process that never ends, and it is important for managers to acknowledge this.

External change agents

7.3 *Johnson, Scholes and Whittington* argue that 'outsiders' are important in the change process. An organisation may introduce a new chief executive or manager(s) from outside, to enhance its capability for change, or may contract external consultants to plan and facilitate change programmes.

7.4 The advantages of using external resources to perform such roles are as follows.

- They are more likely to be objective and dispassionate, without the 'cultural baggage' or personal and factional interests that might bias insiders.
- They may better represent the interests of other stakeholders in the change process and outcomes. (Customers, suppliers and others may themselves act as external change agents, in the sense that they may have influence in the process.)
- They are better able to ask questions and perform analyses which challenge the *status quo* and its constraints, and broaden the range of options.
- They may have technical expertise in carrying out research and change interventions which in-house managers lack.
- They are dedicated to the change programme, where internal managers' focus is likely to be dissipated by their workload and other competing priorities.
- They represent a significant, focused investment in change, and may help to signal to stakeholders that the organisation is taking the change process seriously.

Chapter summary

- Evolutionary (or incremental) change is a proactive approach, building on the existing situation in small steps over a long period of time. It is the basis of continuous improvement (*kaizen*) and total quality management strategies. Revolutionary (fundamental or transformational) change is often a reactive approach, responding to disruptive change, crisis or the need for a completely new paradigm. It involves radical change in a relatively short period of time (eg via business process re-engineering).

- Change may be caused by internal triggers (such as questioning, poor performance, innovators, changes in goals, processes, structures or new knowledge and resources) or by external forces (political, economic, socio-cultural, technological, legal or ecological).

- Although attention is paid to 'resistance to change', organisational conditions can favour change: financial viability; adaptable organisational structures; good communication systems; vision and leadership; supportive HR systems and culture.

- An influential tool in analysing the dynamics of change is Lewin's force field analysis, which enables managers to map the nature and strength of various forces which support change (driving forces) or resist it (restraining forces).

- A compelling vision is shared, widespread, motivating, meaningful and vivid. Such a vision can be communicated and modelled in various ways, and reinforced by the HR systems of the organisation.

- In so far as objectives are set in advance for a change programme, they must be aligned, SMART (specific, measurable, attainable, relevant and time-bounded), bought-into by stakeholders and flexible enough to absorb contingencies.

- Four main causes of resistance to change are self-interest, misunderstanding, contradictory assessments and low tolerance of change. Individual responses to change will be affected not just by the facts, but also by beliefs, feelings and values about change.

- Strategies for overcoming resistance to change (Kotter and Schlesinger) include: education and communication; facilitation and support; participation and involvement; negotiation and agreement; manipulation and co-optation; and explicit and implicit coercion.

- Dunphy and Stace identify four categories of change leadership style: coercion, direction, consultation and collaboration. These will be exercised differently, according to the scale and pace of the desired change.

- Lewin and Schein developed a three-stage approach to implementing change: unfreeze the *status quo*; create an imbalance in driving and restraining factors in order to change behaviour and attitudes; and refreeze the new *status quo*.

- Change agents require a skill set including: conflict management; interpersonal skills; project management skills; leadership and flexibility; managing processes; managing strategy; and managing personal development.

8

Self-test questions

Numbers in brackets refer to the paragraphs where you can check your answers.

1 List possible internal triggers for change. (1.3)

2 What are the benefits of incremental change? (1.9)

3 Distinguish between emergent and planned change. (1.14)

4 Describe Lewin's force field model. (2.7)

5 List methods by which a leader's vision may be communicated. (3.5)

6 List aims of consultation processes during change management. (3.15)

7 Describe possible reactions to proposed changes. (4.3)

8 Describe sources of resistance to change. (4.6)

9 List six possible approaches to dealing with resistance to change. (4.8)

10 Explain the stages in Lewin's three-step model for introducing change. (5.2)

11 List possible reasons for the failure of change programmes. (5.12)

12 List attributes of a successful change agent. (7.1)

CHAPTER 9

Managing Conflict

Assessment criteria and indicative content

 Critically assess the main methods for resolving conflict with internal and external stakeholders to support change in the supply chain

- Contingency models of organisations
- The functions of the informal organisation
- The positive and negative outcomes of organisational conflict
- Strategies for resolving conflict

Section headings

1. Contingency models of organisation
2. The informal organisation
3. The nature of organisational conflict
4. Causes of conflict
5. Strategies for resolving conflict
6. Conflict handling styles

Introduction

One of the key roles of leadership is to develop and maintain co-operative working in the organisation (and supply chain), through the process of change.

In an interpersonal sense, this involves a complex, ongoing process of managing diversity and difference. 'Diversity', because change situations involve a range of stakeholders with potentially very varied perspectives and interests. 'Difference', because those areas of diversity will inevitably, from time to time, cause misunderstandings, disagreements, competition and perhaps hostility. This is the kind of difference we generally call 'conflict' – although conflict itself is a complex term which can be seen from a number of different points of view.

In this chapter we discuss what conflict might mean in relation to internal and external stakeholders, and whether it is a good or bad thing. We outline common causes (why conflict arises) and symptoms (how you can know it when you see it) and how it can be prevented, controlled and resolved.

1 Contingency models of organisation

1.1 The syllabus indicative content draws this caption from a short section in Mullins, where conflict is covered as part of a chapter on 'the nature and context of organisations'. We have assumed, for the purposes of this chapter, that contingency models of organisation (such as mechanistic and organismic structures, socio-technical systems and the work of Trist and Bamforth, Lawrence and Lorsch and Joan Woodward) are in fact beyond the intended scope of the syllabus. (They were covered as part of *Management in Procurement and Supply* at Advanced Diploma Level.)

1.2 As we have already seen in relation to leadership styles, however, contingency theory is a class of behavioural theory which argues that there is no 'one best way' to organise, manage or lead an organisation (compare Fiedler's contingency theory or Hersey & Blanchard's situational model) or to make decisions (compare the Vroom-Yetton model). A particular approach to organisation, leadership or decision-making may be effective in one situation – but not in another.

1.3 The main relevance of this concept in the context of 'resolving conflict with internal and external stakeholders to support change in the supply chain' (the assessment criterion on which this chapter is focused) is to highlight:

- The range of organisational and supply chain contexts within which conflict and change may be managed (and hence, the need to contextualise your recommended approaches to the particular details of the case study scenario or example you are addressing: there is no 'one best way' to approach all situations)
- The complex 'web' of inter-related factors in a supply chain conflict leadership situation (and hence, the need to appreciate that changes in one area – such as technology, structure or leadership style – may have impacts in another)
- The potentially wide-ranging constituency of stakeholders in a supply chain change situation (and hence, the potentially divergent interests, viewpoints and influencing attempts that may lead to intra- or inter-organisational conflict).

2 The informal organisation

2.1 Again, this syllabus caption is drawn from the Mullins chapter on 'The nature and context of organisations' – but in this case, it has more specific relevance to the management of conflict in change situations, because of the importance of the informal organisation in supporting (and, more often, resisting) change.

The nature of the informal organisation

2.2 Within – or underneath – every formal organisation, there is a complex informal organisation. Formal organisation has a well-defined, fixed structure of task-focused roles and relationships, which remains stable regardless of changes of membership. Informal organisation, in contrast, is a loosely structured, spontaneous, fluctuating network of interpersonal relationships.

2.3 When people work together, they invariably establish:

- *Social networks and groups*, often cutting across the boundaries of units established by the formal organisation. Examples include a group of managers who get together to play golf, a clique of workmates, or a network of regular contacts who call each other when there is a need for information.
- *Informal ways of getting things done*, often different from the formal rules and procedures of the organisation. Examples include procedural short-cuts, work customs, 'the way we do things round here'.
- *Informal communication networks*, often by-passing formal communication channels. This is

sometimes called the 'grapevine'. It includes rumour and gossip, as well as business networking. The grapevine is often much faster than formal channels – but is also notoriously unreliable in terms of accurate information about work matters.

- *Informal power structures*, often different from the formal position-based scalar chain of command or hierarchy of authority. As we saw in Chapter 4, non-managerial individuals may have informal influence over their collleagues (and even over their 'superiors'). A trusted, long-serving employee may be used as a sounding board by management, say (exercising expert power). A charismatic team member may have more influence than a designated team leader (exercising personal power)
- *Personal and collective values, feelings and behavioural norms:* hostilities and friendships, positive and negative emotions and responses, attitudes and assumptions, personal and group agendas and so on.

Functions of the informal organisation

2.4 The informal organisation can serve a number of important functions for its participants – and for the formal organisation.

- Satisfaction of the social needs of members (Abraham Maslow), in the form of opportunities for social interaction, fellowship and belonging (which may not be provided for in the formal organisation)
- Motivating factors (Frederick Herzberg) to enhance job satisfaction, in the form of variety, interest, autonomy, social interaction and learning
- Sources of information valued or required by members: filling information vacuums or gaps left by the formal communication channels of the organisation
- Stability and confidence, through the familiarity and acceptance of informal norms of behaviour
- Mechanisms of social and cultural control, where management can align informal norms, values and leaders with organisational goals
- Solutions or 'work arounds' for performance barriers, inefficiencies or lack of resources in the formal organisation and processes.

2.5 Informal dynamics may support the objectives of the formal organisation. Here are some examples in relation to change management.

- The grapevine can be used to speed up the spread of information through the organisation, perhaps with greater acceptability than if it was formally conveyed by management (and therefore suspected of managerial 'spin').
- Informal communication networks may encourage horizontal and upward communication to a greater extent than complex formal channels, increasing the potential for flexibility, innovation and learning.
- Informal ways of working may actually be more efficient than unwieldly formal procedures – and should be given the opportunity to drive adjustment of formal procedures where this is so.
- An informal leader, who is trusted and influential within a work group, may be co-opted to support a manager or designated team leader in gaining the commitment of the team (eg as a 'change champion').
- Personal and group values, attitudes and sentiments may be aligned with the organisational vision (supporting 'buy-in' and commitment).

2.6 However, there is also potential for the informal organisation to work against the objectives of the formal organisation. When employees are dissatisfied with aspects of the formal organisation, they are likely to rely more heavily on the informal organisation for information, satisfying relationships and less frustrating ways of getting things done.

- Informal activities may therefore divert attention and energy away from the task.
- Informal information is often wildly inaccurate and unnecessarily negative (eg exaggerating the threat of redundancies), causing stress, conflict and resistance to change.
- Informal work methods may cut corners, with negative consequences for quality or health and safety.
- Informal leaders may undermine formal managerial authority.

- Personal and group values, needs, fears and agendas may cause resistance to managers' change management initiatives.

2.7 Formal communication systems, in particular, benefit from the support of a positive informal network – and suffer from undermining by a negative informal network. Leaders might harness the advantages of the grapevine by the following measures.

- Feeding plentiful, accurate and positive information into the informal network (eg through house journals or intranet pages, or 'management by walking around')
- Facilitating informal networking, by encouraging social events and normal work interactions
- Joining the informal network themselves, to be aware of what is going on (and what personnel *think* is going on).

Organisational politics

2.8 The political interests of different individuals or groups in organisations (and supply chains) may include the acquisition of individual power or influence, 'empire building', career advancement, or favourable allocation of organisational resources.

2.9 The techniques for achieving these objectives (referred to as 'games' by Mintzberg and others) include the enhancement of individual power by forming networks, alliances and coalitions, and exercising power to undermine and control others (eg by withholding information, creating red tape and so on).

2.10 Here are some other political strategies.

- *Contracting:* negotiating a *quid pro quo* agreement between groups, making concessions to make gains (eg in collective bargaining)
- *Co-opting:* short-circuiting opposition and criticism by getting potential critics to share responsibility for the decision
- *Forming networks and coalitions:* combining the information and power of individuals or groups by making strategic alliances
- *Influencing decision criteria:* 'moving the goal posts', changing the criteria by which success and failure are judged, to make yourself look good or others bad
- *Controlling information:* selectively giving, withholding or distorting information to strengthen your position ('knowledge is power') or undermine that of others'
- *Coercion and pressure tactics:* threatening or applying negative power (eg withdrawal of labour in industrial action)
- *Rule making:* imposing rules, procedures, restrictions or official requirements on other groups in order to bolster one's own importance

3 The nature of organisational conflict

Different views of conflict

3.1 There are different ideological perspectives on conflict in organisations.

- The **happy family view** (or **unitary perspective**) assumes that organisations are basically co-operative structures, in which there are no systemic conflicts of interest: conflicts are unnatural and exceptional, caused by lack of leadership, poor communication or inflexibility on the part of individuals or interest groups. Strong culture, good communication, co-operative values and motivational leadership should be able to eliminate conflict.
- The **conflict view** (or **pluralist perspective**) assumes that organisations are natural arenas for conflict, as members compete for limited resources, status and rewards, and pursue different goals and professional values. Individual and organisational interests cannot always coincide – but a mutual

survival strategy, involving the control of conflict through compromise, can be made acceptable in varying degrees to all concerned.

- The **evolutionary view** (or **interactionist perspective)** regards conflict as a force for gradual, evolutionary change: it maintains the *status quo* (by balancing competing interests) while also keeping the organisation sensitive to the need for change. (This is in contrast to the **radical perspective**, based on the ideas of thinkers such as Karl Marx, which sees conflict as inevitable and necessary as a force for the destruction of an oppressive social system, in order to introduce revolutionary change.)

Positive and negative outcomes from conflict

3.2 Conflict can be highly desirable. It can energise relationships and clarify issues. John Hunt *(Managing People in Organisations)* suggests that conflict is **constructive**, when its effect is to:

- Introduce different solutions to problems
- Define power relationships more clearly
- Encourage creativity and the testing of ideas
- Focus attention on individual contributions
- Bring emotions out into the open
- Provide opportunity for catharsis (the release of hostile feelings that might otherwise be repressed).

3.3 Conflict can also be **destructive,** negative and damaging to social systems (which the radical perspective still regards as positive and desirable). Hunt suggests that conflict of this kind may act in a group of individuals to:

- Distract attention from the task
- Polarise views and 'dislocate' the group
- Subvert objectives in favour of secondary goals
- Encourage defensive or 'spoiling' behaviour
- Result in disintegration of the group
- Stimulate emotional, win-lose conflicts, or hostility (damaging communication).

3.4 SP Robbins *(Managing Organisational Conflict: a Non-Traditional Approach)* suggests that a contemporary approach to conflict:

- Recognises the inevitability (even necessity) of conflict
- Explicitly encourages opposition and challenge to ideas and the *status quo*
- Defines conflict management to include stimulation as well as resolution of conflict
- Considers the management of conflict as a major responsibility of all managers.

Conflict behaviours

3.5 How do you diagnose conflict in an internal or external stakeholder situation? According to Handy *(Understanding Organisations)*, there will be observable symptoms of conflict.

- Intra-personal struggles or frustration, where an individual has conflicting goals within himself
- Interpersonal friction, hostility or 'personality clashes'
- Poor communication (upward, downward and/or lateral)
- Inter-group rivalry, competition and jealousy (eg in regard to status, power or resources)
- Low morale and frustration
- The proliferation of rules, norms and myths (to protect different positions)
- Widespread use of arbitration, escalation (appeals to higher authority) and grievances or disputes
- Inflexible attitudes towards change
- Poor co-ordination between hostile, non-communicating groups, resulting in work delays (and possibly customer complaints).

4 Causes of conflict

4.1 Gary Dessler *(Human Resource Management)* classifies four major sources of organisational conflict.

- *Interdependence and shared resources.* Conflict is most likely to occur where groups are dependent on each other to achieve their goals and use shared resources in pursuit of these goals.
- *Differences in goals, values and perceptions.* Groups are distinctive social units and will have special interests, particular views of what is important and what is not, and will tend to see the world in a way which supports the maintenance and success of the group. (Overlapping membership – eg if a team member is also a trade-union member – may cause conflict within the individual, as well as within the group.)
- *Authority imbalance.* Where a group has too little authority compared to its responsibilities or prestige, it will aggressively seek more (in competition with other groups): if it has too much, it will be a target of others who attempt to enhance their own authority or prestige. If group contributions are equivalent or substitutable, political conflict may escalate as groups by-pass or replace one another.
- *Ambiguity.* Where a group's responsibilities are ambiguous or unclear, power vacuums arise: competition to fill the vacuum ensues. Similarly, uncertainty about *other* groups' purpose or motives leads to mistrust and political game-playing.

4.2 Mullins summarises the potential sources of organisational conflict: Table 9.1.

Table 9.1 *Mullins's causes of conflict*

Differences in perception	Different people attach different meanings to the same objects or events: different attitudes and value judgements can then become a source of interpersonal conflict
Limited resources	Individuals and groups often have to compete for a share of limited (or scarce) resources, such as budget, staff, space and so on.
Specialisation	Division of labour on the basis of specialisation leads to functional departmentation. Functional departments may have different goals, priorities, methods and culture – creating potential for a 'silo' mentality and self-interested (sub-optimal) behaviour. This can lead to conflict especially where departments need to work together in a co-ordinated manner.
The nature of work activities	Where the task of one person or group is dependent on another, as part of a process, there is potential for conflict due to failure to meet the internal customer's needs (failure to meet agreed schedules or meet output targets, say) – especially if the customer department feels that it is being unfairly judged on results which were 'sabotaged' by the other party.
Role conflict	The failure of people to behave as they are expected to, or to live up to the requirements of their role in the eyes of stakeholders.
Inequitable treatment	Conflict may arise if a person or group feels they have been treated unjustly or unfairly, especially in relation to another person or group
Violation of territory	People tend to be 'territorial' and 'possessive' in regard to resources and responsibilities perceived to be 'theirs'. They may feel resentful or threatened if others 'invade' or 'encroach' on their territory: usurping power, taking over clients, sharing their workspace and so on.
Environmental change	Environmental change can be a catalyst for any of the above sources of conflict: eg economic recession causing intensified competition for scarce resources, or employment legislation causing conflicts of interest between workers and management.

Inter-group conflict

4.3 Various forms of inter-group conflict are therefore common in organisations.

- Institutionalised conflict, such as that between trade unions and management.
- Hierarchy-based conflict, caused by inequalities of positional power.
- Functional conflict, caused by clashing goals and competition for power and resources between different organisational functions.
- Line/staff conflict, such as that between production and sales functions and 'advisory' functions

such as the HR department, Accounts and so on: the power of staff functions is often resented and resisted by line managers as interference, and staff functions have to reassert their authority (often by negative means, such as red-tape and rule enforcement).

- Formal/informal conflict, where the unwritten rules, communication channels and power structures of the informal organisation clash with those of the formal organisation.
- Status conflict, where groups compete for status and prestige.
- Resource conflict, where groups compete for finance, staff, space and other resources. This is often the basis of adversarial negotiations: 'win/lose' competition where one party can gain only at another's expense.
- Political conflict, where 'individuals or interest groups exercise whatever power they can amass to influence the goals, criteria or processes used in organisational decision-making to advance their own interests' (Miles).

Intra-group conflict

4.4 In addition, conflict may arise within a team, project or supplier relationship, because of everyday factors such as the following.

- Disagreement about needs, goals, values, priorities and interests (since individuals may have different agendas – or different perceptions about the team's goals and purposes). This will be made worse by:
  - Lack of direction (from the organisation or team leader) as to what the team's purpose and goals are.
  - Lack of clarity in the roles assigned to team members, leading to stressful role ambiguity (where individuals don't know clearly what they are expected to contribute) and/or frustration and loss of co-ordination, as roles are duplicated or left vacant.
- Poor communication, which is a cause (as well as a symptom) of conflict. The less people communicate, the more potential there is for negative assumptions, stereotypes and misunderstandings. Withholding of information may also escalate conflict, as it is perceived to be a hostile political game.
- Competition for scarce resources. Individuals may compete for power, office space, team-based rewards, the manager's recognition and attention, machine time (or other resources) and so on.
- Interpersonal issues, such as personality clashes, aggression or domination by strong individuals, argumentative or manipulative communication styles and so on.
- Hygiene issues (in the technical sense used by Herzberg in his motivational theory): dissatisfactions with the leadership, working conditions or pay, say, which can cause grievance against the organisation (or leader) and/or spill over into interpersonal conflict in the team (eg if some members feel others are being paid more).

4.5 One of the key roles of the change leader is to resolve conflicts of interest between **stakeholders** (at the programme or project definition stage) and to resolve any conflicts that may arise between collaborators as the programme progresses. Conflicts may arise over disappointed or mismatched expectations; competition for scarce resources; frustration due to the interdependence of activities along the critical path; political competition for influence; and so on.

5 Strategies for resolving conflict

5.1 The suitability of any approach to managing or resolving conflict must be judged according to its relevance to a particular situation. There is no 'right way'. In some situations, the best outcome may be achieved by compromise; in others, imposition of a win-lose solution may be required; in others, the process of seeking a win-win solution, whatever the eventual outcome, may be helpful.

5.2 Some authorities identify two basic approaches to dealing with conflict.

(a) **Conflict management** refers to what Handy calls 'ecological' strategies: creating conditions in which individuals and groups may be better able to interact co-operatively with each other, and in which issues and potential conflicts can be openly discussed with a view to mutual understanding (if not always agreement).

Such strategies are wide-ranging and ongoing, including measures such as: agreeing shared objectives and values; reinforcing the group or team nature of organisational life via cultural mechanisms and supportive leadership; training people in group process skills; setting up mechanisms for multi-directional communication, employee relations and involvement; clarifying territorial and role ambiguities; eliminating unnecessary status barriers and inequalities; distributing resources fairly and with transparency; setting ground rules for group discussion and issues management; and so on.

(b) **Conflict resolution** refers to what Handy calls 'regulation strategies': resolving disputes or conflicts once they emerge. They include: establishing detailed rules and procedures for conduct; appointing liaison or co-ordination officers to manage areas of conflict; using confrontation and negotiation meetings to hammer out differences and reach compromise; providing mechanisms for third-party intervention (eg by mediation, conciliation or arbitration); or separating conflicting individuals.

Strategies for resolving conflict

5.3 Robbins provides the following classification of possible strategies for resolving conflict.

- Problem-solving: the parties are brought together to find a solution to the particular issue
- Superordinate goals: the parties are encouraged to see the bigger picture and identify shared goals that override their differences
- Expansion of resources: resources are freed and mobilised to meet both parties' needs, eliminating the need for competition
- Avoidance: one or both parties withdraws from the conflict or conceals the incompatibility
- Smoothing: one or both parties plays down the differences and 'papers over the cracks'
- Compromise: bargaining, negotiating and conciliating, so that each party makes some concessions in order to obtain some gains
- Authoritative command: an arbitrator with authority over both parties makes a decisive judgement
- Altering the human variable: effort is made to change the attitudes, beliefs and perceptions underlying the conflict
- Altering the structural variable: effort is made to re-organise work relationships in order to minimise the potential for conflict

5.4 Mullins summarises the range of strategies as follows.

- Clarification of goals and objectives, role definitions and performance standards, in order to avoid conflict based on misunderstandings
- Resource distribution: increasing the share of resources, mobilising new resources, or allocating resources in such a way as to maximise perceived fairness and utility
- The use of non-monetary rewards, where financial resources are limited
- Just and equitable human resource management policies and procedures: fair rewards, grievance and disciplinary procedures; positive employee relations; and training managers in coaching and negotiation skills; and so on

- Development of interpersonal and group process skills, to foster self-awareness and self-control, conflict management and problem-solving
- Group selection and development: eg careful selection of members for cross-functional teams; using formal and informal mechanisms to encourage cross-functional communication
- Leadership and management. Mullins suggests that 'a more participative and supportive style of leadership and managerial behaviour is likely to assist in conflict management' (eg fostering interpersonal respect, team values and so on) – but you might also note that more directive styles may be necessary to resolve conflict
- Organisational processes: removing unnecessary stressors from authority structures (eg status barriers); communication channels; decision-making processes; and bureaucratic 'red tape'
- Socio-technical approach: attending to the psycho-social factors of work and organisation, alongside technical and structural requirements.

5.5 In a supply chain context:

- Clear service standards and specifications may be established to avoid conflict due to ambiguity or misunderstanding
- Dispute resolution methods may be built into contracts (including arbitration or alternative dispute resolution mechanisms, in preference to costly and relationship-damaging litigation)
- Differing values, priorities and agendas may be openly confronted and explored, so that parties collaborate in seeking creative and mutually satisfying ('win-win') solutions (or compromise, as a second-best option)
- Negotiation processes may be used to clarify individual and organisational values and priorities. An adversarial, competitive or challenging element may be used as a spur to innovation and improvement, or a test of capability – within a collaborative and problem-solving framework.

6 Conflict handling styles

6.1 The **Thomas-Kilmann instrument** (TKI) is a popular tool in conflict assessment, developed by Kenworth Thomas and Ralph Kilmann (building on earlier work by Thomas and Ruble).

6.2 Thomas ('Conflict & Conflict Management': *Handbook of Industrial and Organisational Psychology*) suggested that individuals' conflict-handling styles could be mapped on two dimensions, according to the intentions of the parties involved: their assertiveness (the extent to which they try to satisfy their own concerns) and their co-operativeness (the extent to which they try to satisfy the other party's concerns).

6.3 The five key points on this map are shown in Figure 9.1.

Figure 9.1 *Model of conflict-handling styles*

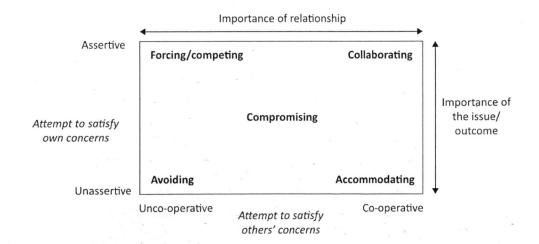

6.4 The five styles can be compared as follows.

- **Avoiding**: you withdraw from the conflict or attempt to sweep it under the carpet. This allows you to avoid dealing with conflict, and avoids immediate tensions: it may be appropriate if the issue is genuinely trivial, or you need a 'cooling off' period, or someone else is better placed to deal with the conflict. However, underlying problems don't get resolved: long-term frustrations and resentments may emerge in other ways.
- **Forcing/competing**: you impose your solution on the problem. This allows you to get your way, and may be appropriate for issues that need winning: breaking down the inflexibility of others or implementing unpopular measures quickly in a crisis, say. However, the other party is likely to feel defeated and demeaned, and this can damage ongoing collaboration and trust.
- **Accommodating**: you concede the issue without a fight, to preserve harmony. This avoids upsetting people, and may be appropriate where maintaining the relationship is more important than the issue (or if you realise you are wrong). However, you are giving permission for the other person to take advantage of the situation, and your authority may be undermined.
- **Compromising**: you use bargaining or negotiation, so that each party trades some concessions for some gains. This reaches an agreement that both parties can live with, and enables you to get on with work: it may be necessary where power is evenly balanced and there is genuine conflict of interest. However, the solution is often more expedient than effective, and may leave both parties unsatisfied.
- **Collaborating**: you work together to find an outcome which meets the clearly stated needs of both parties as far as possible: a problem-solving or 'win-win' approach. This assumes that both positions are important, even if they are not necessarily equally valid. It takes time, but at the end of the process, both parties should be committed to the solution and satisfied that they have been treated fairly. This facilitates learning, generates more creative options and encourages trust. (We examine the 'win-win' approach in more detail below.)

6.5 Note that there is still no one best style: change leaders need behavioural flexibility. Thomas suggests that research backs collaboration as the best way to settle conflict. However, others such as CB Derr ('Managing organisational conflict: collaboration, bargaining, power approaches' in *California Management Review,* 1978) disagree, suggesting that:

- Competition is a valid response to a different set of assumptions than those underlying collaboration. It may be necessary for solving ideological disputes, obtaining flexibility, avoiding vulnerability and establishing autonomy: in other words, sometimes you just have to 'stick to your guns'.
- Collaboration is a useful way to resolve conflict when there is at least a moderate amount of interdependence among the parties (so that a win-lose situation would damage both); a perceived equality of power exists between the two parties (so that both can afford to be as open as collaboration requires); there are mutual advantages to collaboration that can be seen by both parties; and the collaborative process is supported by the organisation.
- Compromise can offer a useful bridge between collaborative approaches and power-plays.

The win-win approach to conflict resolution

6.6 Another useful model for conflict resolution is 'win-win'. Helena Cornelius and Shoshana Faire *(Everyone Can Win)* suggest that there are three basic ways in which a conflict or disagreement can be worked out.

- Win-lose: one party gets what he wants at the expense of the other party. However well justified such a solution is, there is often lingering resentment on the part of the 'losing' party, which may begin to damage working relationships.
- Lose-lose: neither party gets what he really wants. Compromise comes into this category. However logical such a solution is, there is often resentment and dissatisfaction on both sides: even positive compromises only result in half-satisfied needs.
- Win-win: both parties get as close as possible to what they really want. Whether or not the outcome is actually possible, the attempt to pursue it generates more options, more creative problem-solving, more open communication, and enhanced cooperation, as well as preserving working relationships.

6.7   Cornelius and Faire outline a win-win approach as follows.

Step 1   Find out why each party needs what they say they want. Getting to the other party's fears and needs in the situation facilitates meaningful problem-solving. It also encourages communication, supports other people's values, and separates the problem from the personalities involved.

Step 2   Find out where the differences dovetail. Diverging needs may seem like the cause of conflict – but they also offer potential for problem-solving, since the different needs may not be mutually exclusive, but may dovetail at some point.

Step 3   Design new options, where everyone gets more of what they need. Techniques include: brainstorming; chunking (breaking a big problem down into manageable chunks and seeking solutions to those); and devising usable 'currencies' (suggestions and concessions which are easy or low-cost for both parties, and can be traded). The aim is mutual gain.

Step 4   Co-operate. Treat the other person as a partner, not an opponent.

6.8   The example given is of two men fighting over an orange. The win-win approach would ask each man why he needs the orange. One may want to make orange juice, while the other wants the skin of the orange to make candied peel: the conflict disappears. If they both want the juice, other options will be explored: sharing the juice; getting more oranges; diluting the juice; buying one man some bottled orange juice and so on. Even if compromise is settled on, the outcome will be a win-win, because both parties will have been fully assertive and willingly cooperative, enhancing the relationship between them (which adds to the 'win' outcome).

9

Chapter summary

- Within a formal organisation, there is invariably an informal organisation, involving social networks, informal ways of getting things done, informal communication networks, informal power structures, and informal norms. The informal organisation may assist in achievement of organisational goals, or may work against them.
- Conflict within organisations is usually seen as a negative feature, but there are positive aspects to conflict if these can be constructively harnessed.
- Dessler classifies sources of organisational conflict: interdependence and shared resources; differences in goals, values and perceptions; authority imbalance; ambiguity.
- There are two basic approaches to dealing with conflict: conflict management and conflict resolution. Robbins suggests a variety of means for conflict resolution.
- An alternative framework for managing conflict is provided by the Thomas-Kilmann model. This highlights five main approaches to dealing with conflict.

Self-test questions

Numbers in brackets refer to the paragraphs where you can check your answers.

1   Describe elements of the informal organisation. (2.3)

2   In what ways can the informal organisation support the formal organisation in relation to change management? (2.5)

3   In what circumstances may conflict be constructive? (3.2)

4   Describe four sources of organisational conflict, according to Dessler. (4.1)

5   What factors may give rise to intra-group conflict? (4.4)

6   Distinguish between conflict management and conflict resolution. (5.2)

7   Describe the five main styles of handling conflict, according to the Thomas-Kilmann model. (6.4)

8   Describe the four steps in a win-win approach to conflict management (Cornelius and Faire). (6.7)

CHAPTER 10

Delegation and Empowerment

Assessment criteria and indicative content

 4.3 Evaluate the importance of effective delegation to implement change successfully

- Authority, responsibility and accountability
- Benefits of delegation
- A systematic approach to delegation
- The concept of empowerment

Section headings

1. Authority, responsibility, accountability and delegation
2. Benefits of delegation
3. A systematic approach to delegation
4. The concept of empowerment

Introduction

In this chapter we focus on a unique attribute of authority – as opposed to power or influence: the fact that it can be delegated to others, or cascaded down the hierarchy or 'chain' of command. The syllabus raises the topic of delegation in the specific context of change management, highlighting the importance of effective delegation in the successful implementation of change: that is, co-opting and involving team members in implementing change, so that ownership of change goals 'cascades' down through the organisation.

We begin by clarifying the terminology surrounding organisational authority, and the relationship between different concepts. We then focus on delegation: its importance, and how it can best be achieved by managers and leaders.

Finally, we highlight the related topic of 'empowerment', which is often associated with the delegation of authority, and increased responsibility for workers.

1   Authority, responsibility, accountability and delegation

Authority

1.1   If power is the *ability* to exert influence over objects, persons or situations, authority is the *right* to exercise power in a particular context.

1.2   This is an important distinction. Authority refers to the scope and amount of discretion given to a person to make decisions by virtue of the position he holds in the organisation. It is usually conferred 'from the top down' by the process of delegation (although it may also be conferred 'from the bottom up' – by election, for example).

1.3   Once authority is delegated to a subordinate, he has the legitimate right to take actions or decisions that would otherwise be taken by the delegating manager. This supports the 'cascading down' of authority through the organisation. The subordinate can now legitimately issue directions (within the scope of his delegated authority) for others to follow, and expect compliance from them.

Responsibility and accountability

1.4   Responsibility is the obligation of an individual to use the authority assigned to him or her by the organisation, or by a superior within the organisation, appropriately – or to be liable to reprimand for unsatisfactory performance. (The term is also used to mean a duty or activity assigned to a given position of authority: thus a procurement team leader has particular 'responsibilities'.)

1.5   Accountability is the liability of each person who is given authority to give an 'account' or report of their use of that authority (ie their performance) to the person who assigned it to them. It is often associated with 'ultimate responsibility': that is, the place where 'the buck stops'.

1.6   While authority can be delegated (giving the subordinate certain responsibilities), 'ultimate responsibility' (and accountability) remains with the delegating manager. Effective delegation is not 'abdication of responsibility'.

Matching authority and responsibility

1.7   Classical organisation theorists, such as Henri Fayol, placed great emphasis on the need for authority to be commensurate with responsibility.

- IC McGivering *et al* (*Management in Britain,* 1960) argue that: 'It is axiomatic in organisational processes that responsibility should be equal to authority, for power without corresponding responsibility is likely to lead to behaviour uncontrolled by the organisation and hence to unintended and probably undesirable consequences.'
- The opposite situation – in which employees are given responsibility for results without the corresponding authority to take decisions and direct others to achieve them – is equally dysfunctional, because of the inefficiency of struggling to obtain co-operation, and the frustration and stress it is likely to cause the individual. Mullins suggests that 'many problems of delegation stem from failure to delegate sufficient authority to enable subordinates to fulfil their responsibilities'.

1.8   Managers must delegate sufficient authority to enable (empower) subordinates to fulfil their responsibilities. For example, if a category buying team leader is responsible to the procurement manager for the performance of the team, but is not given authority to select team members, set team rewards, allocate team roles and duties, initiate performance improvement interventions (such as counselling or training) or access resources for the team's task – the team leader cannot legitimately be held responsible for the team's performance. The procurement manager is ultimately accountable for the poor performance of the team, and responsible for ensuring that the team leader has the authority and resources required to secure the desired results.

Delegation

1.9 Delegation of authority is the process through which a superior entrusts to a subordinate (or team) part of his or her own authority to make decisions or take actions. Mullins defines delegation as: 'the authorisation to undertake activities that would otherwise be carried out by someone in a more senior position'.

1.10 In Chapter 3, where we explored the nature of power, we noted that all organisations face a dilemma in balancing the need for control, order and predictability with the need for flexibility and responsiveness (especially in customer-facing units). Delegation is the key process by which decision-making authority in an organisation is devolved to:

- *Lower levels of the organisation*, giving front-line employees the autonomy to use their discretion and initiative in pursuit of improved performance and customer value
- *Local units of the organisation*, giving managers the autonomy to respond flexibly to local work site, supply market and product market factors.

1.11 Delegation is thus closely related to the concept of **decentralisation** in formal organisation structures. The term 'decentralisation' can be used to refer to:

- The extent to which decision-making authority is cascaded down to lower levels of the hierarchy – rather than being kept close to the centre or 'apex' of the firm
- The extent to which related tasks, expertise and resources are devolved to, and distributed among, different work sites, business units or line departments – rather than being gathered under a single functional authority (as in a dedicated procurement function) or at a single location (as in a 'head office').

1.12 Alfred Sloan *(My Years with General Motors)* argued that 'From decentralisation we get initiative, responsibility, development of personnel, decisions close to the facts, flexibility – in short, all the qualities necessary for an organisation to adapt to new conditions. From co-ordination [centralised control] we get efficiencies and economies.' Sloan pioneered the concept of 'co-ordinated decentralisation' (balancing order and flexibility), by the delegation of tactical and operational decisions further down the organisation, while retaining strategic policy decisions at corporate headquarters.

1.13 You may remember that delegation is also a **style of leadership** in Hersey and Blanchard's situational model of leadership. Best suited to high-readiness teams (able and willing and/or confident), a delegating style involves a low degree of directive behaviour, and a fairly low degree of supportive behaviour. The leader basically turns over responsibility for decisions and their implementation to the team members, within agreed goals and parameters.

1.14 While delegates are responsible and accountable to the delegator for their use of the authority, the delegator retains ultimate responsibility (and accountability to higher management). This creates what Mullins calls a 'dual responsibility' in delegation: 'The subordinate is responsible to the manager for doing the job, while the manager is responsible for seeing that the job gets done. The manager is accountable to a superior for the actions of his or her subordinates.'

2 Benefits of delegation

Managerial effectiveness

2.1 The purpose of effective delegation is to optimise the use of human resources to support organisational goals. Delegation is necessary, primarily because, as John Adair *(Time Management and Personal Development)* suggests: 'leading managers tend to have responsibilities for more work than they can possibly execute themselves. They need to delegate some of it to others, together with some of their own positional authority.' It is generally recognised that in any large, complex organisation, managers will have to delegate to some extent, because there are physical and mental limitations to the workload of any individual or group in authority.

2.2 The passing of routine or less important decisions down the line also ensures best **use of managerial time**. It frees managers to concentrate on the more distinctive aspects of their work (such as strategic planning, new business development, culture creation, goal articulation, staff development and so on) – while also enhancing the quality of the decisions by involving stakeholders who may be more qualified to make them (by virtue of functional expertise or closeness to the supplier or customer, say). This is partly an issue of cost efficiency: if decisions are made at a higher level than necessary, they cost more than they need to. There is an opportunity cost to failure to delegate.

2.3 By devolving decisions to team members, delegation also supports:

- Quicker response to operational problems, as decisions are taken closer to the operation
- Quicker response to changing supplier and customer requirements, as decisions are taken closer to the interface with external stakeholders.
- 'Today's leaders understand that you have to give up control to get results' (I Gretton, 'Taking the lead in leadership', *Professional Manager,* 1995).

Team member motivation and development

2.4 Influential research by JR Hackman and GR Oldham ('Motivation through the design of work', in *Organisational Behaviour and Human Performance)* suggested that certain core job dimensions contribute to job satisfaction and intrinsic motivation. Job satisfaction is related to the experience of three psychological states, each of which is aroused by key job characteristics: Table 10.1.

Table 10.1 *Hackman and Oldham's core job dimensions*

STATE	JOB DIMENSIONS
Meaningfulness of work	Skill variety: the opportunity to exercise different skills and perform different operations – as opposed to micro-specialisation and repetition, which cause monotony and boredom
	Task identity: the integration of operations into a 'whole' task (or a meaningful 'chunk' of a task), as opposed to task fragmentation
	Task significance: the task has a role, purpose, meaning and worth, according to the values of the organisation and the individual
Responsibility	Autonomy: the opportunity to exercise discretion or self-management in areas such as target-setting, scheduling and choice of work methods
Knowledge of outcomes	Feedback: the availability of information by which the individual can assess progress and performance in relation to expectations and targets – and the opportunity to give feedback and have a voice in performance improvement.

2.5 Such models suggest that delegation is a key tool for motivating team members and increasing their job satisfaction, loyalty and commitment.

2.6 By enhancing opportunities for lower-level employees to exercise new skills and responsibilities, delegation also contributes to other desirable outcomes.

- The development of individual employees and teams, with enhanced capabilities in problem-solving, decision-making and self-management
- The development of wider and deeper organisational capabilities, competencies and competitive strengths
- Management succession planning: identifying and 'grooming' individuals with potential for promotion to managerial positions
- Avoidance of the 'Peter Principle', whereby individuals are promoted on the basis of achievements in

a current role, until they are promoted to a role beyond their competence. Delegation gives managers the opportunity to preview how individuals perform at higher levels of responsibility.

2.7 Delegation should not be seen merely as a mechanism by which management-made decisions flow down the organisation. It is designed to devolve decision-making authority to lower levels of the organisation. This is particularly important in a change management context.

The importance of delegation in the implementation of change

2.8 Here are some key points about delegation in the implementation of change.

- Delegation ensures that key participant stakeholders are given genuine involvement in the process, and are therefore more likely to own and commit to it, and to implement changes effectively.
- Delegation is part of a 'facilitate-and-empower' style of leadership which may be less aversive (resented and resisted) than a 'command-and-control' style, because it builds understanding, confidence, resources and a sense of control to support change.
- The scope of change initiatives may be very wide, encompassing a large number of stakeholders and tasks. Delegation ensures that no individual manager has responsibility for the management of more stakeholders and programme elements than he can effectively handle.
- Delegation supports the allocation of authority for stakeholder engagement and liaison to individuals and teams best placed (eg by virtue of existing contacts and relationships) to manage them: for example, to line managers, category buyers or account managers.
- By increasing team members' understanding, engagement and initiative in the change process, and increasing multi-directional communication around the change, delegation can encourage innovative problem-solving and improvements to the change plan, based on team-members' front-line knowledge and expertise, access to supplier and customer feedback and so on.

Why don't managers delegate, or delegate successfully?

2.9 In practice, many managers are reluctant to delegate and retain a routine workload in addition to their leading and managing functions.

- The manager may have low confidence in the abilities of team members. ('If you want something done, do it yourself.') This may be in the manager's perception (eg as a result of 'Theory X' assumptions) – or may be due to poor selection, training and/or motivation of personnel, resulting in genuine problems of competence or attitude. (As we saw in Hersey & Blanchard's situational leadership model such problems make 'delegating' a less appropriate leadership style.)
- The burden of responsibility and accountability for the mistakes of the team may put pressure on the leader to retain control.
- The manager may want to 'stay in touch' with team relationships and with the familiarities of the routine workload (particularly if he is new to, or uncomfortable with, the leadership role).
- The leader may feel threatened by the perception that the team could 'do the job' without his or her input, failing to understand the complexity of the leadership role. Empowerment implies the need for managers to change from 'commanders and controllers' to coaches, facilitators, communication hubs and entrepreneurial resource mobilisers on behalf of the team. If the team performs well, this should be understood as reflecting well on the manager's leadership.
- The leader may lack skills in time management (which fosters an appreciation of the need for delegation), assertiveness (to distinguish delegation from loss of control), training and development of staff, or delegation itself. As we will see below, a number of intra- and inter-personal skills are required for effective delegation.
- The organisation culture may be resistant to delegation: failing to promote or reward effective delegation, or regarding it as 'shirking responsibility' or 'loss of control'.

10

2.10 The essence of leadership – as we have seen throughout this Course Book – is to get things done *through other people*. 'Managers who think about what can be done only in terms of what they can do, cannot be effective. Managers must learn to accept their dependence upon people.' (Rosemary Stewart, *The Reality of Management*).

2.11 Encouraging managers to delegate therefore involves measures such as the following.

- Training managers in delegation-related skills (such as time management, assertiveness, staff coaching and development and delegation itself)
- Senior management modelling of effective delegation
- Recognising and rewarding positive and effective delegation: emphasising that initiative and effective self-management by the team reflects well on its manager
- Increasing trust, by: training and developing team members so that they are capable of handling delegated authority; and establishing monitoring, communication and control systems to manage the risks of delegation.

3 · A systematic approach to delegation ·

3.1 Management literature emphasises both the *importance* of delegation and the need for *effective* delegation. Mullins argues that setting up a successful system of delegation involves a manager examining four basic questions.

- What tasks could be performed better (or more cost efficiently) by other staff?
- What opportunities are there for staff to learn and develop by undertaking delegated tasks and responsibilities?
- How should the increased responsibilities be implemented and to whom should they be given?
- What forms of monitoring and control system would be most appropriate (in order to balance flexibility and autonomy with the need to maintain co-ordination, control and the chain of command)?

When to delegate

3.2 Knowing when to delegate is the first skill of effective delegation. Delegation may be possible – or positively advantageous – when trust can be placed in the competence and reliability of subordinates *and*:

- The work to be delegated is routine, repetitive or of low consequence; *or*
- The quality of the work or decision will be improved by the input of subordinates; *or*
- Subordinates' involvement in, or acceptance of, a decision is important for staff morale and commitment to its implementation. (This may be the case in many changes that will affect subordinates' work or working conditions.)
- There is an opportunity cost involved in having a higher manager take the decision or action, when it could effectively be taken at a lower level.

The delegation process

3.3 Delegation is an interpersonal process which balances control and support (so that the superior can be confident the work will be done as required) and empowerment and challenge (so that the subordinate can exercise genuine initiative and discretion within the bounds of task requirements). The process is shown in Figure 10.1

Figure 10.1 *The process of delegation*

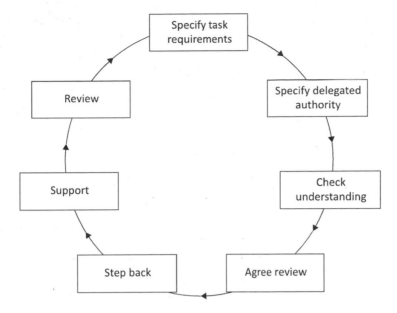

Briefing and resourcing

3.4 The leader must first specify the task, the contexts and levels of performance required, and the timescale for performance. There are two issues here.

- Subordinates must know exactly what is expected of them. Clear direction or sponsorship is required, particularly in delegating to teams or networks: unity of direction depends on someone initiating and co-ordinating multiple contributions.
- Expectations must be reasonable. Appropriate resources (including information flow, contacts, use of equipment, training and development, assistance and so on) must be devoted to the task. Adequate timescales must be allowed to complete tasks to the standard required. (This may be monitored and renegotiated, if necessary, as challenges or difficulties emerge and additional time or resources are required.)

3.5 Next, the leader must clearly specify the terms of reference, and the scope and limits of the authority being delegated: setting out parameters for reporting by exception, and defining what subordinates can and cannot do without reference to the manager. A clear authority or mandate is required for team members to move forward without having constantly to refer decisions back: this allows genuine initiative and flexibility, which support change.

3.6 It will be important to check subordinates' understanding and agreement: seek feedback, give opportunities for questions and input and so on. This may be the point at which learning or training needs emerge, in order to equip subordinates to take on the task or responsibility.

Balancing trust and control

3.7 The leader and delegate(s) should agree in advance on methods and timescales for **monitoring, reporting, progress review** and so on. Here are some possible methods of monitoring and review.

- Periodic work or activity sampling or observation by the leader
- Formal and informal reporting back (on a periodic or exception basis)
- Team meetings for progress assessment, feedback and problem-solving
- Gathering feedback (eg 360-degree feedback or supplier surveys)
- Measuring progress against defined goals or project gates or milestones

3.8   A key principle of delegation is: 'not buying a dog and barking yourself'. Having delegated, the leader must **allow freedom of action** within the agreed terms of reference: letting team members get on with the delegated tasks and responsibilities, without unnecessary interference or conspicuous monitoring (which can interfere with performance). Micro-management implies lack of trust.

3.9   The leader should, however, be available to **support and facilitate** (with additional information or instruction) where asked or required to do so, using where possible a non-directive approach to develop the subordinate's problem-solving skills.

3.10   Monitoring and reviewing performance at the agreed intervals, the leader should be alert to both negative feedback (suggesting that things are going wrong) and positive feedback (suggesting that things are going right). He should offer constructive criticism where necessary to aid learning, *and* acknowledge successes and improvements. Many writers on leadership emphasise that it is more motivating to catch people doing things right than doing things wrong.

3.11   If performance feedback indicates an unforeseen or escalating problem, the leader may need to take **corrective action.** This may take various forms.

- Facilitating subordinates in problem-solving, by offering information or guidance – and where necessary, additional time or resources. This can be a powerful demonstration of trust, and a valuable developmental experience.
- Giving more directive leadership: extra instruction and closer monitoring until the problem is solved – particularly where time is short and the stakes are high
- Re-directing the tasks to others (possibly the leader himself) with the authority and expertise to take fast remedial action. This can be demotivating for the original delegates, and will have to be handled constructively, with the emphasis on problem-solving, feedback and learning. However, in a crisis, it may be necessary.

3.12   Successful delivery of delegated activities and outcomes should be recognised and **rewarded**. Formal individual and team rewards may be available as part of the organisation's reward system: financial bonuses on project completion, awards for change management excellence, opportunities for development and further responsibility, and so on. However, informal rewards – acknowledgement, praise, 'hero' status, symbolic tokens, celebrations – should not be underestimated.

4   The concept of empowerment

Job design and performance

4.1   The question of job design acquired its prominence when human relations theorists became interested in the motivational aspects of the job and the role of 'job satisfaction' in worker performance.

4.2   Motivation researcher Frederick Herzberg was among the first to suggest a systematic approach to job satisfaction and its relationship to job design. Herzberg's 'two factor' theory argued that the job itself can be a source of satisfaction, offering various ways of meeting the individual's needs for personal growth (motivator factors). Huczynski and Buchanan *(Introduction to Organisational Behaviour)* explain this by pointing out that 'the design of an individual's job determines both the kind of rewards that are available and what the individual has to do to get those rewards.'

4.3   Herzberg *(Work and the Nature of Man)* recommended three basic approaches to increasing worker satisfaction and motivation through job design: job rotation, job enlargement and job enrichment.

- **Job rotation** is the planned transfer of staff between jobs to give greater task variety. (The documented example quotes a warehouse gang of four workers, where the worst job was seen as tying the necks of the sacks at the base of the hopper, and the best job as being the forklift truck driver: job rotation would ensure that individuals spent equal time on all jobs.) It is generally admitted that the developmental value of job rotation is limited, but it can reduce the monotony of repetitive work.

- **Job enlargement** is an attempt to widen jobs by increasing the number of operations or tasks in which the worker is involved. This is a 'horizontal extension' of the job (Chris Argyris). The lengthened time cycle of repeated operations may reduce monotony. However, Herzberg himself noted that asking a worker to complete three separate tedious, unchallenging tasks is unlikely to motivate him more than asking him to fulfil one single tedious, unchallenging task.
- **Job enrichment** is a planned, deliberate action to build greater responsibility, breadth and challenge of work into a job. This is a 'vertical extension' of the job (Arygris), which is often equated with 'empowerment'. It may include removing controls over workers' actions; increasing responsibility and accountability; providing more regular feedback on performance; introducing new tasks; or allocating special assignments. This will clearly impact more powerfully on employees' experience in the core job dimensions discussed earlier.

Empowerment

4.4 Empowerment involves both giving workers greater **authority** (scope and discretion) to make decisions about how to organise their work *and* giving workers greater **responsibility** for their own actions – and their contribution to unit and organisational objectives.

4.5 The term 'empowerment' is often used interchangeably with delegation. However, it may be argued that:

- Empowerment is more proactive and wide-ranging than delegation of tasks or authority: empowered individuals and teams may effectively become self-managing (within broad guidelines set by management)
- Empowerment implies giving team members the power, resources and tools to make and implement decisions – not just the *authority* to do so. It is more supportive and facilitative than delegation, with a broader impact on team development and capability.
- Delegation is a practical expression and tool of a management style and culture based on empowerment.

4.6 Empowerment may be seen within a broader view of the managerial role, which has been referred to as the 'inverted pyramid'.

4.7 In the traditional view of management, the organisation should support the objectives of management: each level of the hierarchy facilitating the activities of the one above it. Today, it is often considered that managerial activity should support the objectives of the organisation: each level of the hierarchy facilitating the activities of the one below it: Figure 10.2.

Figure 10.2 *The inverted pyramid*

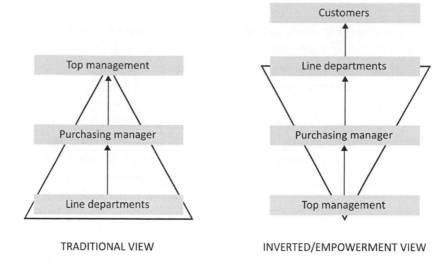

TRADITIONAL VIEW   INVERTED/EMPOWERMENT VIEW

4.8 An interesting early case study on empowerment in the UK was provided by Harvester Restaurants, where the management structure comprised a branch manager and a 'coach' – with everyone else as 'team members'. All members have one or more accountabilities (recruitment, drawing up rosters, keeping track of sales targets) which are shared out by the team members at a weekly team meeting. The job of 'co-ordinator' (responsible for taking non-routine decisions) is shared by all team members on a rotating basis. J Pickard ('The real meaning of empowerment,' *Personnel Management,* 1993) described improved job satisfaction and staff commitment to customer service arising from this approach.

Empowerment in practice: facilitating team member initiative

4.9 Effective leaders seek to foster initiative in team members: welcoming and guiding the development of team-generated suggestions and solutions. Whetten and Cameron *(Developing Management Skills)* suggest the following behavioural guidelines for leaders wanting to support initiative in a team.

- Create a supportive climate by emphasising that you have a shared stake in the work and its results, and will support team members' efforts. ('How are we going to do this?' 'How would you like me to contribute?')
- Draw out factual information, by asking open questions and showing interest.
- Encourage team members to analyse and evaluate their own proposals, by asking for their best judgement on potential issues. ('What costs have you factored in?' 'What risks have you identified?')
- If improvements or adjustments need to be made, guide team members in resolving issues themselves: present facts to which they may not have access (eg about corporate objectives, policy constraints).
- If team members have overlooked or overemphasised some points, ask them to analyse further and suggest a revised plan: don't correct the plan for them.

Empowerment in practice: facilitating team member development

4.10 Leaders support and encourage the continuous learning and development of team members, to equip them for progressive empowerment. Apart from helping team members to access formal learning and development opportunities within or outside the organisation, a team leader can create a learning-supportive climate in the following ways.

- Role modelling and encouraging the questioning of assumptions, the voicing of divergent views, and reinterpretation of problems in new ways
- Role modelling and welcoming trial and error learning: affirming mistakes as learning opportunities, and coaching team members in problem-solving so they can draw out the learning from problems

- Supporting knowledge-sharing and information-sharing within the team, particularly on performance issues; encouraging more experienced members to coach and mentor others; encouraging the capturing of ideas and information from other sources; and so on
- Acting as coach and/or mentor to team members, to identify learning opportunities, provide feedback and help access resources for development
- Delegating tasks, taking on 'assistants', appointing team members to committees and project teams, and facilitating role shadowing – maximising opportunities for learning by doing
- Avoiding micro-management of performance, to encourage team members in initiative and self-management

Evaluating empowerment

4.11   Empowerment is intended to enhance organisational effectiveness in the following ways.

- Increasing employees' motivation and job satisfaction (in terms of immediate motivator factors, and also by offering greater autonomy and responsibility in delayered organisations where promotions up a career ladder may not be available)
- Harnessing employees' creativity and 'front-line' expertise for problem-solving, improvement and innovation
- Shortening response times at the interface with customers and suppliers, especially in regard to improving customer service – and seizing opportunities that are too local or 'on the spot' to be responded to centrally or at a higher level.

4.12   However, there are acknowledged barriers and drawbacks to empowerment in practice.

- If handled ineffectively, there may be loss of control and co-ordination, and a breakdown of respect for authority and the chain of command.
- Stress, conflict and delay may be caused by lack of clarity about where responsibility lies in a given situation or task.
- Not all employees desire more challenge or responsibility. Some will fear the learning and accountability that accompanies extra responsibilities. Some will not be suited to the ambiguity and uncertainty that may accompany empowerment.
- Not all employees are capable of exercising greater responsibility or undertaking the necessary skill development.
- Managers may struggle to release control and/or to change role and style.
- The organisation culture, or environment, may not be supportive of empowerment, which requires transparent information-sharing, flexibility and tolerance of mistakes in support of learning.
- Empowerment is not a substitute for other rewards: it must be reinforced by recognition and/ or financial rewards for exercising increased responsibility. (As Charles Handy points out, 'Even those who want their jobs enriched will expect to be rewarded with more than job satisfaction. Job enrichment is not a cheaper way to greater productivity. Its pay-off will come in the less visible costs of morale, climate and working relationships.')
- Empowerment may be perceived as a poor alternative to promotion or career development.
- Empowerment cannot simply be 'implemented': it has to be developed over time, as both managers and subordinates develop trust, confidence and capability.

10

Chapter summary

- Classical organisation theory emphasises the importance of matching authority and responsibility.
- Delegation of authority is the process through which a leader hands over to another person part of his or her own authority to make decisions or take actions. It overcomes the limitations imposed by the leader's workload — and encourages delegates to develop ownership and initiative.
- The delegation process is one of briefing and resourcing subordinates; checking understanding; agreeing monitoring and review procedures — and then stepping back, providing support when needed and reviewing when agreed.
- Empowerment involves both giving workers greater authority to make decisions regarding their work, and giving them responsibility for their actions. The aim is to enhance organisational effectiveness.

Self-test questions

Numbers in brackets refer to the paragraphs where you can check your answers.

1   What happens if authority is given without responsibility? What happens in the opposite situation? (1.7)

2   Summarise benefits of decentralisation and centralisation. (1.12)

3   List desirable outcomes of delegation. (2.6)

4   Explain reasons why managers fail to delegate successfully. (2.9)

5   According to Mullins, what four questions must a manager address in setting up a successful system of delegation? (3.1)

6   List stages in the process of delegation. (Figure 10.1)

7   Describe job rotation, job enlargement and job enrichment. (4.3)

8   In what ways may empowerment enhance organisational effectiveness? (4.11)

Subject Index